COLERIDGE'S VARIETY

Bicentenary Studies

COLERIDGE'S VARIETY

Bicentenary Studies

Edited by
JOHN BEER

With an Introduction by
L. C. KNIGHTS

First published 1974 by
THE MACMILLAN PRESS LTD
London and Basingstoke
Associated companies in New York
Dublin Melbourne Johannesburg and Madras

SBN 333 16906 9

Printed in Great Britain by
WESTERN PRINTING SERVICES LTD
Bristol

Contents

Preface and Acknowledgements

Shortly before the bicentenary of Coleridge's birth, several members of the English Faculty in Cambridge felt that it would be appropriate to commemorate the occasion not only in his College, but in the Faculty as well. This feeling was prompted partly by the fact that while no geographical centre is closely associated with him (in the way that Grasmere, for example, is associated with Wordsworth) Cambridge has had a series of intellectual links with his thought and work, both through theologians such as Julius Hare and F. J. A. Hort in the nineteenth century and through a line of distinguished literary critics, beginning with Quiller-Couch and Richards, in the twentieth. Accordingly, it was agreed that, in addition to the commemorative lecture to be given in Jesus College, a series should be arranged to which distinguished scholars outside the Faculty should be invited to contribute.

The Committee which was set up was greatly impressed by the response to its invitations. A number of scholars proved willing to rearrange their plans or otherwise put themselves to inconvenience, even at short notice, in order to come to Cambridge during the Michaelmas Term of 1972. Professor Kathleen Coburn, who was committed to lecture elsewhere, was able to offer an informal seminar, and Professor David Erdman gave an informal lecture on Coleridge's journalism, based on his work as editor of *Essays on his Times* in the *Collected Coleridge*.

Far from being, as we had feared, a deterrent, the lack of a geographical focus proved to be a positive stimulus to commemoration. Events were arranged at Christ's Hospital, Bristol, The Royal Institution, The British Museum and Highgate (to mention only those known to us). Some of the lectures included in the various programmes were committed for exclusive publication elsewhere; but those which were not proved to complement each other remarkably well and to constitute, in the sum, an interesting and unusual conspectus of approaches to Coleridge. This is not, perhaps, surprising. It may be that a man of Coleridge's mercurial and multifarious gifts is best apprehended through the contributions of a group of critics, each in turn recording what he or she has gained from a sustained engagement with his intelligence.

One further topical event may be mentioned for the benefit of future readers. It happened that the chief publishing event to mark the bicentenary in England was the publication of Norman Fruman's book, *Coleridge, the Damaged Archangel*. Some of those associated with the lectures had already reviewed the book on its appearance in the U.S.A. (see, e.g., Owen Barfield, 'Abysses of Incomprehension', *The Nation*, 12 June 1972; L. C. Knights, 'Coleridge: the Wound without the Bow', *New York Review of Books*, 4 May 1972); others felt the need to make some reference to Mr Fruman's charges in so far as they related to the topics of their particular lectures.

The original lectures took place in October and November 1972, and except where the place of delivery is otherwise indicated in a footnote, they were given before the University of Cambridge. Some are printed as delivered, others have been extensively revised; some, therefore, show the immediacy of the lecture-room, others are in the more reflective mode of the written article.

The editor and contributors would like to express their thanks to the Master and Fellows of Jesus College, Cambridge; the Headmaster and Governors of Christ's Hospital; the President and Members of the Royal Institution; the Trustees of the Coleridge Memorial Trust at Highgate; and the Faculty Board of English in the University of Cambridge, for both sponsoring particular lectures and giving permission for their publication. We should also like to thank the Master and Fellows of Peterhouse, the President and Fellows of Clare Hall and the following individuals for their help in arranging the lectures and accompanying events: Professor J. A. W. Bennett; Professor M. C. Bradbrook; Dr Howard Erskine-Hill; Professor John Holloway; Professor Graham Hough; Dr Ian Jack; Dr Duncan McKie; Mrs Sita Narasimhan; Sir Denys and Lady Page; Lady Radzinowitz; Mr Basil Savage; Dr Elinor Shaffer; Mrs Sheila Sibson-Turnbull; Mr Graham Storey; Mr Richard Tuck; Mr George Watson and

Dr Raymond Williams. Several people gave ready assistance with a few problems of annotation which overtook us in the final stages; we are particularly grateful to Professor R. L. Brett, Professor Craig Miller, Mr Basil Savage, Dr Donald Sultana, Dr Judith Wardle and Professor Basil Willey – and more especially so to Dr A. J. Harding who, in addition, constructed the index at very short notice.

Among the many other Coleridgeans whom we should have liked to include in the list of lecturers, two in particular should be mentioned. Professor I. A. Richards had originally hoped to contribute a paper but later found that it would be impossible for him to be in Cambridge at that time; Professor Basil Willey, with characteristic modesty, declined our invitation on the grounds that his new book had just appeared. No acknowledgements would be complete, nevertheless, which did not mention how much Coleridge studies owe to them. It also gives us great pleasure that Professor L. C. Knights, whose name should head the list of those who have given the lectures their encouragement, who has been constantly active in Coleridge studies both in and out of the university, and for whom the Coleridge bicentenary coincided with his concluding year as King Edward VII Professor of English at Cambridge, has consented to introduce the collection with a short essay of his own.

J. B. B.

Notes on Contributors

M. H. Abrams, Class of 1916 Professor of English Literature at Cornell University, is the author of The Milk of Paradise, The Mirror and the Lamp: Romantic Theory and the Critical Tradition, and Natural Supernaturalism: Tradition and Revolution in Romantic Literature, and editor, among other things, of The Poetry of Pope, Literature and Belief, English Romantic Poets: Modern Essays in Criticism and Wordsworth: A Collection of Critical Essays.

Owen Barfield is author of What Coleridge Thought, History in English Words, Poetic Diction, Saving the Appearances and other books. Mr Barfield has spent the greater part of his active life in the practice of the law. Since retiring about ten years ago he has from time to time resided at Brandeis and other American universities as a Visiting Professor in Literature and Philosophy.

John Beer is Lecturer in English at Cambridge and Fellow of Peterhouse. In addition to writing Coleridge the Visionary, The Achievement of E. M. Forster, Blake's Humanism and Blake's Visionary Universe, he has edited Coleridge's Poems for Everyman's University Library and is editing Aids to Reflection for The Collected Coleridge. Further studies, now in preparation, concentrate on Wordsworth, and on Coleridge's psychological theories.

Kathleen Coburn, editor of the Notebooks of Samuel Taylor Coleridge and General Editor of the Bollingen edition of the Collected Works, has also edited a volume of Coleridge's hitherto unpublished Philosophical Lectures 1818–19, and a selection from his prose writings, published and unpublished, entitled Inquiring Spirit, in addition to her various articles on

Coleridge, Wordsworth and Hazlitt. She is Professor Emeritus in Victoria College in the University of Toronto and Hon. Fellow of St Hugh's College, Oxford.

Dorothy Emmet, Emeritus Professor of Philosophy in the University of Manchester, Fellow of Lucy Cavendish College, Cambridge and Honorary Fellow of Lady Margaret Hall, Oxford, has published *Whitehead's Philosophy of Organism; The Nature of Metaphysical Thinking; Function, Purpose and Powers; Rules, Roles and Relations*, and a number of articles, including 'Coleridge on the Growth of the Mind' (*Bulletin of the John Rylands Library* 1952) and 'Coleridge and Philosophy' (in *S. T. Coleridge*, ed. R. L. Brett, 'Writers and their Background' Series).

Earl Leslie Griggs was, before his recent retirement, Professor of English at the University of California at Los Angeles. In addition to his edition of Coleridge's *Collected Letters*, his publications include biographies of Hartley Coleridge and of Sara Coleridge (*Coleridge Fille*), the *Letters of Hartley Coleridge* and over forty other books and articles on Coleridgean and related matters.

L. C. Knights is Emeritus King Edward VII Professor of English Literature at Cambridge and Emeritus Fellow of Queens' College. His books include *Drama and Society in the Age of Johnson, Explorations, Further Explorations, Some Shakespearean Themes* and *Public Voices: Literature and Politics with special reference to the Seventeenth Century*; among his other essays and reviews are several on Coleridge.

Thomas McFarland is Distinguished Professor of English Literature at the Graduate Center of the City University of New York. He is the author of *Coleridge and the Pantheist Tradition* and is editing Coleridge's *Opus Maximum* and Coleridge's *Philosophical Lectures* for *The Collected Coleridge*.

D. M. MacKinnon is Norris-Hulse Professor of Divinity at Cambridge and Fellow of Corpus Christi College. His publications include *The Notion of a Philosophy of History, A Study in*

Ethical Theory, The Resurrection, Borderlands of Theology and other papers and *The Stripping of the Altars.*

George Whalley is Professor of English at Queen's University, Kingston, Ontario. His published work includes *Poetic Process* and *Coleridge and Sara Hutchinson.* He is now completing the edition of Coleridge's marginalia for the *Collected Works of Samuel Taylor Coleridge.*

Abbreviations

(Place of publication is London unless otherwise stated.)

AR	S. T. Coleridge, *Aids to Reflection* (1825).
BL	S. T. Coleridge, *Biographia Literaria*, ed. J. Shawcross (1907).
BM	British Museum
C & S	S. T. Coleridge, *On the Constitution of the Church and State, According to the Idea of Each*, 2nd ed. (1830).
Carlyle	Thomas Carlyle, *Life of John Sterling* (1851).
CL	*Collected Letters of Samuel Taylor Coleridge*, ed. Earl Leslie Griggs, 6 vols (Oxford, 1956–71).
CN	*The Notebooks of Samuel Taylor Coleridge* ed. Kathleen Coburn (1957–).
CT	*Coleridge the Talker*, ed. R. W. Armour and R. F. Howes (Ithaca, N.Y., 1940).
Deschamps	Paul Deschamps, *La Formation de la pensée de Coleridge 1772–1804* (Paris, 1964).
DQW	*The Collected Works of Thomas de Quincey*, ed. David Masson, 14 vols (Edinburgh, 1889–90).
DW	*Collected Works of Sir Humphry Davy, Bart*, ed. John Davy, 9 vols (1839–40).
DWJ	*Journals of Dorothy Wordsworth*, ed. Ernest de Selincourt, 2 vols (Oxford, 1941).
Freud	*Complete Psychological Works of Sigmund Freud*, Standard Edition, ed. J. Strachey et al., 23 vols (1953–64).
Friend	S. T. Coleridge, *The Friend*, ed. Barbara Rooke, 2 vols (1969) (*Collected Coleridge*).

Fruman	Norman Fruman, *Coleridge, the Damaged Archangel* (New York 1971, London 1972).
Gillman	James Gillman, *Life of Samuel Taylor Coleridge* (1838).
HCR	*Henry Crabb Robinson on Books and their Writers*, ed. E. J. Morley, 3 vols (1938).
House	Humphry House, *Coleridge, the Clark Lectures* (1953).
HW	*The Complete Works of William Hazlitt*, ed. P. P. Howe, 21 vols (1930–4).
IS	*Inquiring Spirit, a New Presentation of Coleridge from His Published and Unpublished Prose Writings*, ed. Kathleen Coburn (1951) (Cited by page).
LL	*The Letters of Charles Lamb, to which are added Those of His Sister Mary Lamb*, ed. E. V. Lucas, 3 vols (1935).
LR	S. T. Coleridge, *Literary Remains*, ed. H. N. Coleridge, 4 vols (1836–9).
LS	S. T. Coleridge, *Lay Sermons*, ed. R. J. White (1972) (*Collected Coleridge*).
LW	*The Works of Charles and Mary Lamb*, ed. E. V. Lucas, 7 vols (1903–5).
Misc C	S. T. Coleridge, *Miscellaneous Criticism*, ed. T. M. Raysor (1936).
N	S. T. Coleridge, Unpublished MS notebooks in the B.M.
PL	S. T. Coleridge, *Philosophical Lectures*, ed. Kathleen Coburn (1949).
PW	*The Complete Poetical Works of Samuel Taylor Coleridge* ed E. H. Coleridge, 2 vols (Oxford, 1912).
Sh C	S. T. Coleridge, *Shakespearean Criticism*, ed. T. M. Raysor, 2 vols (1930).
TL	S. T. Coleridge, *Hints Towards the Formation of a More Comprehensive Theory of Life*, ed. Seth B. Watson (1848; reprinted 1970).
TT	*Specimens of the Table Talk of the late*

S. T. *Coleridge*, ed. H. N. Coleridge, 2 vols (1835).

WLR(1787–1805) *Letters of William and Dorothy Wordsworth, 1787–1805*, ed. E. de Selincourt, 2nd ed. revised C. Shaver (Oxford, 1967).

WLR(1806–1811) *Letters of William and Dorothy Wordsworth, 1806–1811*, ed. E. de Selincourt, 2nd ed. revised M. Moorman, Oxford 1969).

WL(LY) *Letters of William and Dorothy Wordsworth: the later years (1821–50)*, ed. E. de Selincourt, 3 vols (Oxford, 1939).

WPW *The Poetical Works of William Wordsworth*, ed. E. de Selincourt and Helen Darbishire, 5 vols, (Oxford, 1940–9).

WPrW W. Wordsworth, *Prose Works*, ed. A. B. Grosart, 3 vols (1876).

W Prel W. Wordsworth, *The Prelude*, ed. E. de Selincourt, 2nd ed. revised. H. Darbishire (Oxford, 1959).

Introduction

L. C. Knights

The lectures presented here were intended as an act of homage to a great man. But inevitably they deal only with selected aspects of a genius that is as multiform and various as it is commanding and, at times, enigmatic. It is not only that, as F. D. Maurice said, 'those who have most profited by what he has taught them, do not and cannot form a school', those who through a lifetime return to his works are likely to find that their understanding stops far short of anything they would care to call finality. Dr Beer, who quotes Maurice's remark, concludes his second lecture by saying: 'Coleridge's career, in its intricate processes and riddling self-contradictions, continually beckons one ... to further thought and investigation rather than to attempts at sweeping evaluation'. I think this is true; but it does not relieve us of the necessity of trying to clear up our minds about why we value Coleridge or to elicit the unifying principles that make his work as a whole so much more than a collection of false starts from which brilliant occasional insights emerge.

I have always thought that Coleridge's literary criticism – occupying, so to speak, a middle place between the poetry and the philosophy and general thought – offers the common reader the best purchase for further investigation. And since the essays collected here say very little about the criticism, it may be appropriate to give it some prominence in this Introduction.

When we try to define the value of Coleridge's literary criticism perhaps the observation to start from is that it is related to deep personal needs: it is not just 'literary criticism' as that phrase is only too often understood. Coleridge as critic is not simply the man of letters whose basic assumptions about life are more or less taken for granted, so that they can be kept outside his discussion of particular literary problems, as Dryden, for example, urbanely and intelligently but without moral resonance, discusses the problems of his craft. And I think it is in general true to say that the criticism that we most often go back to for insight and stimulus is either that of the creative writer urgently exploring the implications of some radically new way of writing that he practises (Eliot, Yeats, Lawrence), or that of a man whose feeling for life as a whole gets into and informs his criticism (Dr Johnson, Matthew Arnold). Coleridge, although he wrote some great poems, and would not have been the critic he was unless he had been capable of writing them, belongs to the second class. His criticism is immethodical, not always of the same high standard, and it can be sadly off the point. But at its best it is of great and permanent value because the question it asks is, How does *this* make for life? to what extent is *this* an expression of the imagination? And behind this, What *is* the imagination, and why is it so important that we should cultivate it? In other words, Coleridge's literary criticism springs from the same source as his thinking about education, psychology, religion, politics. It is part of his total confrontation of human experience, and is connected with the life of feeling and intuitive perception that it is the poet's special task to bring to expression. Coleridge's attempt to define the imagination began when he tried to make clear to himself the distinctive qualities of Wordsworth's poetry. But what invigorates and directs his criticism and, beyond that, his general thought, is not only the experience of an uncommonly sensitive reader of poetry, it is his own experience as a poet.

It is, then, helpful to preface even a brief account of the criticism with a reference to 'Dejection: An Ode'. That poem is, of course, about the loss of joy, the animating principle, 'my shaping spirit of Imagination'; but in the central stanzas, iv and v, there is the paradoxical recognition of joy as a principle of life. Paradoxical, because the poem records a defeat, but records it so faithfully and completely that Coleridge, at a deep level of engagement, *realises* what is meant by the opposite of defeat. To put this in slightly different words, the intensity of the imaginative process – including an un-self-regarding steadiness of contemplation – has set free and established some of the fundamental insights of Coleridge's philosophy.* Professor Dorothy Emmet, in the brilliant paper that she wrote some twenty years ago,[1] says:

> I believe that Coleridge was concerned to explore not only a source of the creative power of imagination shown in genius but also more generally the liberation of the mind from deadness and dereliction, a liberation on which its growth depends ... [His] philosophy was concerned with exploring the conditions which make possible, and the conditions which frustrate this joy which underlies the creative growth of the mind.

And again:

> 'The Ancient Mariner', 'Christabel', 'Kubla Khan', give us above all symbols of dereliction and joy. Joy for Coleridge was not just an 'equipoise of the intellectual and emotional faculties', at any rate if this means the achievement of a balanced temperament, which he sorely lacked. It was a state in which it was possible to bless and be blessed; and to Coleridge there was no half-way house: its absence was like the misery of a curse. And what he learnt about joy came as much from his failure to achieve liberty of spirit as from the rare moments when he did achieve it.

Coleridge's central preoccupation was indeed with growth and creativeness, and with the activity of consciousness, the energy and joy, that are the conditions, the signs and the consequences of creativeness. To grasp the implications of that takes us to the heart of his philosophy and shows us the close connection between his literary criticism and the wider aspects of his thought. As Shawcross put it, in the Preface to his edition of the *Biographia*, 'The search for a criterion of poetry involved him in the wider search for a criterion of life'. The statement could equally well be reversed. What is important is to realise that in Coleridge's thinking the attempt to understand and to find a criterion for poetry is inseparable from the attempt to

---

* I refer of course to the finished, the *worked at*, poem. The original verse letter to Sara Hutchinson is not only very much longer, with a different arrangement of parts, it is full of a self-pity that has been completely eliminated in the re-working.

understand and to find a criterion for all other aspects of life. As he said of his projected book on poetry (in a letter to Humphry Davy, 9 October 1800), 'its Title would be an Essay on the Elements of Poetry', but 'it would be in reality a disguised System of Morals and Politics', adding, a few months later (3 February 1801), 'the Work would supersede all the Books of Metaphysics hitherto written, and all the Books of Morals too'. A rather large claim, but not to be dismissed as the compensatory fantasy – Carlyle's 'bottled moonshine' – of a man who was too indolent, or too troubled, to carry to completion any work he planned.

'Life' of course is somewhat too big to talk about. Coleridge knew as well as Blake that life only reveals itself in – sometimes minute – particulars. If the guiding principles of Coleridge's thought are in fact revealed or intimated in his literary criticism, this is because 'principles' and 'practical criticism' are intimately and necessarily connected: one recalls the significant collocation in the first sentence of Chapter xv of the *Biographia Literaria*. Coleridge was a first-class practical critic. As Professor William Walsh has said – referring to 'the tonic effect' of his criticism – it has a 'fiercely individual and personal bite. . . . It braces and concentrates attention.'[2] Again and again a sure personal judgement – disciplined and sustained, not dissipated, by a remarkable range of reading – goes straight to the mark. He had a very clear perception of Wordsworth's greatness as a poet, and – long before Wordsworth was an accepted classic – his praise was generous, sure and discriminating. He was a pioneer in the rehabilitation of Donne and 'our elder poets' of the early seventeenth century, noting their 'pure and genuine mother English'[3] even in the expression of difficult thoughts. Of George Herbert he wrote,

> the scholar and the poet supplies the material, but the perfect well-bred gentleman the expressions and the arrangement;
>   (BL II 73)

and (ahead even of cultivated taste by a century) of the lively expressiveness of Donne's rhythms:

> Read even Donne's Satires as he meant them to be read, and as the sense and passion demand, and you will find in the lines and manly harmony   (Misc C 67)

His lectures and notes on Shakespeare and the Jacobean dramatists are uneven, but they are a quarry of perceptions that lead
the mind further into particular plays. There is psychological
acumen, as when he notes the contrast between Macbeth's and
Banquo's response to the witches; there is a feeling for the relation between immediate dramatic effect and the unfolding whole
of which it forms a part, as in the superb account of the contrasting opening scenes of *Hamlet, Macbeth* and *King Lear*;[4] and
always attention is focused on the particular, and poetic, use
of words, as when he comments on Lady Macbeth's welcome
to Duncan, 'the very rhythm expresses the insincere overmuch
in [her] answer to the king'.[5] Poetic, one should say, *and* dramatic: a casual remark on Shakespeare's versification anticipates
what is sometimes thought of as a modern discovery:

> Shakespeare never introduces a catalectic line without
> intending an equivalent to the foot omitted, in the pauses, or
> the dwelling emphasis, or the diffused retardation. (ShC 1 24)

Almost everywhere, in short, we find evidence of Coleridge's
feeling for 'the blessed machine of language'[6] – the way in
which it carries within it a human history that can enter into
new, subtle and precise expression. Many years ago I jotted on
a fly-leaf of Owen Barfield's *Poetic Diction* (a book which, with
its companion, *History in English Words*, Coleridge would have
enjoyed) a sentence from *Aids to Reflection*:

> There are cases, in which more knowledge of more value may
> be conveyed by the history of a *word*, than by the history of
> a campaign.   (AR 6n)

Coleridge's criticism, however, is valuable not only for the
particular perceptions that show him coming to grips with and
illuminating what is actually there in front of him, but because
it constantly circles round and refers to certain *principles* or
'organising insights'.[7] Of these the most important are the
conception of poetry as a form of energy – the 'vigour' with 'a
substrate of profound feeling'[8] that he calls attention to in
distinguishing Donne from Cowley – and the belief that in good
poetry 'the poet's ever active mind' is answered by a corresponding 'activity of attention required on the part of the reader'.[9]
I know very well that literary criticism cannot be conducted in
these general terms: when we want to define the excellence of

a particular poem we don't rhapsodise about any access of energy it may give, we point to this or that in the structure and texture of the poem – its 'sound of sense', the choice and order of words, the imagery or the rhythm. But sometimes we need to see what all these things are *for*. Coleridge's principles not only emerge from his own direct experience of literature – both as maker and critic – they help us, once we have grasped them, to organise our thinking about literature, and much else besides; and it is worth noticing in what varied ways, in the *Biographia* and elsewhere, the principle of energy is put to work. The phrases that I have quoted about the activity of the poet's mind and the corresponding activity of the reader are parts of a re-markable account of what modern criticism calls 'realisation', that sense of living actuality that comes about when the mind is called on to do several different things simultaneously, and finds that they cohere in one complex act of attention. We may note in passing that all that needs to be said about the nature of pornography is contained in the remark that 'a mind roused and awakened' cannot be 'brooded on by mean and indistinct emotion'. What is more important is that by associating energy with vividness and precision, and the unformed or indistinct with 'the merely passive of our nature', Coleridge makes explicit and intelligible a fundamental criterion not only for literature but for the general life of the mind. Fanaticism, we may recall – elsewhere associated with a 'debility and dimness of the imaginative power' – is said to 'master the feelings more especially by indistinct watchwords'.[10] It is not simply as a *literary* critic that Coleridge recommends 'the advantage which language alone ... presents to the instructor of impressing modes of intellectual energy'.[11]

In this wide context we should be able to focus more clearly on the famous passage on the imagination at the end of Chapter XIV of the *Biographia*, beginning, 'The poet, described in ideal perfection, brings the whole soul of man into activity....' Professor Wellek has said some hard things about this,[12] but even its 'random eclecticism' cannot obscure the fundamental insights that it contains. The imagination is a form of energy, but it is no undirected *élan vital*; it 'struggles to unify' not only thoughts and feelings that often war unnecessarily with each other, but the different modes of being through which the self, including the subliminal self, exercises its powers. It is a function of the whole person, a dynamic integrating force through which we not only come to know ourselves and the world, but experience that sense of creative freedom which in 'Dejection' is called joy. I do not know any more profound account, any account more suggestive and fertilising, of why poetry matters, or of why 'the cultivation of the judgment is a positive command of the moral law'.[13]

For Coleridge, then, the imagination is not a special faculty cultivated by poets and readers of poetry, it is simply life coming to consciousness. R. J. White, referring to Coleridge's achievement in 'The Ancient Mariner', says that he 'spent the rest of his life translating his experience of the creative mind into terms of a philosophy of life, in showing to men that the way of creative genius is the way of ordinary humanity.'[14] In exploring the ways of poetry and the imagination he is also exploring the life of reason as a whole. Professor Emmet – in the paper to which I have referred and in her contribution to the present volume – brings out how, for Coleridge, thinking is not simply a clearly delimited *mental* activity. It is not merely that, as he puts it in *The Friend*,[15] 'in the moral being lies the source of the intellectual'; moral integrity is related to the sympathies and the feelings, which themselves relate closely to the organic life of the body. In matters of essential concern 'knowledge' is not simply deduction from experience or the end of a logical process, it is a function of being, including that 'unconscious activity' that is 'the genius in the man of genius'.*

* There is no need to make a mystery of this; nor is anything that has been said at variance with Coleridge's known dislike of 'floating and obscure generalities' and his insistence on the virtues of vividness and precision. It is simply that the meaning of the word 'precision' varies with the context within which, or the level at which, it is used. In literary criticism precision refers to a clearly directed energy, springing from and supported by feelings that cannot be entirely brought to light. As Coleridge is reported as saying in the lectures on Shakespeare and Milton, 'the grandest efforts of poetry are where the imagination is called forth, not to produce a distinct form, but *a strong working of the mind*' (my italics). So too, in important regions of our thought, 'meaning' is inseparable from an energetic *reaching out* of the mind, and 'precise' definition may put a stop to that. None of which however relieves us of the need to think as clearly as we can.

Bishop Hort, in his 1856 essay, speaks of the influence of Plato and the New Testament in leading Coleridge 'to a region not unfamiliar to English travellers, the first step in which is the identification, in some sense or other, of knowledge and being'.[16] *Quantum sumus, scimus.* In Chapter XXIV of the *Biographia*, dealing with the question of religious faith, Coleridge speaks of 'what we can only *know* by the act of *becoming*'. *Mutatis mutandis* the same could be said of our knowledge of poetry: 'You feel Shakespeare to be a poet inasmuch as, for a time, he has made you one, an active creative being.'[17] As I have said, there is no compartmentalising in Coleridge's thought. Whether he is dealing with poetry, with religion, with the art of thought, with education or with politics, the same principles are at work, and there is the same fundamental concern for zest of life, vitality, growth and creativeness: all of which he knew – knew in specific and detailed forms – from his direct experience as man, as poet and as critic – though he also knew them (as more than one contributor to this volume points out) from his failures. Some of those principles – 'living Sparks' or 'Kindle-fuel', as Coleridge called the Platonic Recollections[18] – will be found at work in the lectures that follow; though it is entirely in keeping that they should work in such different ways and in different fields of thought.

I

Coleridge's Poetic Sensibility

George Whalley

The Samuel Taylor Coleridge who went down from Jesus College in the spring weather of 1794 – thinking no doubt that he would return, though he never seriously did – was the same young man that Dorothy Wordsworth first saw at Racedown two years later when he jumped over the gate because it would take too long to open it, and ran up across the broad lawn to the house.

> At first I thought him very plain, that is, for about three minutes: he is pale and thin, has a wide mouth, thick lips, and not very good teeth, longish loose-growing half-curling rough black hair. But if you hear him speak for five minutes you think no more of them. His eye is large and full, not dark but grey; such an eye as would receive from a heavy soul the dullest expression; but it speaks every emotion of his animated mind; it has more the 'poet's eye in a fine frenzy rolling' than I ever witnessed. (WLR (1787–1805) 188–9)

Whether or not Dorothy in that instant also meant by this that Coleridge had – in Humphry House's words – 'Exceedingly acute senses and great sensitivity to all sense-experiences',[1] Coleridge immediately noticed those qualities in Dorothy: 'She is a woman indeed – in mind, I mean, and heart. . . Her information various – her eye watchful in minutest observation of nature – and her taste a perfect electrometer – it bends, protrudes, and draws in, at subtlest beauties and most recondite faults.'[2] There is record, during the Alfoxden days, of that grave lyrical sensibility of hers – any example can be chosen at random.

> [23 Jan 1798] Bright sunshine, went out at 3 o'clock. The sea perfectly calm blue, streaked with deeper colour by the

clouds, and tongues or points of sand; on our return of a
gloomy red. The sun gone down. The crescent moon, Jupiter,
and Venus. The sound of the sea distinctly heard on the tops
of the hills, which we could never hear in summer. We attribute this partly to the bareness of the trees, but chiefly to the
absence of the singing of birds, the hum of insects, that noise-
less noise which lives in the summer air. The villages marked
out by beautiful beds of smoke. The turf fading into the mountain road. The scarlet flowers of the moss.   (DWJ 1 2)

The phrase 'poetic sensibility' is at first sight quite plain and
unproblematic: it means presumably the sensibility of a poet, or
the sensibility exhibited in poems. If we endorse what Coleridge
called 'the sandy Sophisms of Locke, and the Mechanic Dog-
matists'[3] we should expect the question of Coleridge's 'poetic
sensibility' to resolve itself into a demonstration that he was an
abnormally sensitive receiver of impressions, a fine reactor to
stimuli, an acute recorder of whatever presented itself to his
senses; and we should expect to find the evidence particularly in
his poems, in the precise rendering there of perceptual experience. Given that evidence, however, would it tell us much either
in general about the quality we call 'poetic' or in particular
about sensibility? Coleridge's later writings would suggest not.
He said that he wished to demonstrate 'that the senses were
living growths and developments of the Mind & spirit in a much
juster as well as higher sense, than the mind can be said to be
formed by the Senses.'[4] And in a well-known section of Biographia
Literaria he was to maintain that 'The primary imagination . . .
[is] the living power and prime agent of all human perception,
and as a repetition in the finite mind of the eternal act of creation
in the infinite I AM.'[5] Nevertheless, those statements are of late
date, and most of Coleridge's poems are a young man's poems.
Evidence of early date should be examined.

'Thought,' Coleridge said, 'is a laborious breaking through the
law of association.'[6] Our minds habitually move from the particular to the general, from the less to the more. If we simply
accept Coleridge's own statements of later date – critical statements the power of which comes from his own reflection upon
his own poetic experience – we may lose the illumination of discovery that his statements embody. To move from the more

to the less, however, from poetry, or a single poem, to single symbolic events and images – that is what the habit of our minds resists; yet that is what reflection is for. I should like therefore to trace a little the path in experience – in poetic experience and practice – along which Coleridge approached his uncanny understanding of perception and the work of perception in imagination, in poetic making, in the whole ambit of the mind's possible activities. To take such a course is also to ask whether indeed 'the shaping spirit of imagination' left Coleridge when he said it had – whether indeed it ever left him, even when poems were infrequent and many of them seem like 'the hard and thorny rind and shell within which the rich fruit was elaborating'.[7]

Let us begin then by supposing that there *is* some poetic virtue in a refined sensibility – the 'more than usual organic sensibility' that Wordsworth postulated for the poet – and that there is some virtue in rendering such a sensibility in poems. At least that gives us the comfortable illusion that, having ourselves eyes and ears and nostrils and fingertips, we can judge how well Coleridge sees and hears and feels.

In looking through the early poems I am struck by the general absence of vivid sensory images until the *annus mirabilis* and the conversation poems. Coleridge's literary perception was subtle enough to catch, even at Christ's Hospital, a glimpse of his own poetic destiny in the bloodless languor of William Lisle Bowles's *Sonnets*, and while he was still at Cambridge to rejoice in 'an original poetic genius' as soon as he read Wordsworth's *Descriptive Sketches*. Here and there in the Bristol poems we catch occasionally a turn of phrase, a rhythm, a fragmentary inkling of the fine poems that were soon to come. But in the poems before 1796 it is clear – now that we have his best poems – what a long hard pull Coleridge had in verse against the rhetorical formality and sententiousness ingrained in his youth and reinforced by his precocious facility, his impetuous self-abandonment, his need for approval. Very little evidence of an exceptional sensibility breaks the opaque surface of a multifarious but received poetic manner until 'This Lime-Tree Bower'; and even there, in the first version of July 1797, the recommended coomb that was to achieve opulent specificity in *Sibylline Leaves* is a 'rifted dell' where he promises that 'ferny

rock' will be found, and 'plumy ferns'. The poeticising habit
encumbers much else, yet the poem opens with a stride that
presages the opening of 'Dejection: An Ode' –

> Well, they are gone, and here must I remain—

and whatever the tradition of his training it did not prevent him
from being faithful to eye, ear and nostrils in choosing words
which had not yet been canonised by poetic use.

> I watch'd
> The sunshine of each broad transparent Leaf
> Broke by the shadows of the Leaf or Stem,
> Which hung above it: and that Wall-nut Tree
> Was richly ting'd: and a deep radiance lay
> Full on the ancient ivy ...   (CL I 335)

The 'solitary humble-bee/Sings in the bean flower' and 'the last
Rook' that 'Beat it's straight path along the dusky air', 'Flew
creaking o'er your heads'. But altogether the evidence for an
exceptional sensibility is not overwhelming if it is sought in the
wording of the early poems – until the end of 1797 if not later.

The evidence of the notebooks is much less uncertain than the
poems, even though at the beginning, in the 'Gutch Memorandum Book', Coleridge often had the uses of poetry in the front
of his mind. He would sometimes record a sharp sensory flash in
epigrammatic form, or put it into a fine phrase for a poem not
yet written; and indeed several of these little scraps, circum-
veilloped in his mind no doubt with much that was not written
down in those early trenchant notes, did find their way into
poems. A sequence of entries, almost unbroken, written
apparently from late 1796 to perhaps September 1797, begins
with what appears to be material for the never-written poem
'The Brook' and end with a draft of a passage for 'The Nightingale'.

> The swallows interweaving there mid the paired
> Sea-mews, at distance wildly-wailing.—

> The brook runs over Sea-weeds.—

> Sabbath day – from the Miller's mossy wheel
> the waterdrops dripp'd leisurely—

On the broad mountain-top
The neighing wild-colt races with the wind
O'er fern & heath-flowers—

A long deep Lane
So overshadow'd, it might seem one bower –
The damp Clay banks were furr'd with mouldy moss

[Is this the coomb recommended for the walk in 'This Lime-tree Bower'?]

Broad-breasted Pollards with broad-branching head.

And one or two poor melancholy Joys
Pass by on flimsy wing in Hope's cold gleam,
Moths in the Moonlight.—

'Twas sweet to know it only possible –
Some *wishes* cross'd my mind & dimly cheer'd it –
And one or two poor melancholy Pleasures
In these, the pale unwarming light of Hope
Silvring their flimsy wing flew silent by,
Moths in the moonlight—

Behind the thin
Grey cloud that cover'd but not hid the sky
The round full moon look'd small.—

The subtle snow in every breeze rose curling from the Grove, like pillars of cottage smoke.

Hartley fell down & hurt himself – I caught him up crying & screaming – & ran out of doors with him – The Moon caught his eye – he ceased crying immediately – & his eyes & the tears in them, how they glittered in the Moonlight!

– Some wilderness-plot, green & fountainous & unviolated by Man.

The Infant playing with its mother's Shadow – Rocking its little sister's cradle & singing to her with inarticulate voice.—

> The flat pink-colour'd stone painted over in jagged circles
> & strange parallelograms with the greenish black-spotted
> lichens.—
>
> The Sun-shine lies on the cottage-wall
> Ashining thro' the snow –
>
> – The merry nightingale
> That crowds & hurries & precipitates
> With fast thick warble his delicious notes;
> As he were fearful, that an April Night
> Would be too short for him to utter forth
> His love-chant, and disburden his full soul
> Of all its music!—[8]

What happened to these fragments? In April 1798 the last
fragment made its way into 'The Nightingale' without a
syllable changed, and when he was writing the poem he was
able to extend even further his virtuoso rendering of the bird's
song.

> But never elsewhere in one place I knew
> So many nightingales; and far and near,
> In wood and thicket, over the wide grove,
> They answer and provoke each other's song,
> With skirmish and capricious passagings,
> And murmurs musical and swift jug jug,
> And one low piping sound more sweet than all –
> Stirring the air with such a harmony,
> That should you close your eyes, you might almost
> Forget it was not day!   (PW I 265–6)

The surprising detail of the nightingales sitting 'on moonlight
bushes' and their eyes glistening in the moonlight is not so
sharply rendered. Is that why it was omitted from *Lyrical
Ballads* (1800)? – yet it was later restored. And the poetical
version (in the same poem) of the baby Hartley silenced by the
moonlight shows how difficult it is to assimilate into poetry a
vivid record of heightened perception, how like a Deianeira's
shirt the singing robes can be.—

> and once, when he awoke
> In most distressful mood (some inward pain
> Had made up that strange thing, an infant's dream –)

I hurried with him to our orchard-plot,
And he beheld the moon, and, hushed at once,
Suspends his sobs, and laughs most silently,
While his fair eyes, that swam with undropped tears,
Did glitter in the yellow moon-beam!   (PW I 266)

That note turned up again in more sententious form in the
Conclusion to Part I of *Christabel* –

                    and tears she sheds –
            Large tears that leave the lashes bright!
            And oft the while she seems to smile
            As infants at a sudden light![9]

The 'Moths in the Moonlight' never found a home, but 'the
thin/Grey cloud that cover'd but not hid the sky' appears with
only slight change in the opening lines of *Christabel*. The
'wilderness-plot, green & fountainous & unviolated by Man' had
its origin – like other material interspersed through these entries
– in Bartram's *Travels* and feels like a glimpse of the mental
landscape that was to be realised in *Kubla Khan*.

One must admit that the hiatus between the actual perceptual
experience and the wording of it in a notebook jotting, and
between the notebook jotting (when it exists) and the rendering
of it in verse, are both of them unfathomable. These notebook
entries are presumably personal and trenchant mnemonics that
can evoke in the writer of them a far more complex and extended state of mind than the notes themselves delineate or
define; each note could indeed call back a whole event of experience. A poet can never get very far from words. As long as the
writer is concerned – as Coleridge evidently was in those months
– to embody his primary perceptual experience in verse, the
projection is consistently towards poetic rendering *in language*;
and in Coleridge's case, as we can see from the first versions of
'This Lime-Tree Bower' and 'Frost at Midnight', there could be
a wide gap between the acuity of his perceptions and a wording
subtle and flexible enough to catch the symbolic cutting edge of
the original perception. The miracles of 'Frost at Midnight' are
poetic miracles, not miracles of perception; here, perceptions so
merged and complex that they elude descriptive notation
have been transfigured into shapely words. That Coleridge's
sensibility was in fact, like Dorothy's, 'a perfect [goldleaf]

electrometer' there can be no question. His senses – all of them –
were exquisitely responsive, subtle, discriminating, and they induced joyous meditative activity. Even though (in the notebooks),
if we are to see in detail his full capacity for 'armed vision', we
have to wait for the records of the voyage to Hamburg, the Harz-
reise, and the several walks through the Lakes before leaving for
Malta, there are clear enough evidences of earlier date. Yet if
we look forward to the triumphs of perceptual rendering in his
poems – in *The Ancient Mariner* and *Kubla Khan*, with
Christabel in an intermediate position – here the perceptions are
often fictions, images transformed through the evocative written
witness of others and fused both with his own direct observations
and with the inward turning of his attention upon the very
substantial landscape of his own mind. And his mind, being a
poet's mind, is populated not simply with vivid perceptual fragments – perceptual raw material (so to speak), visual, auditory,
tactual, olfactory – but with the words and rhythms that body
forth the acts themselves of perceiving, and ideas and mental
events apprehended in what Whitehead would call the perceptual mode.

Looking back at Dorothy Wordsworth's journal we find no
discontinuity of manner, it seems; no tension between observing
and wording, but a grave, naïve, sustained musicality, perpetually sure-footed, tinged with a marvellous delicacy of feeling.

[1 Feb 1798]   About two hours before dinner, set forward
towards Mr Bartholomew's. The wind blew so keen in our
faces that we felt ourselves inclined to seek the covert of the
wood. There we had a warm shelter, gathered a burthen of
large rotten boughs blown down by the wind of the preceding
night. The sun shone clear, but all at once a heavy blackness
hung over the sea. The trees almost *roared*, and the ground
seemed in motion with the multitude of dancing leaves, which
made a rustling sound, distinct from that of the trees. Still
the asses pastured in quietness under the hollies, undisturbed
by these forerunners of the storm. The wind beat furiously
against us as we returned. Full moon. She rose in uncommon
majesty over the sea, slowly ascending through the clouds.
Sat with the window open an hour in the moonlight.

(DWJ 1 6)

To take Dorothy's writing as a naïve datum for sensory acuity is itself to adopt a naïve assumption: it leaves out of account her skill at writing. But at least it was spontaneous writing, for her eye and William's only, not intended for publication. If Coleridge's impulse towards verse in the early years prevented his perceptual notation in verse from reaching consistently the sensitive and muted instrumentation of Dorothy's journal, it was before long to take him much farther than she could go, simply because of his superior sense of language, his insistence that language can and must be taken where it had not been before, his conviction that whatever seized his attention in the outer world and held it imperiously was in a vivid sense – at times, in an ominous sense – a symbol in a language that he was on the verge of being able to interpret.[10]

The lichened stone noticed in the Gutch Memorandum Book is an instance. It falls into resonance with an even more curious stone which he found at the Oderteich in the Harz mountains in May 1799 – noted in a letter to his wife but not in his notebook.

> Here & else where we found large rocks of violet Stone which when rubbed or when the Sun shines strong on them, emit a scent which I could not [have] distinguished from violet. It is yellow-red in colou[r.]   (CL I 503)

In the *Biographia*, where he spoke of 'the perfect truth of nature in [Wordsworth's] images and descriptions as taken immediately from nature, and proving a long and genial intimacy with the very spirit which gives the physiognomic expression to all the works of nature', he remarked: 'Like the moisture or the polish on a pebble, genius neither distorts nor false-colours its objects; but on the contrary brings out many a vein and many a tint, which escapes the eye of common observation, thus raising to the rank of gems, what had been often kicked away by the hurrying foot of the traveller on the dusty high road of custom.'[11] It turns up again many years later in a grimly jocular letter about the conflict between the Mind and Nature in youth and age. 'For a while the Mind seems to have the better in the contest, and makes of Nature what it likes; takes her Lichens and Weather-stains for Types & Printer's Ink and prints Maps & Fac Similes of Arabic and Sanscrit Mss. on her rocks.'[12]

To take another instance. In January 1802 Coleridge wrote to Godwin:

> Partly from ill-health, & partly from an unhealthy & reverie like vividness of *Thoughts*, & (pardon the pedantry of the phrase) a diminished Impressibility from *Things*, my ideas, wishes, & feelings are to a diseased degree disconnected from *motion* & *action*. In plain & natural English, I am a dreaming & therefore an indolent man − . I am a Starling self-incaged, & always in the Moult, & my whole Note is, Tomorrow, & tomorrow, & tomorrow.   (CL II 782)

This might call to mind the many occasions, later, when he was to see himself in the emblem of a bird encaged, bird-limed, moulting, even self-encaged; and in that setting the word 'starling' might recall the passage in the *Inferno* (V 40–98) where the movement of the carnal sinners is described in the figure of a flight of starlings. But, whether or not Coleridge knew and remembered the Dante passage, the germ of his use of the word *starling* here is an actual observation made as he approached London by coach at dawn on 27 November 1799.

> Awoke from the uneasy Doze-dream of the Coach/ a rich orange sky like that of a winter Evening save that the fleecy dark Blue that rippled above showed it to be morning/ − soon became a glowing Brass colour, fleeces of Brass like sand − convolves high up in to the Sky − the Sun rose o'er the plain like a Kite/ rose wholly, & a column in the waters, and soon after, a Hill meeting with it, rose thro' other clouds − with a different Glory − Starlings—

> Starlings in vast flights drove along like smoke, mist, or any thing misty [without] volition − now a circular area inclined [in an] arc − now a globe − [now from a complete orb into an] elipse & oblong − [now] a balloon with the [car suspend]ed, now a concaved [sem]icircle & [still] it expands & condenses, some [moments] glimmering & shivering, dim & shadowy, now thickening, deepening, blackening!—
>   (CN I 581, 582)

In October 1803 he included this among a series of observations entitled 'Images', and reworked it a little − the flight was 'like a

body unindued with voluntary Power', and he revised the closing phrase to read: 'still expanding, or contracting, thinning or
condensing, now glimmering and shivering, now thickening,
deepening, blackening!'[13] But he had already used the image of
the starlings in telling Sara Hutchinson of a hazardous because
uncircumspect descent from Sca Fell on 5 August 1802. He was
in the situation that all rock-climbers have experienced at some
time or another; he was committed to going down, the slightest
slip would mean death, and his 'limbs were all in a tremble'
from exertion. He was able to stop on a ledge and lay on his
back to rest, looking up at the crags he had come down, at the
rapidly moving clouds, laughed at himself 'for a Madman', and
'lay in a state of almost prophetic Trance and Delight and
blessed God aloud for the powers of Reason and the Will, which
remaining no Danger can overpower us!' 'If this Reality were
a Dream,' he said to himself, 'if I were asleep, what agonies had
I suffered! what screams!

> When the Reason and the Will are away, what remain to us
> but Darkness and Dimness and a bewildering Shame, and Pain
> that is utterly Lord over us, or fantastic Pleasure that draws
> the Soul along swimming through the air in many shapes,
> even as a Flight of Starlings in a wind.—　　　(IS 235–6)

Dwelling for a little in the memory, the image of coherent
indirection had found the body it was looking for. At a certain
point it ceases to describe; it defines and affirms the 'aimless
activity and unregulated accumulation' of the heuristic mind,[14]
as in December 1803 in a fragment of verse that bears the context of the initial imprinting, yet never found a home for itself.

> My Spirit with a fixed yet leisurely gaze
> Following its ever yet quietly changing Clusters of Thoughts,
> As the outward Eye of a happy Traveller a flock of Starlings.
> 　　　　　　　　　　　　　　(CN I 1779)

'How doth the old instinct bring back the old names.' The
invocation is sometimes in thematic and verbal echoes as from
The Ancient Mariner to 'Dejection', when the Mariner's crisis
of grace is transformed into a crisis of sensibility. Sometimes it
appears in the reiteration of a rhythmic pattern, a syntax turned
liturgical in catching the anguish of regret.

> Alas! they had been friends in youth;
> But whispering tongues can poison truth;
> And constancy lives in realms above;
> And life is thorny; and youth is vain;
> And to be wroth with one we love
> Doth work like madness in the brain.   (PW I 229)

This ritual tread, greatly varied and intrinsicated – distantly echoing, it may be, a similar ravelling-out in 'Tintern Abbey' – returns in the poem 'To William Wordsworth'.

> Ah! as I listened with a heart forlorn,
> The pulses of my being beat anew:
> And even as Life returns upon the drowned,
> Life's joys rekindling roused a throng of pains –
> Keen pangs of Love, awakening as a babe
> Turbulent, with an outcry in the heart;
> And fears self-willed, that shunned the eye of Hope;
> And Hope that scarce would know itself from Fear;
> Sense of past Youth, and Manhood come in vain,
> And Genius given, and Knowledge won in vain;
> And all which I had culled in wood-walks wild,
> And all which patient toil had reared, and all,
> Commune with thee had opened out – but flowers
> Strewed on my corse, and borne upon my bier,
> In the same coffin, for the self-same grave!
>
>   (PW I 407)

The fascination with birds that singled out the flight of starlings and earlier in Bristol had induced him to set down (from the not very reliable authority of Theophrastus at second remove by way of *Nicholson's Journal*) 'Prognostics of the Weather from the Flight of Birds', played its part in the composition of 'The Nightingale'; and it was the poet's eye – an instant apprehension of possibilities dropping into a void that hungered to be filled – that recognised at a glance the albatross he needed for *The Ancient Mariner* when Wordsworth reported it from Shelvocke's *Voyage round the World*. The nightingales that haunted the Quantocks of his youth, and were to delight him and trouble his sleep in Highgate in advanced age – these he was to catch up in a vivid but not conventionally 'poetic' record of a May evening in Göttingen when he was a student there.

The nightingales in a ⟨cluster or little wood of⟩ blossomed Trees singing – and a bat wheeling incessantly round & round. – The noise of the Frogs not unpleasant – resemble the humming of spinning wheels in a large manufactury, now & then a distinct sound, sometimes like a Duck, & sometimes like the shrill note of Sea-fowls.—   (CN I 421)

And when, in Highgate, at 10 o'clock on Wednesday morning, 10 September 1823, he set down the first tentative draft of 'Youth and Age' it was the tune of the verse that haunted him, a tune still to be given body; the haunting calls back the nightingales and the Quantocks, and the exuberant delight he had surely felt in rendering the bird's song in 'The Nightingale'; and the way he locates the source of the skylark's song has the same excruciating tactual specificity as Keats's tracing of a bird's flight at the close of his 'Ode to a Nightingale'.

An *Air* that whizzed δια ἐγκεφάλου (right across the diameter of my Brain) exactly like a Hummel Bee, *alias* Dumbeldore, the gentleman with Rappee Spenser, with bands of Red, and Orange Plush Breeches, close by my ear, at once sharp and burry, right over the summit of Quantock at earliest Dawn just between the Nightingale that I stopt to hear in the Copse at the Foot of Quantock, and the first Sky-Lark that was a Song-Fountain, dashing up and sparkling to the Ear's eye, in full column, or ornamented Shaft of sound in the order of Gothic Extravaganza, out of Sight, over the Cornfields on the Descent of the Mountain on the other side – out of sight, tho' twice I beheld its *mute* shoot downward in the sunshine like a falling star of silver:

And the "*Air*" begins –

> Flowers are lovely, Love is flower-like,
> Friendship is a shelt'ring tree –

                                        (PW II 1084–5)

Like Gerard Manley Hopkins impelled to compose *The Wreck of the Deutschland*,[15] Coleridge was haunted by an 'Air', a tune. He was no trained musician, but his ear was good enough to choose for him as favourite composers Purcell, Cimarosa, Mozart, Handel, Beethoven. And although his power of visual observation was refined and acute, one cannot reckon it superior to his auditory sense, whether in the shaping of a cadence in words or in recording with the most exact refinement particularities of sound.

> In the Lawn by the Wilderness of Rocks an Oak bush with oblong carrotty Leaves – heard as I came near it, a noise like a spinning wheel or grasshopper – observed one leaf in brisk motion, from whence this noise proceeded – only one of all the bush – thought it must be some bird, woodpecker pecking, but no! – this one Leaf was by the bending of its sides a complete scollop shell, & so placed as to catch the wind – hence the upheaval. (CN 1 856)

In many parts of *The Ancient Mariner*, and particularly in *Kubla Khan*, the appeal is not to any one sense but to an inter-inanimation of all the senses combined into a tactual impression of great power – a condition that psychologists call synaesthesia. This may well be a prime characteristic of all poetic perception, of the poetic sense of language, and perhaps of all our refined and developed sensory experience. Synaesthesia is a state, not a process; it is not what David Hartley popularised as 'Association of Ideas'. But a remarkable instance of Coleridge's sustained process of association shows how much it is like the dreaming in which we construct for an intrusive physical sensation a compelling rationale in the form of images or words – a mental process intrinsic to poetry altogether.

> [10 Mar 1810]   I had been talking of the association of Ideas, and endeavoring to convince an Idolator of Hume & Hartley, that this was strictly speaking a law only of the memory & imagination, of the *Stuff out* of which we make our conceptions & perceptions, not of the thinking faculty, by which we make them – that it was as the force of gravitation to leaping to any given point – without gravitation this would be impossible, and yet equally impossible to leap except by a *power* counteracting first, and then using the *force* of gravitation.... And yet to shew him that I was neither ignorant, nor idle in observing, the vast extent and multifold activity of the *Associative Force* I entered into a curious and tho fanciful yet strictly true and actual, exemplification. Many of my Instances recalled to my mind my little poem on *Lewti*,

the Circassian (and as by this same force joined with the assent of the will most often, tho' often too vainly because weakly opposed by it, I inevitably by some link or other return to you, or (say rather) bring some fuel of thought to the ceaseless Yearning for you at my Inmost, which like a steady fire attracts constantly the air which constantly feeds it) I began strictly and as matter of fact to examine that subtle Vulcanian Spider-web Net of Steel – strong as Steel yet subtle as the Ether, in which my soul flutters inclosed with the Idea of your's – to pass rapidly as in a catalogue thro' the Images only, exclusive of the thousand Thoughts that possess the same force, which never fail instantly to awake into vivider flame the for ever and ever Feeling of you/ – The fire/ Mary, you, and I at Gallow-Hill/ – or if flamy, reflected in children's round faces – ah whose children? – a dog – that dog whose restless eyes oft catching the light of the fire used to watch your face, as you leaned with your head on your hand and arm, & your feet on the *fender*/ the fender thence/ – Fowls at Table – the last dinner at Gallow Hill, when you drest the two fowls in that delicious white Sauce which when very ill is the only idea of food that does not make me *sicker*/ all natural Scenery – ten thousand links, and if it please me, the very spasm & drawing-back of a pleasure which is half-pain, you not being there – Cheese – at Middleham, too salt/ horses, my ride to Scarborough – asses, to that large living 2 or 3 miles from Middleham/ All Books – my Study at Keswick/ – the Ceiling or Head of a Bed – the green watered Mazarine! – a Candle in its socket, with its alternate fits & dying flashes of lingering Light – O *God! O God!* – Books of abstruse Know-ledge – the Thomas Aquinas & Suarez from the Durham Library/ – a peony faced cottage Girl – little Jane/ all articles of female dress – music – the opening of a Street door – when you first came to Keswick – ... Letters, year, the very paper on which one might be written – or from the habit of half unconsciously writing your name or its Symbol invented by me to express it – all Travels/ my yearning Absence/ all books of natural History – ... the Heavens/ your name in those bright Stars, or an M or W recalling those Stars – Aurora borealis – at Keswick by the corner parlour window/ ... any eye fixed kindly on me when I am talking—. . .[16]

This is an exceptionally sustained instance, not a special instance; it is the heart of the matter at a curious, even unique, pitch. Here the individual sharply apprehended images intrinsicate and resolve, each bearing no less physically than the sensory detail itself the imprint of distinct and complex feeling; they dispose themselves in a psychic matrix as inscrutable in the mind as the symbolic language that alphabets the sky. This notebook entry is not in any accepted sense a poem, or even a poem in the making; it is 'The *Stuff* out of which we make our conceptions & perceptions', a lucid delineation of the activity of mind that produced it, its tracings as abstract as glass, its momentum ineluctable. All Coleridge's major poems, and most of his prose, bear witness to this process of the definitive self-exposition of the mind. 'What is a Thought but another word for "I-thinking"?' he asked in a marginal note.[17] Yet, of 'the greater & perhaps nobler certainly all the subtler parts of one's nature' he could say: 'how much lies *below* his own Consciousness.'[18]

What we thought we were at first looking for was instances of poetic sensibility – the picking out, isolating, giving identity to, and rendering into words moments of heightened sensibility that could be tested for reliability because of the identifiable natural objects, sources of impressions, or remembered images at the heart of them. But recognition of a more complex process has supervened; we were obliged to notice a certain enriching and cumulative activity in the personal history of particular images that – by extension into time, as it were – provided the intensity of epiphany. In short, that the more intensely perceived the image – and with that intensity the stronger and more complex the feeling – the more the rendering of the intense image became not so much a symbol *of* something as a generative symbol acting as its own expository definition. Eventually Coleridge was to say in the *Statesman's Manual* – at the very time that he almost stopped saying anything much in public about poetry – that 'a symbol [which is always self-declarative] ... always partakes of the reality which it renders intelligible; and while it enunciates the whole, abides itself as a living part in that unity of which it is the representative.'* Symbols, then, are neither

* *Statesman's Manual* in LS 30. The rendering of Coleridge's parenthetic phrase, ὅ ἐστιν ἀεὶ ταυτηγόρικον, is mine, White correctly,

distinguishable items nor conventional marks in a denotative system, but centres rather of finely disposed shaping energy that command a wider or narrower field of poetic activity. By partaking of the reality that they render intelligible they are patient of very detailed analogical exploration – as the image of the flight of starlings is – and this is the delight and duty of critical inquiry. Yet they transcend the abstract parallelism of analogy because they are active in a field where the centrifugal force of recognition is opposed by the centripetal activity of evocation or 'association'; and this in itself ensures that inter-pretation will normally be peripheral to critical inquiry. It is better to ask of a symbolic event, not 'What does it mean?' but 'What is it doing?' We expect (if our poetic experience has any depth) that a symbol will not be single but manifold – that its true simplicity will disclose an astonishing complexity. It is in symbolic process that the *data* of perception (if there are such things) are transformed into the *données* of poems.

Images achieve symbolic character only under certain condi-tions. Acute observation is not in itself enough, partly because the observation has to be worded in order to become poetry at all, partly because a peculiar interinanimation of the senses is needed to achieve the functional richness and power that invests symbolic events. Coleridge had noticed this as early as September 1801, as can be seen in a much-obliterated analysis of his wife's coldness.

> ... The cant phrase, 'tangible sensation' – which ought to be tactual – is not a mere moment of sensation – but it is the blending & unifying of the sensations that inhere in the mani-fold goings on of the Life of the whole man. ... All appetites that do not diffuse themselves & evidence their existence in

---

and for the first time, explains that Coleridge has coined the word *tautegorical* in order to mark a distinction from *allegorical*, and so translates the phrase 'which is always tautegorical'. But that only puts into condensed form (by transliterating the Greek version of an English word coined from Greek roots) what Coleridge then says by way of a gloss on ταυτηγόρικον – that a symbol 'partakes of the reality which it renders intelligible'. In order to break this circular definition, and to emphasise the importance of not representing a poetic symbol as patient of allegorical interpretation, I have used a phrase that looks forward to the passage from CN III 4397 quoted on p. 24 below.

all diversities of gradation & combination, have no effect on
the *Tactual* – Why? they are always *local* in the body itself –
an object of sight or visual idea – not to mention the immedi-
ateness of their application to some distinct separate, visible
part of some other Body external to theirs.   (CN I 979)

Much later, in the *Biographia Literaria*, he was to say that

Images, however beautiful, though faithfully copied from
nature ... do not of themselves characterize the poet. They
become proofs of original genius only as far as they are modified by a predominant passion ... or when they have the
effect of reducing multitude to unity ... or when a human
and intellectual life is transferred to them from the poet's
own spirit.   (BL II 16)

If there is one word – one *sensory* word – by which Coleridge
tends to identify that transformation, either in the poet or in
the reader, it is the word *tact* – the sense of touch.

... a great Poet must be, implicitè if not explicitè, a profound Metaphysician. He may not have it in logical coherence,
in his Brain & Tongue; but he must have it by *Tact*/ for all
sounds, & forms of human nature he must have the *ear* of a
wild Arab listening in the silent Desart, the eye of a North
American Indian tracing the footsteps of an Enemy upon the
Leaves that strew the Forest—; the *Touch* of a Blind Man
feeling the face of a darling Child—   (CL II 810)

Fortunately we can to some extent watch the actual process
of symbolising through the records of the notebooks – the
cumulative patterns of sensory impressions, the flux and reflux
of feeling, the thinking that occurs when 'a succession of perceptions [is] accompanied by a sense of *nisus* & purpose',[19] the
thinking that is held firmly in the perceptual mode, 'the images
of Memory flowing in on the impulses of immediate Impression'[20]
in progressive emotional enrichment and definition, as clarity
of apprehension gathers impressions into a luminous focus. The
following notebook entries are taken in sequence (with omission
of other matter intervening) from 25 October to 2 November
1803, in those last days of restless and dismayed waiting at
Greta Hall before he set off for the Mediterranean. Here can be

clearly seen the distinction too often ignored in considerations of perception and sensibility – the shift from seeing and hearing to gazing and listening.

(*a*)   The moon setting over the Mountain pale – the Sky very dim & marbled or water stained as blue Ma[za]rine Canopy – and in the blue Interspaces the Stars all dim & lustreless ⟨& until I looked steadily at them, *one* only of all the Stars *twinkled.*⟩ – the Water between me & it, & the few House-roofs are bright. The water is the only Sound/ the Moon is more than a half moon/ it sank to a rude [half-disc] – then to a crescent, its bow stiffly & imperfect & still keeping this shape, thinned & thinned & thinned, till *once* it became a star, at its vanishing – but immediately after sent up a *throb* of Light in its former Shape & dimension – & so for several Seconds it throbbed & heaved, a soft Boiling up or restlessness of a Fluid in carrying – / and now all is alike thro' the vale, the vast Ellipse of mountain suffused with dim Hoariness, & the Sky where white & where blue, still dim are both/ save only that the whole range of mountains behind which the Moon sate, from Bonitas under Grisedale Pile to Rowling End under Causey Pike are blacker & more definite than all the rest, the white Clouds stains, or Cloud–Inlays, brighter, the blue more genuinely blue. Tuesday Midnight – it wants 15 minutes of One o'clock. Oct. 25.   (CN I 1614)

(*b*)   Thursday Morning, 40 minutes past One o'clock – a perfect calm – now & then a breeze shakes the heads of the two Poplars, ⟨& disturbs⟩ the murmur of the moonlight Greta, that in almost a direct Line from the moon to me is all silver – Motion and Wrinkle & Light – & under the arch of the Bridge a wave ever & anon leaps up in Light. – & the evergreens are bright, under my window/. The Moon now hangs midway over Cowdale Halse – in a line, & resting on each of the divergent Legs of its Triangle a fish-head-shaped Cloud – the whole area of the Triangle blue Sky – but above the cloud, & ⟨in⟩ the interspaces between it and the Moon little cloudlets, scarcely larger than large Stars – Wrinkles/ – long roundish floating Braids of Hair floating & making its single Hairs distinguishable as it wantons on some regular Breeze/ ... black smooth Space of Shade – silver mirror/

gleaming of moonlight Reeds beyond – as the moon sets the water from Silver becomes a rich yellow. – Sadly do I need to have my Imagination enriched with appropriate Images for Shapes – / Read Architecture, & Ichthyology—

(CN I 1616)

(At a quarter past two he watched the moon set – 'so barred & cross-barred, over its whole face, as I never before saw – '. At three he was 'not yet asleep' and thought a little about Hartley's education; and went over at some length 'A most unpleasant Dispute with W. & Hazlitt' that had occurred that afternoon; then added: 'This is the Day, quo primum illam vidi! [when I first saw her]! – Let me try for a Song.' But he did not achieve a song; and at forty minutes past three he wrote after a long reflection on the source of vice and misery in the world:)

(c)   . . . the Sky covered with one Cloud, that yet lies in dark & light Shades, & tho' one smooth Cloud, by the Dark Colour it appears to be *steppy*. – A sad night – went to bed after Tea – & in about 2 hours absolutely summoned the whole Household to me by my Screams, from all the chambers – & I continued screaming even after Mrs. Coleridge was sitting & speaking to me! – O me! O me!—   (CN I 1619)

(d)   Sat. Morn. Oct. 29. 1803. Three o'clock. The Moon hangs high over Greta, & the Bridge, on the first step of her Descent, & three hours at least from the Mountains, behind which she is to sink: nearly full – not a Cloud in Heaven, the Sky deep sable blue, the Stars many & white in the height of the Sky, but above, around, & beneath the Moon, not a Star; she is starless as the Sun. Yet there is no gleam, much less silver whiteness, on the Lake: simply it is easily seen; & even the Greta stretching strait in an oblique line underneath is not ⟨silver⟩–bright, or any where brilliant; but rather the gleam of some baser Composition imitating Silver, it is a grey brightness like the colour of an ash grove in keenest December Moonlight. The Mountains are dark, low, all compact together, quiet, silent, asleep – the white Houses are bright throughout the vale, & the evergreens in the garden. The only Sound is the murmur of the Greta, perpetual Voice of the Vale—   (CN I 1624) (*e*) Oct. 31. 1803. The full moon glided behind a black cloud/ & what then? & who cared? – It was past 7 °clock in the morning – There is a small Cloud in the East, not larger than the Moon, & ten times brighter than she! So passes Night & all her favors vanish in our minds, ungrateful!—

(CN I 1625)

(*f*) Wednesday Morning, 20 minutes past 2 °clock. November 2nd, 1803. The Voice of the Greta, and the Cock-crowing: the Voice seems to grow, like a Flower on or about the water beyond the Bridge, while the Cock crowing is nowhere particular, it is at any place I imagine & do not distinctly see. A most remarkable Sky! The Moon, now waned to a perfect Ostrich's Eggs, hangs over our House almost – only so much beyond it, garden-ward, that I can see it, holding my Head out of the smaller Study window. The Sky is covered with whitish, & with dingy *Cloudage*, thin dingiest Scud close under the moon & one side of it moving, all else moveless: but there are two great Breaks of Blue Sky – the one stretching over our House, & away toward Castlerigg, & this is speckled & blotched with white Cloud – the other hangs over the road, in the line of the Road in the shape of a . . . I do not know what to call [it] . . . this is unspeckled, all blue – 3 Stars in it/ more in the former Break – all unmoving. The water leaden white, even as the grey gleam of Water is in latest Twilight. – Now while I have been writing this & gazing between whiles (it is 40 M. past Two) the Break over the road is swallowed up, & the Stars gone, the Break over the House is narrowed into a rude Circle, & on the edge of its circumference one very bright Star – see! already the white mass thinning at its edge fights with its Brilliance – see! it has bedimmed it – & now it is gone – & the Moon is gone. The Cock-crowing too has ceased. The Greta sounds on, for ever. But I hear only the Ticking of my Watch, in the Pen-place of my Writing Desk, & the far lower note of the noise of the Fire – perpetual, yet seeming uncertain/ it is the low voice of quiet change, of Destruction doing its work by little & little.   (CN I 1635)

Coleridge was ten days past his thirty-first birthday when he wrote that last entry. Although many poems were still to be written and published, and many drafted and abandoned, there

were to be no more poems that could encompass such material
as this. Where did it go, the gradual gathering and concentrating
of power closing on the commanding rhythms of that last entry?
Unlike the distinct figures of the lichened stone and the flight
of starlings, nowhere identifiable – unless we could believe that
that last note did later inform the Moon-gloss to *The Ancient
Mariner*. When the Mariner was at the crisis of his desolation,
and for seven days and nights had seen the curse of the dead
men's eyes yet could not die, the poem reads:

> The moving Moon went up the sky,
> And no where did abide:
> Softly she was going up,
> And a star or two beside—

At this place in *Sibylline Leaves* Coleridge caused to be printed
in the margin these words:

> In his loneliness and fixedness he yearneth towards the
> journeying Moon, and the stars that still sojourn, yet still
> move onward; and every where the blue sky belongs to them,
> and is their appointed rest, and their native country and their
> own natural homes, which they enter unannounced, as lords
> that are certainly expected and yet there is a silent joy at
> their arrival.   (PW I 197)

In the *Biographia Literaria* Coleridge asserted that when
things and selves are 'not only coherent but identical, and one
and the same thing with our own immediate self-consciousness'
we discover 'the truest and most binding realism'.[21] As for
Coleridge's 'true and original realism', the dynamic philosophy
that he evolved from the starting-point of his own intense
experience of making poems, persons more learned and more
subtle than I will no doubt be unfolding in its metaphysical,
psychological and theological implications later in this series of
lectures. My argument so far has sought to make only three
points: (*a*) that the evidence for the quality of a poet's sensibility is to be seen in his specific wording of it; (*b*) that
the records of a poet's sensibility, particularly when given
final articulation, evince a complexity of 'poetic perception'
that assails the mechanistic (or behavioural) view that perception is simply an upper order of 'sensation'; and (*c*) that

fully articulated poems force us to consider perception as a
shaping, unifying, energetic process; in short, that the poet's
'more than usual organic sensibility' – and peculiarly Coleridge's – is indeed a *poetic*, a *poietic*, *making* activity of
mind that flows seamlessly from perception if it is instantly being
worded in rhythmic and sonic forms, complex, subtle and stable
enough. One of Coleridge's axioms for imagination is thoroughly
Aristotelian – *nihil in intellectu quod non prius in sensu*. Another
set of axioms for the relation between the whole and parts in
poetry is no less Aristotelian: the whole is logically prior to the
parts, the whole inheres in every part, a poem is unity in multeity. At a single stroke, in discussing Milton's use of the word
'sensuous' in the account of poetry as 'simple, sensuous, and
passionate', Coleridge identified perception with the ineradicable
human *nisus* of poetry.

> . . . sensuousness insures that framework of objectivity, that
> definiteness and articulation of imagery, and that modification
> of the images themselves, without which poetry becomes
> flattened into mere didactic practice or evaporates into a hazy,
> unthoughtful, day-dreaming; and . . . passion provides that
> neither thought nor imagery shall be simply objective, but
> that the *passio vera* of humanity shall warm and animate
> both.*

Coleridge's understanding of these matters, however, goes far
beyond a gnomic declaration of them.

The sensitive faculty is the power of being affected and modified by *Things*, so as to receive impressions from them. The
Quality of these Impressions is determined partly by the
nature of the sensitive faculty itself and its organs, and partly
by the nature of the Things. These impressions are in the first
instant *immediate Sensations*: as soon as the *attention* is
directed to them, and they are taken up into the *Consciousness*, they become *Perceptions*. The repetition of past Perceptions in the Consciousness is Imagination. The Object of the
Attention *during* Perception may be aptly termed a *Presentation*, during Imagination a Representation. All Sensations

---

* Sh C I 149. The original manuscript from which H. N. Coleridge
took this observation has not been identified.

and their correspondent Objects have doubtless something in common; but it is impossible to abstract it, that is, to discover what that is in Sensation ⟨in general⟩ which causes it to produce perception, or what it is in any given sensation which causes it to produce a certain particular perception. Equally impossible is it with regard to the Objects of past or present perception – i.e. the presentations or representations of Things, to distinguish by determinate boundaries, what part proceeds from the sensitive faculty itself, and what from the outward Causes or the Things acting on the faculty.... The cause of this impossibility is that we become conscious both of the one and of the other in one & the same way; namely, as modifications of our own Being. What precedes the modification as its cause, we can never know; because our consciousness originates in the modification.   (CN III 3065)

A marginal note written in Schelling's *Darlegung der wahren Verhältnisse der Naturphilosophie zu der verbesserte Fichte'schen Lehre* was carefully considered and seriously intended: 'All that I read refers me to this desideratum of a Critique on *Perception*. Idealism & Materialism both are ground[ed] on the assertion, that Perception is but the affection in modification.'

In dealing with such matters in the field of poetry 'perhaps the greatest obstacle to the apprehension ... arises in the tendency to look abroad, *out* of the thing in question, in order by means of some *other* thing analogous to understand the former. But this is impossible – for the thing in question *is* the act, we are describing – '[22] And of poetry altogether Coleridge was to say:

Man communicates by articulation of Sounds, and paramountly by the memory in the Ear – ... the Artist must first *eloign* himself from Nature ... he must out of his own mind create forms according to the several Laws of the Intellect, in order to produce in himself that co-ordination of Freedom & Law, that involution of the Obedience in the Prescript, and of the Prescript in the impulse to obey, which assimilates him to Nature – enables him to understand her – ... Each thing, that lives, has its moment of *self-exposition*, and *each* period of each thing – if we remove the disturbing forces of accident – and this is the business of ideal Art.   (CN III 4397)

Coleridge knew well how we can be repaid 'by linking our sweetest but of themselves perishable feelings to distinct & vivid Images, which we ourselves at times & which a thousand casual associations will often recall to our memory.'[23] He spoke from his own experience when he made note that when 'Speaking of the original unific Consciousness, the primary Perception, & its extreme difficulty' he would 'take occasion to draw a lively picture of the energies, self-denials, sacrifices, toils, trembling knees, & sweat-drops on the Brow, of a philosopher who has really been sounding the depths of our being – & to compare it with the greatest & most perseverant Labors of Travellers, Soldiers, and whomever else Men honor & admire – how trifling the latter!'[24] Thinking 'what ample materials exist for a true & nobly-minded Psychologist' in tracing the various stages of self-deception, he added: 'for in order to make fit use of these materials he must love and honor, as well as understand, human nature – rather, he must love in order to understand it.'[25]

In his recently published *Introduction to 'The Rime of the Ancient Mariner'* David Jones says that 'Sensitivity, that first and absolute requirement without which nothing whatever [in art] can be accomplished, is in itself a kind of exactitude'.[26] Few men would be better entitled to make such a statement than David Jones – or Coleridge. My last instance of Coleridge's exactitude shows the tension between the actual and the reality of the imagined in the field of poetic perception. In the 1809–10 *Friend* Coleridge published some of the letters he had written home from Germany in 1798–99 under the title of 'Satyrane's Letters'. In the first letter, written some months after completing *The Ancient Mariner*, he gave a detailed account of the voyage from Yarmouth to Hamburg including this detail:

The Ocean is a noble Thing by night; a beautiful white cloud of foam at momently intervals roars & rushes by the side of the Vessel, and Stars of Flame dance & sparkle & go out in it – & every now and then light Detachments of Foam dart away from the Vessel's side with their galaxies of stars, & scour out of sight, like a Tartar Troop over a Wilderness! – What these Stars are, I cannot say – the sailors say that they are Fish Spawn which is phosphorescent.—[27]

This was the first time the author of *The Ancient Mariner* had ever been to sea. Once the giddiness had passed – for it was a rough passage – he suffered 'a feverish Inappetence of Food' (from the stink of the bilge-water, he thought), but he had his eyes very much about him. He had not expected to encounter in the waters of the cold North Sea a phenomenon that he would have thought occurred only in the tropics; he noted it with absorbed interest. He also noticed exactly how the wake looked from the deck and in 1815 was to alter the line 'The furrow followed free' to 'The furrow stream'd off free' with the note:

> ...I had not been long on board a ship, before I perceived that this was the image as seen by a spectator from the shore, or from another vessel. From the ship itself, the W*ake* appears like a brook flowing off from the stern.*

Thereafter his ear got the better of verisimilitude; he restored the original version. The passage of particular interest to us, however, is in the account of the first afternoon at sea.

> At four o'clock I observed a Wild Duck swimming on the waves, a single solitary wild duck. It is not easy to conceive, how interesting a Thing it looked in that round objectless Desart of Waters. ⟨I had associated such a feeling of immensity with the Ocean, that I felt exceedingly disappointed, when I was out of sight of all land, at the narrowness and *nearness*, as it were, of the circle of the Horizon. So little are images capable of satisfying the obscure feelings connected with words.⟩   (*Friend* II 193)

The last two sentences, about the nearness and narrowness of the horizon, do not appear in the original letter, nor in the briefer journal in the *Notebooks*. When did he actually first notice the peculiar sensation that sailors know well, of the

---

* PW I 190n. In 1799, in the second volume of the new *Naval Chronicle* – a periodical that was to receive original contributions from Nelson, Collingwood, and a succession of notable naval commanders – *The Ancient Mariner* was enthusiastically reviewed and a substantial part of the poem reprinted. In the preface to that volume the editor identified the anonymous author of the poem as Coleridge and 'particularly recommend[ed]' the poem 'to our professional Correspondents'. Presumably Coleridge's seafaring contemporaries found no nautical solecisms in the poem.

nearness of the horizon – from the deck of a ship perhaps no more than seven or eight miles away, or less; the sense of standing not at the centre of a limitless expanse of water but rather of being inside the rim of a shallow saucer, the sea a hollow that curves upward to the horizon? Was it on that first voyage to Hamburg, or on the voyage to Malta six years later, that Coleridge first noticed this? Considering the accuracy of his emotional recall, the chances are that it was on the voyage to Hamburg and that that is why, when it found its way into print on the earliest possible occasion, it appeared in 'Satyrane's Letters'. Is it possible that, if *The Rime of the Ancient Mariner* had been written from actual experience of seafaring rather than out of a fragmentary but glowing imaginative construct from undesignedly absorbed written accounts, the poem would not have conveyed to us as it does the immensity, the infinitude of the ocean? – 'We were the first that ever burst/Into that silent sea' and 'Alone, alone, all, all alone,/Alone on a wide wide sea!'? Can the mind know sometimes better than the eye? Surely these phrases, however achieved, strike us with the frisson of a primordial recognition.

Questions about poetic sensibility, then, are not to be answered simply by an appeal to matter-of-factness or 'truth to nature'; at least, not as far as Coleridge is concerned, and scrupulous modern Coleridge scholarship endorses this. The appeal is rather to 'the truth *of* nature' – his phrase in the *Biographia*. For Coleridge was acutely aware of the dynamic nature of perception and of thinking; of how the eye is reinforced '& supported by the images of Memory flowing in on the impulses of immediate Impression –'* He spoke of 'a succession of perceptions accompanied by a sense of *nisus* & purpose'.[28] Intellectual effort, flowing in upon perception, or in philosophical quest even, had for him the quality of yearning – πόθος – sexual longing; and

> Sometimes when I earnestly look at a beautiful Object or Landscape, it seems as if I were on the *brink* of a Fruition still denied – as if Vision were an *appetite*: even as a man would feel, who having put forth all his muscular strength in an act

* CN I 1648. The last part of the phrase translates a phrase of Wolff's noted in CN I 905 two and a half years earlier.

of prosilience, is at that very moment *held back* – he leaps &
yet moves not from his place.   (CN III 3767)

Out of such recognitions his conviction grew that 'Extremes
meet', and the grounds of his whole dynamic philosophy. When
he gave his Philosophical Lectures in 1818–19 he conceived of
the history of philosophy as 'an essential part of the history of
man, and as if it were the striving of a single mind'.[29] In *The
Theory of Life* he was to maintain that 'the power of sensibility'
at its highest level of development achieves in man 'the highest
realization and reconciliation of both her tendencies, that of the
most perfect detachment with the greatest possible union. . . . In
social and political life this acme is inter-dependence; in moral
life it is independence; in intellectual life it is genius.[30]

In *The Friend* of 23 November 1809, Coleridge offered an
engaging and detailed, if thinly disguised, self-portrait under the
name of Satyrane. Satyrane, made 'pensive and gloomy' by
disappointment at 'the state of morals and intellect of his contemporaries', 'as if he sought a refuge from his own sensibility,
. . . attached himself to the most abstruse researches, and seemed
to derive his purest delight from subjects that exercised the
strength and subtlety of his understanding without awakening
the feelings of his heart'.[31] This echoes back to 'Dejection: An
Ode' and April 1802.

> For not to think of what I needs must feel,
>   But to be still and patient, all I can;
> And haply by abstruse research to steal
>   From my own nature all the natural man –
>   This was my sole resource, my only plan:
> Till that which suits a part infects the whole,
> And now is almost grown the habit of my soul.
>
> (PW I 367)

The Satyrane portrait was not included in the 1818 *Friend*: the
disguise had been forsaken in the opening chapter of the
Biographia.

Well were it for me perhaps, had I never relapsed into the
same mental disease; if I had continued to pluck the flower
and reap the harvest from the cultivated surface, instead of
delving in the unwholesome quicksilver mines of metaphysic

depths. But if in after time I have sought a refuge from bodily pain and mismanaged sensibility in abstruse researches, which exercised the strength and subtlety of the understanding without awakening the feelings of the heart; still there was a long and blessed interval, during which my natural faculties were allowed to expand, and my original tendencies to develope themselves: my fancy, and the love of nature, and the sense of beauty in forms and sounds.   (BL I 10)

Was there in fact such a desolate and desperate drying up of his 'natural faculties', in April 1802? In January 1807 when he heard Wordsworth read aloud the first *Prelude*? In the dark middle years in London, Bristol and Calne before life returned upon the drowned and he could put together *Sibylline Leaves* and *Biographia Literaria*? At times he was to feel again 'that sort of stirring warmth about the Heart, which is with me the robe of incarnation of my [poetic] genius, such as it is.'[32] *Christabel* was never to be finished, but much else was; and much else – not in verse – was conceived, unravelled, desynonymised, disintrinsicated, set down, flowing out of a mind marvellously nourished with a sensibility for language, for ideas, for the ways of the mind and the movements of the mind, a sense of the living presence of the minds of men long dead and their work fragmentary; and all with an energy of seeing and thinking that would not let him rest. For him, intuition – the seeing of the mind – was νοερὰ συναφή, the touch of the intellect;[33] and language, tactile as it came to his call, allowed him to frame, shape, give body to the ceaseless heurism of his thinking, his mind achieving the tact of a blind man's fingers feeling the face of a beloved child.

The ocean of *The Ancient Mariner* was a poet's ocean, not a seafarer's; the peril and grace of that ocean is extended immensely by what he had not yet seen when he wrote the poem. When he had done some seafaring in the double ordeal of the Malta voyage, his eye turned not to the sea then but to that ocean, even more intense and interior, even more curiously figured, the mind, where through the transfiguration of language pure action can be separated even from the matter that gives it body. So to construct and reconstruct, within the lyrical forms of the mind's own working and its self-modifying self-exposition – this is perhaps to transcend even poetry, even though for most of us poetry above all declares and discloses that clarifying and shaping energy. Whether that is to be called 'philosophy' I cannot say; it is a most rare preoccupation, and that is perhaps what Coleridge himself meant by philosophy. Whatever it is to be called, that is what commanded almost the whole of Coleridge's life, making him – through a most refined sensibility and the exquisite tact of the mind – in all things, a poet.

2

Coleridge as Revealed in his Letters

Earl Leslie Griggs

Samuel Taylor Coleridge was born on 21 October 1772 and died on 25 July 1834. Every mood, every thought, everything he ever did, perhaps, is mirrored in his correspondence. Indeed, the almost 2,000 letters in the *Collected Edition* are so varied in subject-matter, so revealing of this 'man of vast Intellect & almost portentous Variety & Depth of Learning',* that their full richness cannot be conveyed in a single lecture. Yet after editing this voluminous correspondence, I can say that a self-drawn portrait emerges from the letters. In them we find, in the words of Henry James, a 'rare, anomalous, magnificent, interesting, curious, tremendously suggestive character, vices and all, with all its imperfections on its head'.[1] Were there no other sources available for the study of Coleridge as a man and as a thinker, the letters would provide an insight into his mind and the main biographical facts of his life. The five autobiographical letters to Poole written in 1797 and 1798, for example, furnish an invaluable account of his family background and earliest childhood.

In one of these autobiographical letters Coleridge says that his father 'was not a first-rate Genius – he was however a first-rate Christian. . . . In learning, good-heartedness, absentness of mind, & excessive ignorance of the world, he was a perfect *Parson Adams*.'[2] Another letter deals in part with the influence of Coleridge's father, who died not long before his son's ninth birthday. On an evening walk, Coleridge wrote, 'he told me

---

* Coleridge's description of the Hebrew scholar Aben Ezra, CL VI 689.

the names of the stars – and how Jupiter was a thousand times larger than our world – and that the other twinkling stars were Suns that had worlds rolling round them – & when I came home, he shewed me how they rolled round. I heard him', Coleridge commented, 'with a profound delight & admiration; but without the least mixture of wonder or incredulity. For from my early reading of Faery Tales, & Genii &c &c – my mind had been habituated to the Vast.' Unlike those who depend on 'the constant testimony of their senses' and to whom 'the Universe ... is but a mass of little things', Coleridge had early become a lover of 'the Great & the Whole'.[3] In 1825 he referred to his father as 'that venerable Countenance and Name which form my earliest recollections and make them *religious*'. In a later letter he said he was a 'very *facsimile*' of his father 'both in body and mind'.[4]

Although Coleridge tried to attune himself to the ability and interests of his correspondents, he usually wrote of what occupied his attention at the moment. His grandson sums up the letters very pertinently:

Coleridge 'wore his heart on his sleeve,' and, now to one friend, now to another, sometimes to two or three friends on the same day, he would seek to unburthen himself of his hopes and fears, his thoughts and fancies, his bodily sufferings, and the keener pangs of the soul. It is, to quote Coleridge's own words, these 'profound touches of the human heart' which command our interest in Coleridge's Letters, and invest them with their peculiar charm.[5]

The letters, we may add, present the Coleridge whom his contemporaries knew and loved, the Coleridge whose conversation held them spellbound, the Coleridge whom they admired and with whom they were at times disappointed.

An insatiable intellectual curiosity, a restless and inquiring mind, led Coleridge to range over almost the whole of man's knowledge, and his letters reflect his preoccupation with a wide variety of subjects – poetry, philosophy, science, politics, literary criticism, theology. His 'Idea-pot'[6] bubbled over with literary plans, and scattered through the letters are the titles and grandiose schemes for books, essays, poems, and dramas, conceived and promised, but many of them never executed.

He recognised the weakness of 'waverings' about many works. 'That is the disease of my mind,' he wrote to a friend: 'it is comprehensive in it's conceptions & wastes itself in the contemplations of the many things which it might do.'[7]

Letter-writing was to Coleridge a means of self-expression, and his epistolary style, now sparkling with poetic language, now overflowing with amplifications and qualifications, varies with mood and subject. His formal prose, as the late E. K. Chambers remarked, 'yields but few examples of that swift felicity of phrase which often illumines his private correspondence'.[8]

At his best, indeed, Coleridge touched his letters with magical expression. Consider the memorable description of Hazlitt: 'brow-hanging, shoe-contemplative, *strange!* . . . He sends well-headed & well-feathered Thoughts straight forwards to the mark with a Twang of the Bow-string.' Or note the comment on Dorothy Wordsworth: 'her eye watchful in minutest observation of nature – and her taste a perfect electrometer – it bends, protrudes, and draws in, at subtlest beauties & most recondite faults'. Or turn to the tender descriptions of his infant daughter, who 'smiles, as if she were basking in a sunshine, as mild as moonlight, of her own quiet Happiness;' and of his young son Hartley, as 'a spirit of Joy dancing on an Aspen Leaf'.[9]

Sometimes the epithets are less poetic than pithy and apropos. In one letter Coleridge characterised William Cobbett as a 'political Rhinoceros, with . . . his one Horn of brutal strength on the Nose of Scorn and Hate – not to forget the fleaing *Rasp* of his Tongue'. In another he referred to the Reform Bill of 1832 as the 'Catalinarian Riff-Raff-form Bill'. He called his Highgate Thursday Evening Conversazioni 'Attic nights' and spoke of them as '*On*eversazioni'.[10]

In contrast to his power of making himself clear with a few well-chosen words stands his tendency to write long involved sentences in a veritable plethora of words. His use of parentheses became habitual: 'Of Parentheses', he wrote to a friend,

I may be too fond – and will be on my guard in this respect—. But I am certain that no work of empassioned & eloquent reasoning ever did or could subsist without them – They are the *drama* of Reason – & present the thought growing, instead of a mere Hortus siccus. The aversion to them is one of the numberless symptoms of a feeble Frenchified Public.

(CL III 282)

An inimitable description of Coleridge's epistolary style is to be found in the following sentences taken from an essay by Virginia Woolf:

> The 'gallop scrawl' of the letters. . . . The great sentences pocketed with parentheses, expanded with dash after dash, break their walls under the strain of including and qualifying and suggesting all that Coleridge feels, fears and glimpses. Often he is prolix to the verge of incoherence, and his meaning dwindles and fades to a wisp on the mind's horizon. Yet in our tongue-tied age there is a joy in this reckless abandonment to the glory of words. Cajoled, caressed, tossed up in handfuls, words yield those flashing phrases that hang like ripe fruit in the many-leaved tree of his immense volubility.[11]

In writing of Archbishop Leighton's prose style Coleridge seems to be unconsciously describing his own way of expressing himself in his letters:

> I need not enlarge . . . on the high and peculiar Merits of Leighton – on his persuasive and penetrating eloquence, or the fine Fancy and profound Reflection which seem trying to hide themselves in the earnest simplicity and if I may so express myself, in the cordiality and *conversingness* of his style and manner.
> (CL V 290)

The letters are as many-sided as Coleridge himself – a potpourri of personal, literary and philosophical ingredients. 'Anything', as Virginia Woolf observed, 'may tumble out of that great maw; the subtlest criticism, the wildest jest, the exact condition of his intestines.'[12] At times Coleridge is a suffering and tormented man caught in a quagmire of debts, domestic woes and ill health, and his letters, filled with frustration and despair, become wearisome outpourings of excuses, resolves, self-condemnation and morbid introspection; at other times, as 'undisturbed as a Toad in a Rock',[13] he can write of the abstruse subjects so dear to his heart. The poetic or the reflective Coleridge is never far to seek; even when he is most vexatious in practical affairs, he yet retains his greatness in contemplative studies. Nothing escapes his attention, and the lofty and the mundane jostle each other for ascendancy. Surely, no letter writer ever served up a stranger mixture of earth and heaven, of grim desperation and hilarious good humour.

Coleridge was capable of redeeming the most tedious matter with flashes of singular beauty or profound insight. Among the most important of these are the critical comments, often brilliant and suggestive, sprinkled here and there throughout the letters. The observation may be brief – 'the divine Chit chat of Cowper'; or 'I love Plato – his dear *gorgeous* Nonsense!'; 'I *think* too much for a *Poet*; he [Southey] too little for a *great* Poet'; it may be an explanation of the allegorical significance of the word 'Haemony' as used in *Comus*; or it may be a letter entirely devoted to literary criticism, as the remarkable appreciation of Sir Thomas Browne written in 1804.[14] No one, perhaps, has ever dealt with the *Hydriotaphia* and *The Garden of Cyrus* with greater sympathetic insight; indeed, the letter reveals as much of Coleridge as of the 'whimsical Knight' of Norwich. Equally impressive are Coleridge's comments on Chapman's translation of the *Odyssey*:

> Chapman writes & feels as a Poet – as Homer might have written had he lived in England in the reign of Queen Elizabeth – in short, it is an exquisite poem, in spite of its frequent & perverse quaintnesses & harshnesses, which are however amply repaid by almost unexampled sweetness & beauty of language, all over spirit & feeling. In the main it is an English Heroic Poem, the *tale* of which is borrowed from the Greek.
> (CL III 68)

Note, too, Coleridge's objection to the phrase, 'the American Sir Walter' in reference to James Fenimore Cooper: 'It would be no less unjust than injurious to Mr Cooper to institute a comparison between him and Sir W[alter] S[cott] (and comparisons generally are in bad taste, weeds of Criticism indigenous to shallow & coarse Soils). If I mistake not, Mr Cooper's Genius would fit him better to fiction of a more avowedly imaginative kind: the farther he is from Society, the more he seems at home.'[15]

It is important to note that Coleridge came to suspect a

'*radical* Difference'[16] between his own opinions concerning poetry and those of Wordsworth. Twice during the summer of 1802 he expressed disagreement with parts of the Preface to *Lyrical Ballads*, and he found himself disturbed by 'a daring Humbleness of Language & Versification, and a strict adherence to matter of fact, even to prolixity',[17] in certain of Wordsworth's poems, thereby anticipating the superb criticism of the *Biographia Literaria*. The famous distinction between imagination and fancy is likewise foreshadowed. In 1802, in illustrating the superiority of Hebrew to Greek poetry, he speaks of the 'Fancy, or the aggregating Faculty of the mind', as opposed to the '*Imagination*, or the *modifying*, and *co-adunating* Faculty'; and in 1804, in an appreciation of Wordsworth, he employs almost the same phrases.[18] The letters not only include many examples of excellent literary criticism, but afford evidence of Coleridge's early maturity and development as a critic.

Occasionally, Coleridge deliberately described himself in his letters. Consider, for example, the self-portrait he sent to a correspondent when he was twenty-four years of age:

> As to me, my face, unless when animated by immediate eloquence, expresses great Sloth, & great, indeed almost ideotic, good nature. 'Tis a mere carcase of a face: fat, flabby, & expressive chiefly of inexpression. Yet, I am told, that my eyes, eyebrows, & forehead are physiognomically good.... As to my shape, 'tis a good shape enough, if measured – but my gait is awkward, & the walk, & the *Whole man* indicates *indolence capable of energies*. I am, & ever have been, a great reader – & have read almost every thing – a library-cormorant – I am *deep* in all out of the way books, whether of the monkish times, or of the puritanical aera – I have read & digested most of the Historical Writers – but I do not *like* History. Metaphysics, & Poetry, & 'Facts of mind' – (i.e. Accounts of all the strange phantasms that ever possessed your philosophy-dreamers from Tauth, [Thoth] the Egyptian to Taylor, the English Pagan,) are my darling Studies. – In short, ... I am almost always reading.... I compose very little – & I absolutely hate composition. Such is my dislike, that even a sense of Duty is sometimes too weak to overpower it.... In conversation I am impassioned, and oppose what I

deem [error] with an eagerness, which is often mistaken for personal asperity – but I am ever so swallowed up in the *thing*, that I perfectly forget my *opponent*. Such am I.

(CL I 259–60)

In 1820, Coleridge presented a vivid contrast between his own habits of mind and those of Southey:

Southey once said to me: You are nosing every nettle along the Hedge, while the Greyhound (meaning himself, I presume) wants only to get sight of the Hare, & FLASH! – strait as a line! – he has it in his mouth! – Even so, I replied, might a Cannibal say to an Anatomist, whom he had watched dissecting a body. But the fact is – I do not care twopence for the *Hare*; but I value most highly the excellencies of scent, patience, discrimination, free Activity; and find a Hare in every Nettle, I make myself acquainted with. I follow the Chamois-Hunters, and seem to set out with the same Object. But I am no Hunter of *that* Chamois Goat; but avail myself of the Chace in order to a nobler purpose – that of making a road across the Mountains, on which Common Sense may hereafter pass backward and forward. (CL v 98)

In 1826 Coleridge colourfully described his inability to clarify his thoughts sufficiently to express them in writing:

In this bleak World of Mutabilities, & where what is not changed, is chilled, and in this winter-time of my own Being, I resemble a Bottle of Brandy in Spitzbergen – a Dram of alcoholic Fire in the center of a Cake of Ice. . . . I [now] find greater difficulty in making my own thoughts sufficiently distinct and clear to communicate them, connectedly and consecutively, in writing. They are mature enough to climb up & chirp on the edge of their Birth-nest; but not fledged enough to fly away, tho' it were but to perch on the next branch. (CL vi 532)

Coleridge's addiction to opium, as the letters show, was the major tragedy of his life. By way of introduction to a brief account of that addiction, it should be pointed out that in Coleridge's day opium was regarded as a panacea for most human ailments. It was freely prescribed in the treatment of such afflictions as rheumatism, gout, dysentery, and diarrhoea, disorders which Coleridge frequently mentions in his letters. Physicians apparently paid little attention to its habit-forming characteristics. Nor was adequate information available concerning the cure of an addict. Furthermore, opium and laudanum, an alcoholic tincture of opium, were obtainable at chemists' shops throughout the country. 'The practice of taking Opium is dreadfully spread,' Coleridge wrote in 1808. 'Throughout Lancashire & Yorkshire it is the common Dram of the lower orders of People – in the small Town of Thorpe the Druggist informed me, that he commonly sold on market days two or three Pound of Opium, & a Gallon of Laudanum – all among the labouring Classes. Surely, this demands legislative Interference.'[19] In 1816 after referring to Wilberforce, who had been 'for a long series of years' under the 'necessity' of taking opium, Coleridge went on to say: 'Talk with any eminent druggist or medical practitioner, especially at the West End of the town, concerning the frequency of this calamity among men and women of eminence.'[20]

The first reference to opium in the correspondence appears in a letter which Coleridge wrote to his brother, George, in November 1791 during his first term at Jesus College, Cambridge. After describing a severe attack of rheumatism which had 'nailed' him to his bed, Coleridge added: 'Opium never used to have any disagreeable effects on me – but it has upon many.'[21] This statement would imply that he had recently taken opium and that the drug had previously been given to him at Christ's Hospital during a severe attack of rheumatic fever.

In February–March 1796 Coleridge himself resorted to laudanum, not to assuage pain, but to relieve mental distress. Driven almost to madness by his wife's illness, the blunders of his printer, etc., he wrote to a friend on 12 March:

> Such has been my situation for this last fortnight – I have been obliged to take Laudanum almost every night.
>
> (CL I 188)

Fortunately, he was able to add, 'Blessed be God! the prospect begins to clear up', for he was in danger of becoming an addict at that time.

In November 1796 Coleridge 'took between 60 & 70 drops of Laudanum' to relieve an 'intolerable pain from my right temple to the tip of my right shoulder', and continued to take '25 drops of Laudanum every five hours'. His medical attendant thought the complaint to be 'altogether nervous' and that it originated either in 'severe application, or excessive anxiety'. To this opinion Coleridge added: 'In excessive anxiety, I believe, it might originate.'[22] Referring to a continuation of this illness, Coleridge wrote on 17 December:

> A nervous Affection from my right temple to the extremity of my right shoulder almost distracted me, & made the frequent use of Laudanum absolutely necessary. And since I have subdued this, a Rheumatic Complaint in the back of my Head & Shoulders, accompanied with sore throat, and depression of the animal Spirits, has convinced me that a man may change bad Lodgers without bettering himself.   (CL I 276)

In March 1798 Coleridge wrote to his brother of an illness which had confined him to his bed:

> My indisposition originated in the stump of a tooth over which some matter had formed: this affected my eye, my eye my stomach, my stomach my head; and the consequence was a general fever – and the sum of pain was considerably increased by the vain attempts of our Surgeon to extract the offending stump. Laudanum gave me repose, not sleep: but YOU, I believe, know how divine that repose is – what a spot of inchantment, a green spot of fountains, & flowers & trees, in the very heart of a waste of Sands![23]

Finally, in a letter of 2 January 1800 to Thomas Wedgwood, Coleridge had this to say: 'Life were so flat a thing without Enthusiasm – that if for a moment it leave me, I have a sort of stomach-sensation attached to all my Thoughts, like those which succeed to the pleasurable operation of a dose of Opium'.[24]

The frank and open manner in which Coleridge occasionally alluded to his use of opiates during these early years, the casual way in which he reminded his brother of the 'divine' repose induced by laudanum, and his passing reference to the disagreeable after-effects of opium indicate that he was wholly unaware of any imminent danger of becoming an addict.

In the light of his later addiction, however, it is ominous that he resorted to laudanum for a fortnight to relieve agitated spirits

in February–March 1796. Ominous, too, was his use of laudanum during a long period of illness brought on by 'excessive
anxiety' during November and December of the same year.

In letters of 1814, 1816, and 1820[25] Coleridge himself associated the beginning of his 'slavery' to opium with 'nine dreary
months'[26] of wretched health, which began in the autumn of
1800 soon after he settled at Greta Hall, Keswick, and continued,
except for brief intervals, during the first half of the following
year. A letter written on 17 May 1801 in the midst of his illness
tends to confirm his after-statements:

> There is no Doubt, that it is irregular Gout combined with
> frequent nephritic attacks...it made it's outward shews
> sometimes in one or other of my fingers, sometimes in one or
> more of my Toes, sometimes in my right Knee & Ancle; but
> in general it was in my left Knee and Ancle...& gave me
> night after night pain enough....All this was mere nothing –
> but O dear Poole! the attacks on my stomach, & the nephritic
> pains in my back which almost alternated with the stomach
> fits – they were terrible! – The Disgust, the Loathing, that
> followed these Fits & no doubt in part too the use of the
> Brandy & Laudanum which they rendered necessary – this
> Disgust, Despondency, & utter Prostration of Strength, &
> the strange sensibility to every change in the atmosphere even
> while in my bed – enough!　　　　　　　　　(CL II 731–2)

A further factor in the continued use of opium arose from the
dissension between Coleridge and his wife. This was due in large
measure to his love for Sara Hutchinson, whom he first met in
October 1799. Believing, however, in the 'indissolubleness' of
marriage,[27] Coleridge was thrown into a state of constant turmoil
and a dependence on laudanum for relief. While away from home
in November 1802 he informed his wife: 'Once in the 24 hours
(but not always at the same hour) I take half a grain of purified
opium, equal to 12 drops of Laudanum – which is not more than
an 8th part of what I took at Keswick.'[28] A week later, after
hastily reading a letter from Mrs Coleridge, a 'fluttering' of his
heart came on. This 'ended (as usual)' he wrote, 'in a sudden &
violent Diarrhoea – I could scarcely touch my Dinner, & was
obliged at last to take 20 drops of Laudanum – which now that I
have for 10 days left off all stimulus of all kinds, excepting ⅓rd

of a grain of opium, at night, acted upon me more powerfully than 80 or 100 drops would have done at Keswick. . . . You must see by this, what absolute necessity I am under of *dieting* myself – & if possible, the still greater Importance of *Tranquillity* to me.'[29]

During the years 1801–04 Coleridge became increasingly aware of the hold opium had upon him. On some occasions he freely admits to resorting to opiates, twice to taking 100 drops of laudanum a day, but in many instances he refers to brief periods of disuse or to smaller doses. By 1803, too, he convinced himself that he could discontinue his use of opium if he could live in a more equable climate. In 1801 he had thought of migrating to the Azores,[30] where he believed the climate would be beneficial to his health. In February 1803 he told Southey:

> My only medicine is an universal & regular Stimulus – Brandy, Laudanum, &c &c make me well, during their first operation; but the secondary Effects increase the cause of the Disease. Heat in a hot climate is the only regular & universal Stimulus of the external world; to which if I can add Tranquillity, the equivalent, & Italian climate, of the world within, I do not despair to be a healthy man.   (CL II 930)

Apparently, Coleridge did not realise that the craving for narcotics, which he had mentioned in a letter of January 1803, was not to cease in a milder climate.

However sanguine Coleridge may have been when he left for Malta in April 1804, he soon discovered that he could not of his own volition leave off opium. Continuing ill-health, frustration over his love for Sara Hutchinson, and knowing that he could not live with his wife reduced him to a pitiable condition. In 1806 he returned to his native land, his mind 'halting between Despondency and Despair'.[31]

During the years 1808 to 1816 Coleridge was to seek the help of a number of physicians. In 1812, for example, he was for a time to benefit by Gooch's prescription of 'a known & measured quantity of Stimulant, with an attempt to diminish the Opiate part of it by little and little, if it were only a single Drop in two days'.[32] Gooch, indeed, entertained 'strong hopes' that Coleridge would be able either wholly to 'emancipate' himself, or if not 'that', to bring himself to such an 'arrangement' as would not very materially affect his 'health or longaevity'.[33] That trial, like all others, was only temporarily successful.

In April 1814 Coleridge fell almost completely under the domination of opium. By his own admission he was taking 'from 4 to 5 ounces a day of Laudanum'; once he took 'near a Pint'.[34] In desperation he suggested confinement in a private 'Establishment', where he could 'procure nothing but what a Physician thought proper' and where a medical attendant would be constantly with him for two or three months.[35] This step was not taken, but William Hood called in a physician, Henry Daniel; and Josiah Wade, with whom Coleridge was then living, employed a 'Keeper' to superintend him. Such was the 'direful state' of his mind that 'every possible instrument of Suicide' was removed from his room. Before long the doses of laudanum had been reduced to 'four tea-spoonfuls in the 24 Hours', and Coleridge was able to say that 'the terror & the indefinite craving' were gone. Daniel was '*sanguine*' of effecting a 'total recovery', but his efforts were to prove unavailing.[36]

In May 1814, while still living at Wade's, Coleridge sent Daniel an extract from *The Pains of Sleep*:

> as an exact and most faithful portraiture of the state of my mind under influences of incipient bodily derangement from the use of Opium, at the time that I yet remained ignorant of the cause, & still *mighty proud* of my supposed grand discovery of Laudanum, as the Remedy or Palliative of Evils, which itself had mainly produced, & at every dose was reproducing. . . . [The lines were] part of a long letter in verse written to a friend [in 1803] while I yet remained ignorant that the direful sufferings, I so complained of, were the mere effects of Opium.   (CL III 495–6)

In late December 1815 Coleridge wrote as follows to Dr Brabant, his physician while he was at Calne:

> Should I have such success in my dramatic enterprizes as to be able to say – 'for six months to come I am not under the *necessity* of doing any thing!' – I have strong hopes that I should emancipate myself altogether from this most pitiable Slavery, the fetters of which do indeed eat into the Soul. In my present circumstances, and under the disquieting uncer-

tainty, in which I am, concerning my place of residence for the ensuing year, all I can do is to be quite regular, and never to exceed the smallest dose of Poison that will suffice to keep me tranquil and capable of literary labor. (CL IV 612)

On the recommendation of Dr Joseph Adams, in April 1816 Coleridge placed himself in the household of James Gillman, a physician at Highgate, in the hope that strict supervision might lead to his cure. Although he planned to try the experiment for a month, he remained with the Gillmans for the rest of his life. In early May 1816, Morgan reported: 'Coleridge goes on exceedingly well – he is reduced to 20 drops a dose.'[37]
A letter of June 1816 affords an insight into the regimen which Gillman proposed:

On Wednesday night about an hour before bed time I was taken as by surprize, with a sensation of indefinite *Fear* over my whole Frame; but it was not accompanied with any craving for Laudanum, and I fought up against it and went to bed. I had a wretched night — and next morning the few drops, I now take, only increasing my irritability, about noon I called on G[illman] for the performance of *his* part of our mutual Engagement, & took enough and *barely* enough (for more, I am certain, would have been better) to break the commencing Cycle before the actual Craving came on. – To day I am much better. (CL VI 1041–2)

'More, I am certain, would have been better' – the words are ominous, for Coleridge soon found a means of surreptitiously obtaining additional supplies of laudanum from a Highgate chemist.* Although it would seem that he tried to limit himself to what he, not Gillman, deemed 'essential to life & usefulness',[38] undue stress and mental agitation in the years which followed certainly led him on occasion to take laudanum in excess of the sustaining doses he ordinarily allowed himself. To the end of his life, however, Coleridge never ceased to deplore his use of opium, 'the Poison', he wrote as late as 1832, 'which for more than 30 years has been the guilt, debasement, and misery of my Existence'.[39]

* For an account of Coleridge's relations with T. H. Dunn, a chemist at Highgate, see E. L. Griggs, 'Samuel Taylor Coleridge and Opium', *Huntington Library Quarterly* (1954) XVII 357–78.

Perhaps we may leave this tragic subject with a request which Coleridge made in 1814:

> After my death, I earnestly entreat, that a full and unqualified narration of my wretchedness, and of its guilty cause, may be made public, that at least some little good may be effected by the direful example! (CL III 511)

The early association of Coleridge and Wordsworth, especially from June 1797 to September 1798 when they left for Germany, served as a stimulus to creative activity for both men. During this period Coleridge wrote most of the poems for which he is remembered, but he said little of them in his letters. Instead, at that time and for many years afterwards, he spoke enthusiastically of Wordsworth's genius and character. In March 1798 Wordsworth wrote to a correspondent that he had written 1,300 lines of a poem on 'Nature, Man, and Society',[40] referring to his long-projected but never-completed 'Recluse'. Indeed, it is to a letter which Coleridge sent to Wordsworth in May 1815 that we must look for a description of what he believed to have been the proposed contents of 'The Recluse' 'as the *first* and *only* true Phil[osophical] Poem in existence'.[41] As the late Helen Darbishire so pertinently observed: 'All that was accomplished of the great philosophical poem, apart from Book I and the magnificent Prospectus, was a Prelude to the main theme, and an Excursion from it. Wordsworth's genius could not express itself in Coleridge's terms: he could not write the true philosophical poem. Perhaps', she concluded, 'no poet can.'[42]

Many years ago the late Sir Walter Raleigh summed up the importance of the early association in fostering the genius of both Coleridge and Wordsworth. His statement is at once true and profound.

> Much of the best work of either poet took its origin from the companionship of 1797 and 1798. . . . Coleridge was the apter, no doubt, to receive impressions. . . . But the chief benefit . . . [Wordsworth] received from Coleridge's friendship lay, after all, in the strength that comes from early appreciation.[43]

Mr Jonathan Wordsworth in a recent study is more specific:

> Coleridge's prose shows the influence of Wordsworth, Wordsworth's verse the influence of Coleridge. Clearly each had

learned much from the other; but Coleridge, though regarding
Wordsworth quite seriously as his teacher, had given far
more than he gained. He learned perhaps a fuller humanity,
moving via the negative position of *Lines Left upon a Seat in a
Yew-tree* – . . . to the new positive love which underlies *The
Ancient Mariner*. But in return he gave Wordsworth a
philosophical basis for his response to Nature, and in doing
so made available to him the material of much of his greatest
poetry.[44]

In June 1800, less than a year after his return from Germany,
Coleridge followed Wordsworth to the Lake Country and on
24 July settled at Keswick. His idolatry continued, but whereas
the early friendship with Wordsworth had set in motion his own
creative genius, soon he noted a decline in his poetic ability. 'The
Poet is dead in me' – he wrote to Godwin in March 1801 in a
letter overflowing with poetic expressions:

> my imagination (or rather the Somewhat that had been
> imaginative) lies, like a Cold Snuff on the circular Rim of a
> Brass Candle-stick, without even a stink of Tallow to remind
> you that it was once cloathed & mitred with Flame. That is
> past by! – I was once a Volume of Gold Leaf, rising & riding
> on every breath of Fancy. . . . If I die, and the Booksellers will
> give you any thing for my Life, be sure to say – 'Wordsworth
> descended upon him, like the Γνῶθι σεαυτόν [Know Thyself]
> from Heaven; by shewing to him what true Poetry was, he
> made him know, that he himself was no Poet.'   (CL II 714)

It may be of interest to mention here a manuscript note of
1828 which Coleridge scribbled in the margins of a letter from
Lady Beaumont:

> Lady B. in this letter urges me to resume Poetry. – Alas!
> how can I? – Is the power extinct? No! No! As in a still
> Summer Noon, when the lulled Air at irregular intervals
> wakes up with a startled *Hush-st* that seems to re-demand
> the silence which it breaks, or heaves a long profound Sigh
> in it's Sleep, and an Æolian Harp has been left in the chink
> of the not quite shut Casement – even so – how often! – scarce
> a week of my Life shuffles by, that does not at some moment
> feel the spur of the old genial impulse – even so do there fall

on my inward Ear swells, and broken snatches of sweet Melody, reminding me that I still have that within me which is both Harp and Breeze. But in the same moment awakes the Sense of C[*hange*] *without* – Life *unendeared*. The tenderest Strings no longer thrill'd.

In order to poetic composition I need the *varied* feeling – Thought charmed to sleep; and the too great *continuity* of mind broken up, to begin anew, with *new*-power seeking & finding *new* themes. (CL VI 731 n.)

And in another marginal note written less than a year before his death, Coleridge expressed what was probably his conviction since 1801:

I have too clearly before me the idea of a poet's genius to deem myself other than a very humble poet; but in the very possession of the idea, I know myself so far a poet as to feel assured that I can understand and interpret a poem in the spirit of poetry, and with the poet's spirit. (LR III 170)

Mention should be made of Coleridge's untiring efforts in the preparation of the second edition of *Lyrical Ballads*, 1800, including sending directions to the printers and laboriously copying out a number of Wordsworth's poems. What is more important is his utter subordination of himself. He did not object to the publication of the two volumes of *Lyrical Ballads* under Wordsworth's name, even though five of his own poems were included. In the Preface Wordsworth merely referred to them as contributed by 'a Friend'. Wordsworth believed that 'the old words and the strangeness' of *The Ancient Mariner*, the first poem in the edition of 1798, had 'deterred readers from going on'.[45] Coleridge responded to this criticism and carefully revised the poem in a letter to the printers. There is no evidence at this time that he was annoyed by the ungenerous note outlining the 'great defects' in *The Ancient Mariner* which Wordsworth inserted in the new edition of *Lyrical Ballads*. Although it was at first proposed that *Christabel* was to be included, Coleridge accepted with equanimity Wordsworth's decision to exclude the poem, even though part of it was then in proof. Coleridge pointed out to Humphry Davy that Wordsworth 'thought it indelicate to print two Volumes with *his name* in which so much of another man's was included – & which was of more consequence – the poem was in direct opposition to the very purpose for which the Lyrical Ballads were published'.[46]

Over the years the intimacy which had characterised the early association of Coleridge and Wordsworth gradually lessened, but it was not until late October 1810 that an open rupture occurred and all communication between them ceased for more than eighteen months. Although a reconciliation was effected through the mediation of Crabb Robinson in May 1812, the former relations were never re-established. As Coleridge afterwards explained:

A Reconciliation has taken place – but the *Feeling*, which I had previous to that moment, when the ¾ths Calumny burst like a Thunder-storm from a blue Sky on my Soul – after 15 years of such religious, almost superstitious, Idolatry & Self-sacrifice – O no! no! that I fear, never can return. All outward actions, all inward Wishes, all Thoughts & Admirations, will be the same – *are* the same – but – aye there remains an immedicable *But*. (CL III 437)

Writing to T. Allsop in 1818 Coleridge expressed his feelings:

But alas! during the prime manhood of my intellect I had nothing but cold water thrown on my efforts. . . . I have loved with enthusiastic self-oblivion those who had been so well pleased that I should, year after year, flow with a hundred nameless Rills into *their* Main Stream, that they could find nothing but cold praise and effective discouragement of every attempt of mine to roll onward in a distinct current of my own – who *admitted* that the Ancient Mariner [and] the Christabel . . . were not without merit, but were abundantly anxious to acquit their judgements of any blindness to the very numerous defects. (CL IV 888)

In another letter, in which Wordsworth is referred to as *Atticus*, Coleridge declared:

Oh, what a heartless, hopeless, almost wishless barrenness of spirit, may not an affectionate and believing mind be reduced to by another, not perhaps the superior in the total sum of their gifts, but whom he has accustomed himself to idolize –

because, only too conscious of the baser mixture in himself, *he* had separated that friend's excellencies from their dross or alloy, in the glow of his attachment, and then recast them into a whole, in the mould of his own imagination. It is a downright *Marattan*, . . . a sand-blast from the desert.

(CL IV 967–8)

Although the break with Wordsworth came as a crippling blow to Coleridge, once he had regained his composure, it was probably beneficial to him in the long run. It brought to a close his servile idolatry and unhealthy dependence and put an end to his association with Sara Hutchinson, Wordsworth's sister-in-law, with whom he had been hopelessly in love for over a decade.

From 1811 to 1819 Coleridge delivered a number of courses of lectures on literature and philosophy, details of which may be gleaned from his letters. In 1813 his *Remorse* was produced at Drury Lane; in 1816 the volume containing *Christabel*, *Kubla Khan*, and *The Pains of Sleep* was published; and during his eighteen-year residence with the Gillmans at Highgate, he published *Sibylline Leaves*, 1817, three editions of his poems and dramas in 1828, 1829 and 1834, and several prose works. Thus he established his reputation as poet, literary critic, political thinker, philosopher and theologian. He was not 'the sole unbusy thing' described in one of his poems.[47]

Reference should be made to the correspondence between Coleridge and Byron. The two men met only once. 'He has', Coleridge wrote after their meeting in April 1816, 'the sweetest Countenance that I ever beheld – his eyes are really Portals of the Sun, things for Light to go in and out of. – I mean to read all his works together: & shall then form my opinion.'[48] During this visit Coleridge recited *Kubla Khan* to Byron, who was 'highly struck' by the poem.

In March 1815 Coleridge sought Byron's assistance in finding a publisher for his poems in two volumes.[49] (Later in that year he determined to publish his poems in a single volume entitled *Sibylline Leaves*.) Byron responded enthusiastically and afterwards took occasion to refer to the poem *Christabel*, which Scott had repeated to him, though without mentioning its name. Calling the poem 'the wildest and finest I ever heard in that

kind of composition', Byron added: 'I think the heroine's name
was Geraldine. At all events, the "toothless mastiff bitch" and
the "witch Lady," the description of the hall, the lamp suspended from the image, and more particularly of the girl herself
as she went forth in the evening – all took a hold on my imagination which I never shall wish to shake off.'[50] John Murray
published the *Christabel* volume on Byron's recommendation,
and it was owing to Byron that *Kubla Khan* was included. In
February 1816, on learning that Coleridge was 'in great distress',
Byron sent him a hundred pounds, 'at a time', he wrote later,
'when I could not command 150 in the world'.[51]

Lovable and affectionate, tolerant and placable, humble and
forgiving, Coleridge basked in the warmth of friendship. If he
felt the need of compassion and understanding on the part of
those whom he loved – 'In Sympathy alone I found at once
Nourishment and Stimulus'[52] – he was always ready, even to a
fault, to sacrifice his own interests to the aspirations and welfare
of others. As he had dedicated himself to forwarding the reputation of Wordsworth, so now in his later years he turned aside
from his own work to assist Hyman Hurwitz, a Hebrew scholar
– Basil Montagu, an editor of Bacon – Edward Irving, a Scottish
preacher – C. A. Tulk, a Swedenborgian – H. F. Cary, a translator of Dante – and Mrs Morgan, the widow of an intimate
friend. 'Be assured', he wrote to G. de' Prati, an Italian patriot
whom he had met only a month earlier, 'that whatever I could
do for a brother, I will do for you.'[53] So, too, in 1828 he reported:
'I have with a sick heart been all this day trotting about to make
up, guinea by guinea,' the sum of twenty pounds to save Mrs
Morgan 'from God knows what'.[54]

During his years at Highgate, Coleridge was to find a whole
new circle of friends. Among those who brought him intellectual
stimulation and affection were three men: John Hookham Frere,
diplomat, poet and translator: Hyman Hurwitz, master of the
Hebrew Academy at Highgate and the first professor of Hebrew
in the newly-founded University of London; and Joseph Henry
Green, a rising young surgeon with philosophical interests.

For Frere, Coleridge felt something of the same admiration
and devotion which Wordsworth had earlier inspired. The
friendly intercourse which began in 1816 was interrupted in
1820 when Frere left for Malta, but was renewed in 1825 on

his return to England for a year. Frere introduced Coleridge to Canning and Lord Liverpool, vainly endeavoured to obtain a sinecure of £200 a year for him, contributed funds for his son, Derwent Coleridge's education at St John's College, Cambridge; and '*at a heavy expence*' had Coleridge's philosophical lectures of 1818–19 taken down in shorthand; but far more than all this, he gave Coleridge encouragement in his literary endeavours. 'It is a great delight to me to be any where with you,' Coleridge wrote to Frere in 1826:

> And more than so – ... it is a source of Strength, and a renewal of hope – and of the hope, I most need – viz. that I am still in a region where the sympathy of sane minds can follow me, and have not been toiling after shadows.
>
> (CL VI 538)

The letters to Hyman Hurwitz, all of them published for the first time in the *Collected Letters of Samuel Taylor Coleridge*, reveal an unbounded admiration for this Hebrew scholar, whom Coleridge once called 'my Christian Neighbor of the Jewish Persuasion',[55] and discovered what he before had not imagined, 'that a learned, unprejudiced, & yet strictly *orthodox* Jew may be much nearer in point of faith & religious principles to a learned & strictly orthodox Christian, of the Church of England, than many called Christians'.[56]

Coleridge translated two Hebrew dirges written by Hurwitz, and prior to the publication of the latter's *Vindiciæ Hebraicæ; or, a Defence of the Hebrew Scriptures*, he read the work 'sentence by sentence'. In recommending its publication to John Murray, he said he considered Hurwitz's 'defence of Revealed Religion itself' of 'greater importance' than even his vindication of the 'Established Version'.[57] Coleridge also suggested the preparation of Hurwitz's *Hebrew Tales*, corrected the manuscript, contributed three *Specimens of Rabbinical Wisdom, selected from the Mishna* which had previously appeared in the *Friend*, and recommended to Murray the publication of the work. Murray did not publish the *Hebrew Tales*, but when Morrison and Watt became the publishers, Coleridge took on the tedious labour of reading the proof-sheets.

The genial friendship between Coleridge and Hurwitz was a truly remarkable one. It brought together two men differing in race, training, and religious affiliation. If Coleridge seems to have been unduly willing to forward his friend's career, Hurwitz made available to him an expert knowledge of the Hebrew Scriptures and led him to a deeper understanding of them.

The intimacy between Coleridge and J. H. Green began soon after their meeting in 1817. At first the relationship was that of 'friend and enlightened Pupil',[58] but it soon became that of two men co-operating in a common objective. In 1820 Coleridge wrote of their '*philosophical* Intercommune',[59] and together they worked on Coleridge's *Opus Maximum*. As premature old age came upon him, Coleridge said in 1828:

> Completely have I been for some time past swallowed up in the one anxiety of arranging and increasing my huge pile of Manuscripts, so that the *substance* at least of the results of my logical, physiological, philosophical, theological, biblical, and I hope I am entitled to add *religious* and *Christian* studies and meditations for the last 20 years of my life might be found in a state capable of being published by my dear Friend Mr Green, who has for ten years devoted the only vacant day of every week to the participation of my labors.   (CL VI 724)

After Coleridge's death in 1834 Green devoted the remainder of his life to an attempt to carry out his friend's wishes. His *Spiritual Philosophy; founded on the Teaching of the late Samuel Taylor Coleridge* was published posthumously in 1865.

The letters make clear the difficulties and delays which accompanied the composition and publication of Coleridge's major prose works. Late in 1814, for example, Coleridge proposed to illustrate by 'fragments of *Auto*-biography' an 'Essay' which was to be 'prefixed' to a theological and philosophical work.[60] Actually, the *Biographia Literaria* grew out of these fragments. In March 1815 he planned to publish his poems in two volumes, with a 'general Preface . . . on the Principles of philosophic and genial criticism relatively to the Fine Arts in general; but especially to Poetry'. Coleridge later decided that a 'detailed publication of my opinions concerning Poetry & Poets, would excite more curiosity and a more immediate Interest than even my Poems'.[61] He determined, therefore, to publish two volumes. The first, the *Biographia Literaria*, was to contain his 'opinions on Religion, Philosophy, Politics, and Poetry',[62] and the second, *Sibylline Leaves*, was to include a collection of his poems.

After having read the comments on imagination and fancy in the Preface to the 1815 edition of Wordsworth's *Poems* and noting that his name had been brought forward and objection made to his own distinction between the two terms, Coleridge was led to expand his *Biographia*. As he wrote to Brabant in July 1815:

> The necessity of extending, what I first intended as a preface, to an Autobiographia literaria, or Sketches of my literary Life & opinions, as far as Poetry and *poetical* Criticism is [are] concerned, has confined me to my Study.... I have given a full account ... of the Controversy concerning Wordsworth's Poems & Theory, in which my name has been so constantly included. (CL IV 578–9)

Ultimately, the *Biographia Literaria* itself was published as a separate work in two volumes in July 1817. *Sibylline Leaves* appeared later in the same month.

The letters exemplify, too, the workings of Coleridge's mind while he was preparing *Aids to Reflection*. First proposed as a book of extracts from Archbishop Leighton, with comments and a life of the author, it turned into a work on the central doctrines of Christianity. As a result, eighteen months elapsed from the time the first proofs were in hand to the appearance of the volume in 1825. 'Thank God!' Coleridge wrote in May 1825, 'I was ... putting down the last sentence of the long-lingering "Aids to Reflection" which was to have been a small volume of Selections from Archbishop Leighton with a few notes by S.T.C. and which has ended in a few pages of Leighton and a large Volume by S.T.C.'[68] Furthermore, even as he was writing *Aids to Reflection*, Coleridge proposed the publication of six Supplementary Disquisitions:

> 1. On Faith; 2. The Eucharist; 3. The philosophy of PRAYER; 4. On the prophetic character of the Old Testament; 5. On the Church plus Establishment, and Dissent – and the true character & danger of the Romish Church; 6. On the right and the superstitious use and estimation of the Sacred Scriptures. (CL V 444)

The fifth of these Disquisitions became a volume, *On the Constitution of the Church and State*, which was published in 1830; the sixth was published posthumously in 1840 under the title, *Confessions of an Inquiring Spirit*. Both works are among the most important of Coleridge's publications.

Among the many projects conceived in Coleridge's teeming brain stands his never completed *Opus Maximum* or *Magnum Opus*. As his letters show, its genesis lies in the religious and metaphysical ideas which were germinating and evolving in his mind during his early manhood. The year 1814, however, really marks the beginning of meaningful comments on the *Opus Maximum*. From April 1814, when Coleridge said he had in his head 'some floating ideas on the *Logos*',[64] to the end of his life, the *Opus* was never far from his thoughts. Indeed, not a year passed in which he failed to refer to it. To this work, he insisted in a letter of 1820, 'all my other writings (unless I except my poems, and these I can exclude in part only) are introductory and preparative'. In 1824 he called his forthcoming *Aids to Reflection* 'a small avant Courier' of his greater work. In 1827 he described his *Opus Maximum* as 'my system of Philosophy and Faith, as the result of all my researches and reflections concerning God, Nature and Man'.[65] Although the title and description varied from time to time, Coleridge's fundamental purpose, the reconciling of the dynamic or constructive philosophy with Christianity, remained the same. Significantly, a work on Logic was to be an integral part of, or at least an introduction to, the *Opus*.

Many of Coleridge's friends have left for posterity their eulogies and estimates of his mind and character. Among them was Basil Montagu, who included his testimony in the Preface to his edition of Bacon. It is dated 17 November 1834 and may serve as a conclusion:

One friend the grave has closed over, who cheered me in my task when I was weary, and better able, from his rich and comprehensive mind, to detect errors, than any man, was always more happy to encourage and to commend. Wise as the serpent, gall-less as the dove, pious and pure of heart, tender, affectionate, and forgiving, this, and more than this, I can say, after the trial of forty years, was my friend and instructor, Samuel Taylor Coleridge.

3

Ice and Spring: Coleridge's Imaginative Education*

John Beer

If the celebration, at his school, of the two-hundredth anniversary of his birth invites us to take yet another look at Coleridge's schooldays, we need not confine ourselves to a detailed account of his career, or of the courses of study that were current in his time – particularly since others, over the years, have written and spoken so well on these topics. It may be better this time to begin with a broader question: What did Coleridge make of the school and what did the school make of him? The question is all the more inviting since the answer might throw some light on some corresponding questions, still unresolved, concerning Coleridge's continuing relationship with the world at large.

To see how complex that relationship remains, even now, we need look no further than to the publications which have marked the bicentenary year. In Great Britain, four studies by distinguished scholars have appeared: Basil Willey has discussed his religious ideas, Owen Barfield his thought more generally, William Empson and David Jones his poetry[1] – and each in so completely different a way as to recall Frederick Denison Maurice's comment: 'I rejoice to think that those who have most profited by what he has taught them, do not and cannot form a school.'[2] A fifth study, a long book by the American scholar Norman Fruman,[3] differs again, but even more radically. After a long and painstaking study of the various cases in which Coleridge can be seen to have acted with something less than strict rectitude in his acknowledgement of sources or his more mundane dealings with the world, Professor Fruman goes on to claim

* A bicentenary lecture given at Christ's Hospital.

that such cases cast doubt on the remainder of Coleridge's achievement; indeed he goes so far as to suggest that Coleridge did not have an original mind at all; that he flourished best as an *entrepreneur* of other men's images and ideas; and that the various stories of his brilliance in childhood and youth stem from fictions invented by himself to disguise a rather mediocre set of achievements. The last claim, at least, is one that will need to be examined rather closely in any consideration of his career at school.

First, however, let us look at the school itself. I suppose that if one were seeking a single word to describe the atmosphere of an English school such as Christ's Hospital at the end of the eighteenth century, that word would, of necessity, be 'severity'. Contemporary records bear witness to the harsh physical conditions under which the boys lived, and Coleridge remembered his headmaster, James Boyer, as a very severe man.* Boyer's floggings were notorious; De Quincey, indeed, was angry with Coleridge for invoking any admiration for a man whom he regarded as a 'grim idol' whose 'altars reeked with Children's blood'.[4]

Yet the portrait of Boyer which appears in an engraving preserved at the school is by no means totally severe. It suggests a strong personality, but one which might as easily expand into humour as into rage. And the same might be said of the school conditions generally. The evidence suggests that in spite of imposing a hard discipline and difficult courses of study, the school did not seek to break the spirit of the boys but expected some flourishing of spirit – perhaps an occasional touch of rebelliousness as well, if it did not go too far.

Even when the school regime is viewed in that larger light, however, Coleridge's personality does not seem to have been well adapted to it. He did not have the basic raw vitality which might have enabled him to either match himself against the system or thrive lustily within it. At the scholastic level, certainly, there were few problems; but to the rough-and-tumble of school life he brought a delicate constitution, a rather feverish temperament and (above all) an easily-stimulated imaginative sense.

That imagination was forced to feed where it could. One of

* For his 'severities' see BL I 6; and cf. LW I 145, II 19–20.

the textbooks used in the classroom at that time was Andrew Tooke's *Pantheon*, a dictionary of classical mythology with the unusual feature that it contained illustrations. Leigh Hunt has mentioned how the boys delighted in 'the Mars, coming on furiously in his car; Apollo, with his radiant head in the midst of shades and fountains; Aurora with hers, a golden dawn; and Venus, very handsome, we thought, and not looking too modest in "a slight cymar"'.[5] Coleridge was equally drawn: forty years later one can still find him classifying the local doctors at Highgate according to symbols in Tooke's plate of Aesculapius.[6] Yet to the modern reader the engravings in the *Pantheon* are really a very staid set: the imaginations of the boys must truly have been starved, one reflects, to find in them the splendours that Leigh Hunt describes – an impression which is perhaps confirmed by Lamb's and Leigh Hunt's accounts of how the boys at that time were obsessed by romances and used to pore over all that they could find.*

Coleridge's imagination, certainly, was working overtime. Consider the well-known story he tells of his experience in walking down a London street:

> Going down the Strand, in one of his day-dreams, fancying himself swimming across the Hellespont, thrusting his hands before him as in the act of swimming, his hand came in contact with a gentleman's pocket; the gentleman seized his hand, turning round and looking at him with some anger, 'What! so young, and so wicked?' at the same time accused him of an attempt to pick his pocket; the frightened boy sobbed out his denial of the intention and explained to him how he thought himself Leander, swimming across the Hellespont. (Gillman 17)

The gentleman was so struck and delighted with 'the novelty of the thing', and with the 'simplicity and intelligence' of the boy, that he took out a subscription for him to a circulating library in Cheapside. That library in Cheapside Coleridge proceeded to ransack, he tells us, devouring everything he could find. At school, meanwhile, there were other severities to contend

---

* CL v 348–9. Coleridge's memory of Tooke may have been refreshed by helping James Gillman's son with his classics (see CL v 492 and cf. p. 210 below).

with, such as the hunger vividly described by Lamb. Coleridge's
reference links it again with the imagination:

> Conceive what I must have been at fourteen; I was in a
> continual low fever. My whole being was, with eyes closed
> to every object of present sense, to crumple myself up in a
> sunny corner and read, read, read – fancy myself on Robinson
> Crusoe's Island, finding a mountain of plum-cake, and eating a
> room for myself, and then eating it into the shapes of tables
> and chairs – hunger and fancy!   (Gillman 20)

The link between fasting and the work of imagination has
long been apparent from records of the ascetic tradition. Quite
recently, moreover, a contemporary artist, Richard Humphry,
gave an interview in which he described how he paints out of an
inner world contained by a glass dome, which he first dreamed
of when at boarding-school. At that time, he said, everything in
it was edible – because 'boys at boarding school are always hungry, so I was always eating the flowers'.

There were other privations, such as the bad food, nause-
atingly described by Lamb,[7] and the bad smells from a shoe
cupboard.* By Coleridge's time the school dungeons (tiny cells
in which boys who ran away more than once had been confined,
and which new boys had been taken to see) were no longer used,
but the memory was no doubt still green, adding further to the
sense of confinement created by the barred windows of the
school proper. For Coleridge, who had been brought up in the
country, the restriction must have been particularly irksome,
and it was not surprising if the evidences of nature outside became linked for him with the idea of human affection. He describes the effects in the first version of 'Dejection':

> Feebly! O feebly! – Yet
> (I well remember it)
> In my first Dawn of Youth that Fancy stole
> With many secret Yearnings on my Soul.
> At eve, sky-gazing in 'ecstatic fit'
> (Alas! for cloister'd in a city School

---

* Gillman 16–17. For a classic account of bad smells at school see
George Orwell, 'Such, Such were the Joys', *Collected Works* (1968)
IV 348.

The Sky was all, I knew, of Beautiful)
At the barr'd window often did I sit,
And oft upon the leaded School-roof lay,
    And to myself would say –
There does not live the Man so stripp'd of good affections
As not to love to see a Maiden's quiet Eyes
Uprais'd, and linking on sweet Dreams by dim Connections
To Moon, or Evening Star, or glorious western Skies –
While yet a Boy, this Thought would so pursue me
That often it became a kind of Vision to me!

(CL II 791–2)

In that passage there is also something else: the suggestion of
a hothouse emotional development. Lamb comments on something of the same sort when he speaks of the strong religious
atmosphere of Christ's Hospital, with so many prayers and
devotions as to be reminiscent of a monastic cloister. A similar
intensity of emotion seems to have communicated itself to all
the elements of warmth. Lamb dwells on the privations of cold:
exclusion from the communal fire was one of the minor punish-
ments.[8] Some lines in Coleridge's 'Frost at Midnight' convey a
memory of the schoolboy huddled over the small fire in his study
while the frost did its work outside, gaining as much warmth as
he could from the glowing coals while dreaming of a hot summer's day in the country. In that age, when the cult of Reason
had been matched by the growth of the cult of sensibility, when
John Wesley had initiated the Wesleyan movement after an
experience of 'heart-warming' among the Moravians, we may
think it not unlikely that a Coleridge who saw the evening star
as like the light in a girl's eye might have seen in his fire an
image of the human heart itself.*

The picture of Coleridge which has emerged so far combines
intellectual precocity with an intensity of emotional and imaginative development in certain spheres. Can we go further? At this
point we are bound to recall the passage in Lamb's essay where
he turns aside from his account of his other contemporaries at
school to apostrophise Coleridge himself:

---

* Cf. Blake's more melodramatic comparison of the human form
to 'a fiery forge', with the human heart 'its hungry gorge', in 'A
Divine Image', Complete Writings, ed. Keynes (1957) p. 221.

Come back into memory, like as thou wert in the day-spring of thy fancies, with hope like a fiery column before thee – the dark pillar not yet turned – Samuel Taylor Coleridge – Logician, Metaphysician, Bard! How have I seen the casual passer through the Cloisters stand still, intranced with admiration (while he weighed the disproportion between the *speech* and the *garb* of the young Mirandula), to hear thee unfold, in thy deep and sweet intonations, the mysteries of Jamblichus, or Plotinus (for even in those years thou waxedst not pale at such philosophic draughts), or reciting Homer in his Greek, or Pindar – while the walls of the old Grey Friars re-echoed to the accents of the *inspired charity-boy!* (LW II 21)

Norman Fruman, who, as I mentioned, is concerned to demonstrate that Coleridge was not a prodigy at school, has some difficulties with this passage, but he finds them eased when he comes across a letter in which Coleridge says that he gave Lamb a good deal of the material for this essay. Clearly, he suggests, Coleridge gave Lamb this picture of himself at school which the guileless Lamb incorporated.[9] That may be so; but one's memory in adolescence can be very tenacious. And Lamb was a canny individual, fully alive to Coleridge's faults and of his habit of 'quizzing the world by lyes, most unaccountable and most disinterested fictions',[10] as he called it. One suspects that if Coleridge managed to convince Lamb that he had heard his friend expounding Iamblichus and Plotinus at school when in fact no such thing had happened, he may have been a greater genius than he is sometimes taken for.

And even if we agree that we should not be totally certain about Iamblichus and Plotinus, it should still be remembered that in the time of Coleridge's schooldays, these philosophers had an unusually topical interest, since Thomas Taylor had just begun his enthusiastic series of translations from the neo-Platonist philosophers. The particular themes of the two in question, moreover, Plotinus' celebration of inward illumination and Iamblichus' accounts of the ways in which the various forms of the creation 'energise', might be expected to appeal particularly to an imaginative adolescent.

The one other piece of evidence that has survived concerning Coleridge's philosophical interests at this time (apart from his

brief mention of a 'rage for metaphysics' brought on by reading
the essays on Liberty and Necessity in Cato's Letters,[11]) comes in
a letter many years later where, insisting on the early date of
many of his ideas, he says of a theory that he is propounding
about the relationship between sound and colour that he had
adopted the idea before his visit to Germany in 1798 and then
adds in parenthesis '(probably from Behmen's *Aurora*, which I
had *conjured over* at school)'.[12] At this point Norman Fruman
is emphatic. 'The evidence is overwhelmingly against Coleridge
having read Jacob Boehme at school', he says,[13] by which he
means that Coleridge said that he read Boehme at school, that
certain other statements about his youth have proved to be
unreliable and that he is known to have read Boehme on various
occasions in his later life.

Since such evidence may legitimately be considered less than
'overwhelming' it will be in order to inquire further. Jacob
Boehme's *Aurora* is not a book that most people find it easy to
read from cover to cover. It contains such an extraordinary
farrago of images and ideas, indeed, that a reader who came to it
in an unsympathetic frame of mind might well think the title-
page description, 'translated from the High Dutch', an accurate
description of the contents. But there are some things about it
which would be very attractive to an adolescent, particularly an
adolescent at the end of the eighteenth century. There are hints
(particularly in the seventeenth-century edition) that mysterious
secrets are being unveiled, that a key to all wisdom is lurking in
the extravagances of the prose. There are also some fine dramatic
touches, as when Boehme begins a chapter:

> Here, *king Lucifer*, pull thy hat down over thy eyes, lest thou
> should'st see how man will take off thy crown away from
> thee, thou canst *no more* rule in heaven . . .[14]

Another feature of Boehme's work which would be likely to
attract an imaginative adolescent is his imagery, particularly
the vivid images which emerge occasionally from his speculations concerning the relationship between nature and the divine.
Such vital and imaginative touches might be expected to appeal
particularly to sensibilities which were baffled by the apparent
gap between the delightful world of the senses in nature and
the contemporary, post-Newtonian scientific world-view, with

its strong suggestion that such delights were local and personal, finding little echo in the universe at large. For Boehme, the realm of nature was rather a realm of correspondences. Whatever its relationship to the Newtonian planetary system (and he was writing before Newton) the sun was for him an all-powerful fountain, its action like that of the heart in human beings.[15] Nature also reflected the fall of Lucifer, its ice and stones embodying the limit which had been set to its own, corresponding fall.[16]

The idea that Coleridge found himself attracted by Boehme's ideas as early as this finds some further support in the anecdote that tells of his having gone off while still at school to apprentice himself to a shoemaker, who subsequently incurred Boyer's full wrath.* It is possible that this egregious fit of impulse was an act of hero-worship, a homage to the fact that Jacob Boehme had himself been a shoemaker.

While the biographical evidence is under examination it should also be mentioned that Lamb's well-known passage is not the only record by a contemporary of Coleridge at school. There is also a short memoir by the Rev. Leapidge Smith, who had been his fag, or study-boy. No man is a hero to his valet, it is said, and Leapidge Smith remembered some of Coleridge's defects very vividly. What is interesting abut his account, however, is that he managed at one and the same time to paint in Coleridge's warts and to give an impression by no means unlike Lamb's. He had been asked to write a piece for a projected new school magazine:

> As you wish for something relative to my old satrap, S. T. Coleridge, permit me to inform you that in my early days I performed the onerous duty, among others, of cleaning his shoes; and well do I remember that they were too often for my comfort very dirty, for he was not very nice in his person or in his dress. He seldom had two garters at one time, in consequence of which his stockings used to drop into a series of not very elegant folds. I have a pleasing remembrance of even Coleridge's old shoes; for as he was not very particular *how*

* TT 27 May 1830. As often with such anecdotes there is an area of uncertainty, since Coleridge claims that he was thirteen and an 'infidel' at the time of the incident; but if he did not have Boehme in mind the choice of a shoemaker is remarkably coincidental.

they were cleaned, and I was not very particular how I cleaned them, the Grecian and myself agreed pretty well on that matter; but woe to my head if he caught me taking the liberty to read in his study. There was not very much there to tempt me, however, for my taste was then in another direction. Instead of Homer and Virgil, I much preferred 'The Seven Champions', or even 'Jack the Giant-killer'. Unluckily, as it happened, he had an odd volume of the 'Arabian Nights' Entertainments' in the vulgar tongue, and one day he caught me very cozily reading this work; on which discovery he most unceremoniously, or perhaps I should say very ceremoniously, kicked me out, prefacing the act with an animated speech. Yes, I well remember his wrath at my impudence, as he angrily called it. What may have increased his indignation on the occasion was, that he found me in the act of eating a remnant of mince-pie, which, in my juvenile innocence, I fancied to be my perquisite as his study boy. Well do I remember the furious look he assumed as he put back his long black curls from his face, and the wrathful curl of his lip in the disappointment of his lost mince-pie, when he hurled the empty plate after me as I quickly retreated from his presence.

I remember his entering his study one afternoon in a state of great irritation against Dr. Boyer, the head master, who had deeply offended his majesty by sneering at his definition of some Greek word, which I have forgotten, and then sending me for a rush candle (the night light of those times). After lighting it, he desired me to go to the doctor's house, immediately opposite, and present it to him with Coleridge's duty, particularly informing the doctor that Coleridge had lighted it. I did not much relish the task, but on presenting myself to the doctor and delivering my message (lighted rush in hand), he laughed most heartily, and replied, 'Tell Colly (he always called him so when pleased) that he is a good fellow.' As from my ignorance of Greek, I never could comprehend this, I must leave the solution thereof to those learned Thebans who may be competent to unriddle the enigma.

Although Coleridge was somewhat of a hard task-master, yet I parted from him, on his leaving for the university, with as deep a regret as a boy could feel for one so superior to himself. In person he was a tall, dark, handsome young man, with

long black flowing hair; eyes, not merely dark, but black and
keenly penetrating; a fine forehead, a deep-toned harmonious
voice; a manner never to be forgotten, full of life, vivacity
and kindness; dignified in his person, and, added to all these,
exhibiting the elements of his future greatness. Yet there was
something awful about him, for all his equals in age and rank
quailed before him. No wonder, therefore, if I did, who was
selected to be his 'boy' or attendant; he was to me the very
impersonation of majesty, and stern indeed he could be when
offended.[17]

There is an appealing honesty about that account, ranging
as it does from Coleridge's carelessness about his appearance and
his despotic behaviour towards his study-boy to the sense of
pleasure and respect that the author evidently still felt for him.
But in some ways the most vivid element in the story is the
anecdote in the middle, conjuring up a picture of the nervous
little boy going across to the headmaster's house and standing
outside with his candle in the darkness; the confrontation with
the fearsome Boyer; and the overwhelming relief when the headmaster took it all in good part.

But what was the point of this gesture of Coleridge's in the
first place? It is a puzzling little conundrum: and for a long time
the best explanation that I could think of was that it might have
emanated from some argument about a Greek word for 'to light'
– whether or not it could be used both transitively and intransi-
tively, or something like that. I have since come to think that the
argument was perhaps about something rather different. There
is a passage in his *Philosophical Lectures*, where, after groping
to find some way of defining life, Coleridge continues:

> but it is easy, when a man is anxious to express his thoughts,
> to take one illustration and pin it down to his literal words
> and to draw from it all the consequence that may be drawn
> from every simile, a sort of procedure which excites my indig-
> nation where it does not excite my ridicule. And as I said to a
> man, 'I have presented a simile as a simile just as I present a
> candle for a light ... or the stench for your pains.'*

* PL 358. For similar images of physical illumination, see TT 21
Sept 1830, and *Coleridge on Shakespeare*, ed. R. A. Foakes (1971)
p. 65.

Unfortunately, the shorthand transcriber missed a passage towards the end, as the dots indicate; but I do not think it is altogether difficult to fill the gap. What Coleridge surely said was something like this:

> I have presented a simile as a simile just as I present a candle for a light: you may either take it and use it for your illumination or you may snuff it out and have the benefit of the darkness – or the stench for your pains.

I also think it likely that Boyer was the 'man' whom Coleridge had been speaking to – that he had been ridiculing some point in one of Coleridge's compositions, say. Coleridge himself has related how he used to take a strong common-sense line in such situations:

> In fancy I can almost hear him now, exclaiming 'Harp? Harp? Lyre? Pen and ink, boy, you mean! Muse, boy, Muse? Your Nurse's daughter, you mean! Pierian spring? Oh aye! the cloister-pump, I suppose!'   (BL I 5)

We need only suppose that Coleridge had been taken to task for using some high-flown simile – in his classical verse, say – and had replied by using the image of the candle as an argument against over-literal criticism, to understand why he might have felt moved to press the point home by sending along a lighted candle to the headmaster's house that evening.

As it happens, also, this is not quite the end of the story. For in turning over the pages of Boehme's *Aurora* I later came across the following passage, which would seem to have been the source of Coleridge's image:

> 14. As when a man kindleth a wax *candle* it giveth light, but when it is put out, then is the snuff or candle darkness: *Thus* also the light shineth from all the powers of the Father; but when the powers are perished or *corrupted*, then the light is extinguished, and the powers would remain in darkness, as is apparent by *Lucifer*.
>
> 15. In God the air also is not of such a kind, but is a lovely, pleasant, still breath or voice, blowing or moving; that is, the *exit*, going forth or moving of the powers is the *original* of the air, in which the Holy Ghost riseth up.

16. Neither is the water of such a kind in God, but it is the *source* or fountain in the powers, *not* of an elementary kind, as in this world; if I should liken it to anything, I must liken it to the sap or *juice* in an apple, but very bright and light-some, like heaven, which is the spirit of all powers.

17. It is lord Lucifer who hath thus *spoiled* it, that it rageth and raveth so in this world, which so runneth and floweth, and is so thick and dark, and moreover *if it runneth not*, it becometh stinking. . . .[18]

If one accepts this further link in the chain; if one takes this as the source in which Coleridge found his image of the illuminating candle, then it would seem that he *was* reading Boehme's *Aurora* at school. Or rather, to use his own expression, 'conjuring over' it: for the interest of that passage lies not only in the new filament of evidence that it brings to a knotty argument, but in the positive insight that it offers into the processes of Coleridge's imagination. We are enabled to glimpse him responding to the vivid images in Boehme's discourse and dwelling on them as a symbolic language in their own right – a language, one might say, for what Keats came to call 'the heart's imagination'. The bright lucency from a wax candle, the crispness and sweetness of an apple, the clear transparency of a running stream; as Boehme's images of the unfallen world join together in the imagination they form themselves into a composite imagery for what Coleridge conceived to be the state of the uncorrupted human heart. They are also mirrored in certain elements of his best imaginative poetry.

If we take this pattern of imagery a stage further, we may begin to see in it a further key to the nature of Coleridge's discourses in the Christ's Hospital cloister. For the writings of Iamblichus and Plotinus contain a not dissimilar imagery: God is seen as the central light of creation, the ever-ebullient fountain of all forms. Instead of a dark God who had set Newton's universe in motion and left it to run its course unimpeded, the eighteenth-century reader could find in these writings the intimations of a God dark only with excess of brightness, who flowed forth for ever as a mighty fountain of light, music and inspiration. To this Boehme's *Aurora* simply added a new dimension, emphasising the relationship between the ideas of

God as an infinite fountain, and of the sun as a similar fountain
of light and heat in the heavens, and the phenomenon of the
actual fountain to be found in every man, woman or child:
the fountain of the human heart.

Other factors, of course, affected Coleridge's thinking between
the time when he left school and the time when he came to
write his greatest poems; of which the only one that calls for
consideration here is the relationship with Wordsworth. Wordsworth came to know Coleridge several years later, when he had
passed through various misfortunes: his despair at college and
subsequent enlistment as a dragoon, his ill-fated marriage, his
illnesses. Wordsworth felt that the conditions of Coleridge's
education had had something to do with all this; that it was the
lack of direct contact with nature at an impressionable age that
had resulted in some of his weaknesses. In *The Prelude* he pictures
Coleridge, accustomed to lie on the leaded roof at Christ's Hospital and gaze at the sky,

> or haply, tired of this,
> To shut thine eyes, and by internal light
> See trees, and meadows, and thy native stream,
> Far distant, thus beheld from year to year
> Of thy long exile . . .
>
> (W Prel (1805) VI 280–4)

This need to make the forms of nature out of his own imagination, he goes on to assert, resulted in Coleridge's later tendency
to live in the world of words and images:

> I have thought
> Of thee, thy learning, gorgeous eloquence,
> And all the strength and plumage of thy youth,
> Thy subtle speculations, toils abstruse
> Among the schoolmen, and Platonic forms
> Of wild ideal pageantry, shaped out
> From things well-matched, or ill, and words for things,
> The self-created sustenance of a mind
> Debarred from Nature's living images,
> Compelled to be a life unto itself
> And unrelentingly possessed by thirst
> Of greatness, love, and beauty.
>
> (Ibid. 305–16)

If he himself had met Coleridge earlier, he suggests, his own nature, nurtured by those powers, might have helped guard Coleridge from excesses of eagerness and impetuosity.

At it was, the period of intense discussion between the two men had not begun in earnest until 1797, when they became neighbours in Somerset. The immediate effects of the dialogue when it did begin can hardly, I believe, be overestimated, though there is no space here for more than an outline of its apparent shape. What Wordsworth held out to Coleridge was, it may be argued, a sense of the consolation to be derived from constant access to the great forms of nature, the permanences which outlast individual human lives. Coleridge, in return, brought a new vividness to all the variegated workings of life; further, we may suppose, he transmitted his ideas (culled, we have argued, from Boehme and others) that there might be in the universe a great series of correspondences between the human heart, the work of all springs and fountains in nature and the sun itself – conceived not as a giant furnace gradually burning itself out over millions of years and running down to darkness and cold, but as a great fountain, taking back energy from the universe even as it emits light and heat – acting indeed like the human heart itself. When this mood was upon him, we may argue, Coleridge could look up at the sun and see it as an image of the splendour of the human heart; he could look down at the smallest spring and see it as an emblem of the heart's pathos. Under that spell, which transformed the whole universe into a universe of life rather than of death, every flower was a miniature fountain, energising from sun and rain, every spring of water an emblem of the life-process.

Wordsworth, we may further argue, was deeply attracted by this idea of Coleridge's, which threw an enchanted light over the whole of nature; but he was equally aware of the darker side to it all; that death no less than life is a reality, and that no amount of contemplation of upsurging life in the universe can change the grief which is felt over the loss of one human being by another. Yet side by side with this he seems to have expressed a further sense which Coleridge may or may not have had before they met: that death no less than life has its forms; that the body of death which a tree presents to us in winter has its own beauty, just as does the body of life which it shows us in spring;

and that everywhere around us, in sea-shells, or leaf skeletons,
or cobwebs, or honeycombs, we can find beautiful forms which
are also, in some sense, forms of death. If I am correct in this
assumption it becomes legitimate to picture Wordsworth and
Coleridge walking over the Quantocks in that year 1797–8 or
wandering by the seashore, looking all the time at things and
seeing them fall apart into their life forms and their death
forms. So Wordsworth contemplates a thorn which seems totally
dead but which is also buried in green life:

> Of leaves it has repaired its loss
> With heavy tufts of dark green moss
>
> (WPW II 240n)

– and goes on to relate that sight to the idea of a desolate mother
weeping for her child. Or he sits in a holly copse, a group of
evergreens, watching a hailstorm dancing in the middle of it,
and reflects on the strange paradox that while it is the holly that
is actually alive there, it is the dance of the lifeless hailstones
which gives one the *sense* of life.[19] Coleridge, meanwhile, is
looking for the minutest manifestations of life, from the dark
row of long dank weeds which drip at a waterspring in a dell,
but which never know any light from the fountain of the sun,
to the weird, creaking sound of a bird flying home at sunset, and
reflecting that 'no sound is dissonant that tells of life'.[20]

In Coleridge's greatest long poem these same extremes meet –
are indeed personified. What death would be without life we
know:

> *His* bones were black with many a crack,
>   All black and bare I ween;
> Jet-black and bare, save where with rust
> Of mouldy damps and charnel crust
>   They're patched with purple and green.
>
> (PW II 1035)

But what would life be without the substantial body which the
power of death makes for itself in us? Something very beautiful,
an entrancing spirit of gaiety and light? Not so, perhaps – and
Coleridge changes suggestively into the present tense:

> *Her* lips are red, *her* looks are free,
>   *Her* locks are yellow as gold:

> Her skin is as white as leprosy,
> And she is far liker Death than he;
> Her flesh makes the still air cold.

(Ibid.)

Nearly twenty years later he names her as 'The Nightmare Life-in-Death' – the essence, perhaps, of life when separated from the warmth of the living body; and she is *more* terrifying than death.

Death, in *The Ancient Mariner*, is fearful, but somewhere in the scale of fearfulness there seems to lurk the reflection that death is also, in some sense, strangely merciful as well – that it might be even more agonising to be forced to live perpetually with a tormented consciousness than to die in physical torments; and this reflection, I suspect, may have been prompted at least in part, by Wordsworth's response to the totality of nature's work.

We may explore the idea more closely by tracing the development of an image which is often associated with death in Coleridge's early work but which later comes to be seen in a more benevolent form: the image of ice. I mentioned earlier the sense of desolation and of physical cold which must often have threatened Coleridge during his schooldays, as he walked the chilly streets or huddled over his fire. And the imagery of ice as one finds it in Coleridge's early poetry normally yields an impression of blank desolation Sometimes he uses it directly, as an emblem of the hardened heart, on which a winter sun shines powerlessly. In the poem on the impending death of his sister (an event which must have affected him very deeply, but which he was not yet able to deal with adequately in verse) he writes of hopes blighted by frost and concludes:

> On me thy icy dart, stern Death, be prov'd; –
> Better to die, than live and not be lov'd!

(PW I 20)

Ice is the correlate of desolation and death. If occasionally he thinks of the attractions of ice in sunlight, it is to speak immediately of its transitoriness or deceitfulness.

Attention was being drawn in Coleridge's time, however, to a fact which has now become a fact of everyday living – that ice actually preserves the life of things. Mrs Barbauld, who as a

Unitarian writer was well known to Coleridge and addressed a
poem to him in the year 1797, had a few years before composed
an 'Inscription for an Ice-House', in which she wrote of the
marvel by which, in the very height of summer, 'stern Winter'
could be made to serve man with a work of benevolence:

> ... here he piles,
> While summer glows around, and southern gales
> Dissolve the fainting world, his treasured snows
> Within the rugged cave ...
>
> The rugged power, fair Pleasure's minister,
> Exerts his art to deck the genial board;
> Congeals the melting peach, the nectarine smooth,
> Burnished and glowing from the sunny wall:
> Darts sudden frost into the crimson veins
> Of the moist berry; moulds the sugared hail:
> Cools with his icy breath our flowing cups;
> Or gives to the fresh dairy's nectared bowls
> A quicker zest.[21]

Discoveries like this placed ice in a rather different light. And
Boehme, as we have seen, had set forward the suggestive theory
that ice and stones represented in nature – perhaps in some
sense *were* – the limits set to the fall of Lucifer.

To the idea of ice as preserver, as well as destroyer, of life we
may add another fact – that in it we may see, in an isolated
and pure form, one element in the whole creative process. Here
is something that looks absolutely lifeless, is lifeless by definition,
and yet if looked at closely it may be seen to embody in itself an
impulse to be found in all life: the impulse to form. The work of
ice on windowpanes which children instinctively humanise by
calling it the work of Jack Frost, or the great icebergs that are
found in northern latitudes are alike mute and vivid witnesses
to the fact that nature, even below the existence of life, still
creates itself into beautiful forms.

This realisation was, I believe, a source of excitement to Coleridge during the period of his great poetry, partly because it
offered him another symbolic language for the work of the
heart's imagination, placing it firmly in a poetic universe of
warmth and cold; a universe pitched between the fountain of

the sun – which is for ever giving itself out in energy and light yet which is always finding itself in its own unity as a mighty sphere – and the world of ice, for ever finding itself in its own form yet never losing its power to respond to the warmth of energy. Somewhere between the two, occupying a mediant position, is the moon, which, although dead, is neither deadening nor freezing; which, while giving out light, gives it (unlike the sun) in a form immediately apprehensible to the human eye. And this universe becomes a universe to which the human heart may fully respond precisely because the heart, too, expands and contracts – expanding in life-sustaining diastole, contracting again to find its own unity.

It was his delight in this idea, I submit, that gave Coleridge for a time an obsessive delight in certain aspects of nature, and in any lore concerning them – causing him, for example, to copy excitedly into his notebook an observation which he found in Maurice's *History of Hindostan*:

> In a cave in the mountains of Cashmere an Image of Ice, which makes its appearance thus – two days before the new *moon* there appears a bubble of Ice: which increases in size every day till the 15th day, at which it is an ell or more in height: then, as the moon decreases, the Image does also till it vanishes.   (CN I 240)

It was this also that made him envision as the supreme triumph for any sort of creative genius the creation of a work which would reproduce in finite terms that infinite dialectic between the expansive sun, finding its own form in the midst of its energy, and the hardened ice, for ever ready to lose or modify its form at the touch of warmth. Not for nothing is it that the 'miracle of rare device' in *Kubla Khan* is 'a sunny pleasure-dome with caves of ice'.

The same excitement, I would further submit, gave him the impulse to create a whole fiction which should take place in such a universe: where a man might pass between extremes of cold and heat and discover, as he experienced the dialectic between them, a key to the nature of the universe. And so he came to figure a story in which a man who did not understand the full significance of the world he lived in, whose behaviour had become hardened and frozen by custom, should have that

significance thrust upon him. The Ancient Mariner set out on his
voyage cheerily and carelessly; but he betrayed the inward state
of his *heart*, its inability to quicken and expand, when he looked
up at the one living being that had followed the ship from the
land of mist and snow and could think of nothing better to do
than to shoot it.

His subsequent experiences are appropriate. Because he has
shown the action of a fixed and frozen heart he is made to live
completely in a world of fixities and definites, where the sun
beats down remorselessly, where the ship stands still, where
there is not even a sense of time. Only when, in the midst of
those fixities, he sees the moon moving up the sky does anything
begin to stir in him; and it is his subsequent sense of expansive
energies at play in the universe that completes the process, causing his hardened heart to turn suddenly into a fountain:

> A spring of love gushed from my heart,
> And I blessed them unaware.

The immediate effects of the experience are a sense of release and
an ability to sleep. He wakes refreshed, to find that it is raining
and that his thirst is at last assuaged. But the relief is uneasy,
broken by fearful sights and sounds, which are followed by a
vision of the sun at dawn, receiving and emitting the sights and
sounds that pass to it from the spirits that visit the dead seamen.
At one time he endures total stasis, the ship being 'fixed' to the
ocean, then a sudden vehemence of motion which flings him into
a swoon. In that second state he hears two voices, which still
seem to be expressing the extremes of the universe into which
he has passed: for while the one knows only the world of ice, of
fixities and definites – yet still sends out its wandering albatrosses
of impulse to aid the creation of moving relationships, the other
speaks out of a more generous knowledge. The first knows only
a realm of experience where the best men can find to do with
divinity is to nail it to a fixed form; the other knows of the
expansive element in humanity, the honey-dew sap, that can
never be contained in this way:

> But ere my living life returned,
> I heard, and in my soul discerned
> Two voices in the air.

'Is it he?' quoth one, 'Is this the man?
By him who died on cross,
With his cruel bow he laid full low
The harmless Albatross.

The spirit who bideth by himself
In the land of mist and snow,
He loved the bird that loved the man
Who shot him with his bow.'

The other was a softer voice,
As soft as honey-dew:
Quoth he, 'The man hath penance done,
And penance more will do.'

And so the Mariner returns to a country where his first impulse
is to find a man who knows the issues of life and death to their
depths, the hermit who kneels at a dead form that is surrounded
by new life, a rotted old oak stump over which fresh moss has
completely grown. But even when he has told his story to the
hermit he does not possess his knowledge; he is merely possessed
by it. He can only retell, over and over again, what happened;
and the only moral that he can draw is a very simple one: that
it is desperately important for human beings to love.

In the years following the composition of his greatest poems
Coleridge continued in a career which was in many outward
respects disastrous. It was as if, like the Mariner himself, he
could not grasp the full significance of what had happened to
him: unable to possess his knowledge fully, he yet remained
strangely possessed by it. Was the universe that he had set up
simply a piece of 'gorgeous nonsense' – as he once described the
speculations of Plato?[22] Sometimes it must have seemed so, yet
there were also things which seemed after all to confirm it,
including some of the assertions of the German transcendentalist
philosophers. Years later, in *Biographia Literaria*, trying to make
sense of his career, we find him eagerly appropriating something
which Schelling had said and giving it prominence in his central
but fragmentary chapter on the imagination:

Des Cartes, speaking as a naturalist and in imitation of Archi-
medes, said, give me matter and motion and I will construct

you the universe ... In the same sense the transcendental philosopher says: grant me a nature having two contrary forces, the one of which tends to expand infinitely, while the other strives to apprehend or find itself in this infinity, and I will cause the world of intelligences with the whole system of their representations to rise up before you. Every other science presupposes intelligence as already existing and complete: the philosopher contemplates it in its growth ...

(BL I 195–6)

The hypothesis which the transcendental philosopher called for was the one that he himself had granted in creating the universe of *The Ancient Mariner*.

It had also facilitated the writing of one of his best other poems. Compared with the exciting rhythms and supernatural events of *The Ancient Mariner*, 'Frost at Midnight' is at first sight totally naturalistic. No hint of the supernatural – apart, perhaps, from the simple superstition surrounding the fluttering film on the grate – falls across its lines. But this simply shows how well Coleridge has here continued to focus such concerns in his descriptions of the real world. What he first does is to introduce the image of ice:

> The Frost performs its secret ministry
> Unhelped by any wind ...

(PW I 240)

The word 'secret' is ambiguous: it can suggest either the sinister or the revelatory. For us, who have been following Coleridge's development, the word 'ministry' gives a better clue: it indicates a benevolence in the strange, silent work by which the frost makes beautiful forms without the aid of movement from the world outside. And if there is something a little disturbing about the silence, broken as it is only by the hoot of an owl, indoors it is mitigated by the poet's awareness of the baby sleeping peacefully by his side, and of the unquivering thin blue flame on the grate, accompanied by the flickering of the film, which extends the sense of ongoing life.

The movement of that film, with the old country superstition that it betokens the arrival of a stranger, makes natural a transition to recollection of the times when, at school, he saw the

same phenomenon, drifted into a warm dream of his birthplace,
and, all next day, found himself subconsciously expectant:

> But O! how oft,
> How oft, at school, with most believing mind,
> Presageful, have I gazed upon the bars,
> To watch that fluttering *stranger*! and as oft
> With unclosed lids, already had I dreamt
> Of my sweet birth-place, and the old church-tower,
> Whose bells, the poor man's only music, rang
> From morn to evening, all the hot Fair-day,
> So sweetly, that they stirred and haunted me
> With a wild pleasure, falling on mine ear
> Most like articulate sounds of things to come!
> So gazed I, till the soothing things, I dreamt,
> Lulled me to sleep, and sleep prolonged my dreams!
> And so I brooded all the following morn,
> Awed by the stern preceptor's face, mine eye
> Fixed with mock study on my swimming book:
> Save if the door half opened, and I snatched
> A hasty glance, and still my heart leaped up,
> For still I hoped to see the *stranger's* face,
> Townsman, or aunt, or sister more beloved,
> My play-mate when we both were clothed alike!

His final thought is of that sister who had succumbed to 'death's
icy dart' in the year he left school. Now that train of thought
prompts him to project an upbringing for the baby by his side
that will fill up the defects of his own early education and teach
him, by Wordsworthian methods, to understand the wholeness
of nature, seeing it as a revelation of the nature of the God that
moves in it.

> Dear Babe, that sleepest cradled by my side
> Whose gentle breathings, heard in this deep calm,
> Fill up the interspersèd vacancies
> And momentary pauses of the thought!
> My babe so beautiful! it thrills my heart
> With tender gladness, thus to look at thee,
> And think that thou shalt learn far other lore,
> And in far other scenes! For I was reared
> In the great city, pent 'mid cloisters dim,

And saw nought lovely but the sky and stars.
But *thou*, my babe! shalt wander like a breeze
By lakes and sandy shores, beneath the crags
Of ancient mountain, and beneath the clouds,
Which image in their bulk both lakes and shores
And mountain crags: so shalt thou see and hear
The lovely shapes and sounds intelligible
Of that eternal language, which thy God
Utters, who from eternity doth teach
Himself in all, and all things in himself.
Great universal Teacher! he shall mould
Thy spirit, and by giving make it ask.

In the vision of nature thus projected for Hartley's future delight, all seasons will be seen to have their own sweetness, so that he will not be able to lose sight of an essential interrelation between the work of life and that of death. A lucency and sweetness like that which we noted in Boehme's images of unfallen nature are here subsumed into a triumphant description of nature as she actually is:

Therefore all seasons shall be sweet to thee,
Whether the summer clothe the general earth
With greenness, or the redbreast sit and sing
Betwixt the tufts of snow on the bare branch
Of mossy apple-tree, while the nigh thatch
Smokes in the sun-thaw; whether the eave-drops fall
Heard only in the trances of the blast,
Or if the secret ministry of frost
Shall hang them up in silent icicles,
Quietly shining to the quiet Moon.

That, in all modern editions, is where the poem ends. When first published, however, it went on to conclude as follows:

Like those, my babe! which ere tomorrow's warmth
Have capp'd their sharp keen points with pendulous drops,
Will catch thine eye, and with their novelty
Suspend thy little soul; then make thee shout
And stretch and flutter from thy mother's arms
As thou wouldst fly for very eagerness.

(PW I 243n)

Humphry House's judgement, that the conclusion of the poem at the earlier point (an alteration made ten years later) was one of Coleridge's best artistic decisions,[23] is at one level indisputable. The effect of the new ending is to round the poem with a sense of mystery. The magic of moonlight on frost is universal to human experience; superimposed now upon the description of the seasons, it replaces the uneasy peace with which the poem began by a final sense of fulfilment. But House also said that the curtailment was justified also because 'once the vista of new domestic detail was opened there was no reason why it should not be indefinitely followed, with increasing shapelessness'.

Here we may legitimately disagree. For if the argument I have been pursuing is acceptable, in 'that imagined moment' next day, when Coleridge would see Hartley first suspend his soul for a moment in entrancement and then open his arms in delight, there was presented an enactment of precisely the same process that Coleridge had been thinking about in other fields: in the first moment of wonder, the baby's heart would momentarily contract, finding a unity in all that it saw; then it would expand violently in an eager access of energy, a desire to reach out, even fly to that beauty. It is, in other words, an emblematic moment in the growth of that intelligence which in Coleridge's view is nourished and finds its growth at a level below that of normal behaviour: and the point that perfects the last line is that the very phenomenon which causes the baby to do this is of the same, or complementary, form: it is the moment when the light of the expansive sun is caught in the formed icicles that excites this corresponding delight in the primal being of the child. The point was however an esoteric one; and in the later edition he was wise to change the poem into a form to which the public reader could immediately respond, even if this involved changing a poem of process, reaching beyond itself, into a more self-contained piece.

There was to be much disillusionment in the years that followed. Coleridge broke his health by intense researches, by drug-taking, by a desperate and hopeless love for Sara Hutchinson. He moved into a stage where he lived between periods of creativity, half-redolent of his old brilliance, a time of torpor and unreality when he would sometimes ease his way through difficult situations by actions with a strong savour of humbug

or dishonesty. Hartley's failure to fulfil the promise that his
father had discerned was an added grief.[24] But even in his ruin,
Coleridge remains a complicated figure, not easily to be put by.

For Wordsworth, particularly, Coleridge remained ambiguous
and haunting: when he came to sum him up after his death,
moreover, he used an expression curiously apposite to all I have
been saying. Two years had not passed, he said,

> Since every mortal power of Coleridge
> Was frozen at its marvellous source.
>
> (WPW IV 277)

It is perhaps significant that it should have been the images of
ice and spring that rose immediately in his imagination.

Certainly the images may be pursued further. For if one is
trying to see Coleridge whole one may simply cast a cold eye
on his products, in which case, as one surveys the things that
went wrong, his whole career may seem to tail off into a long
icy waste; if, on the other hand, one looks into the processes of
his mind, one keeps glimpsing the flash of sun in the ice, the
informing intelligence which insists that its own activity is
itself dialectical and only to be apprehended by similar dialectical
processes in the reader. One thinks again of that epitaph, in
which he asks his reader to pray that

> he who many a year with toil of breath
> Found death in life, may here find life in death!
> Mercy for praise – to be forgiven for fame
> He ask'd, and hoped, through Christ. Do thou the same!
>
> (PW I 492)

For us, also, the issues of life-in-death or death-in-life remain
closely adjacent to those of mercy or praise, when we try to
evaluate Coleridge's achievement. And in one case, as it happens,
they are very literally interrelated. In 1818 Coleridge sent some
verses to an acquaintance, including one entitled 'What is
Life?', which had appeared in an earlier notebook as follows:

> Resembles Life, what once was deem'd of Light,
> Too simple in itself for human Sight?
> An absolute Self? an Element ungrounded?
> All, that we see, all colors of all shade

By incroach of Darkness made?
Is Life itself by consciousness unbounded,
And all the Thoughts, Pains, Joys of mortal Breath
A War-embrace of wrestling Life and Death?

(CN II 2224 f25v)

When Coleridge put that into his letter he said that it had been written 'at the age of 15 or 16' and that he submitted the verses as biographical curiosities, and as 'evidence of my very early Turn to metaphysics and speculative philosophy'.[25] Such evidence as we have, on the other hand, suggests strongly that the verse was written in 1805, when he was thirty-three and in Malta.[26] We cannot be certain that he was not remembering and reworking a schoolboy poem, of course, but in any case it seems clear that his account is not strictly truthful. If it does not do to trust Coleridge wholeheartedly in these matters, however, it does not always do to distrust him, either; and we ought to note one curious feature of the poem. The last lines echo a passage in Boehme's *Aurora*:

the Deity does not stand still, but works and rises up without *Intermission*, as a pleasant Wrestling, Moving, or Struggling.
Like two Creatures which in great Love play together, embracing, struggling and wrestling one with another . . .[27]

Coleridge has changed the love-embrace into a war-embrace (as he also did when he described how 'in Shakespeare's *Poems* the creative power and the intellectual energy wrestle as in a war embrace'),[28] but it is hard to believe that the source of the image as a whole was not in *Aurora* – which we have found some grounds for believing that he was reading (as he himself claimed) in adolescence. In view of this we cannot altogether dismiss the possibility that this sense of dialectic – even perhaps including a sense of it as operating within the life-process itself – was already present to him even in his schooldays, to be revivified and newly pointed during his dialogues with Wordsworth. It is this, perhaps, that is in his mind when he refers to his 'very early Turn to metaphysics and speculative philosophy' and dates the whole poem to his schooldays. When approached with the warmth of sympathy and charity, many of Coleridge's untruths lose their uncompromising frigidity in this way, to suggest some current in his imaginative development – still, apparently, rising up to haunt him in later years.

In such cases, of course, the evidence is often ambiguous rather than firm, its significance dependent upon the attitude of the interpreter. Not always so, however. At what stage Coleridge formulated firmly the mythology of sun god, ice caves, fountains and the inspiring damsel that is to be found deployed in *Kubla Khan*, we do not know. What we do know for certain is that on 31 March 1791, six months before leaving school, he sent a letter to his brother George in which he enclosed a light-hearted poem called 'A Mathematical Problem', and which he prefaced with a statement including the following:

> I have often been surprised that Mathematics, the Quintessence of Truth, should have found admirers so few and so languid. – Frequent consideration and minute scrutiny have at length unravelled the cause – viz – that though Reason is feasted, Imagination is starved: whilst Reason is luxuriating in it's proper Paradise, Imagination is wearily travelling over a dreary desert. To assist *Reason* by the stimulus of *Imagination* is the *Design* of the following Production . . .

> . . . I may justly plume myself that I *first* have drawn the Nymph Mathesis from the visionary caves of Abstracted Idea, and caused her to unite with Harmony. The first-born of this union I now present to you . . .					(CL I 7)

The attempt to match the severity of strict logic with the spontaneous springs of imagination, to make the disciplined nymph Mathesis come forth from the visionary caves to meet the genius of harmony, can be traced through the remainder of Coleridge's thought. (As late as 1830 he could still describe the Pythagorean and Platonic geometricians as 'the great fountains of pure Mathesis'.)[29] Whether in what it did to Coleridge, that relationship is to be regarded as a love embrace or a war embrace, is matter for debate; what is clear is that the need for such a relationship was something that he was already learning and teaching before he left the severe cloisters (and the springing waters of the cloister pump) at Christ's Hospital.

4

Coleridge: A Bridge between Science and Poetry*

Kathleen Coburn

One may reasonably ask at the outset why the Royal Institution should celebrate the bicentenary of an English poet, especially one commonly reputed to be anything but a scientist. The answer lies in the remarkableness of both institutions, Coleridge and the Royal one (for Coleridge is a kind of institution in himself); both are characterised by an imaginative facility in looking at the specific in their field of vision, and also at the wider ranges of more general and complex human considerations. It was natural that Coleridge and the Royal Institution, soon after its founding in 1799, should find each other. The view that Coleridge was anti-science is quite erroneous. Nor did he believe in a world of two cultures.

So far as we know, Coleridge first set foot in the present building in January 1802, to attend the chemistry lectures of his friend from Bristol days, Humphry Davy. Of these lectures as recorded by Coleridge I should like to say something presently, but first a few observations on the context in which Davy and Coleridge met and associated.

It was in Clifton, in the Pneumatic Institution, founded to investigate and minister to a variety of respiratory diseases by the amazing and much too little regarded Dr Thomas Beddoes, father of the better-known Thomas Lovell Beddoes, the melancholy poet. Thomas Beddoes Senior was anything but melancholy – an indefatigable, optimistic man, always pursuing new lines of investigation, distressed by the slave-trade, the neglect

* A Friday evening discourse delivered at The Royal Institution on 27 October 1972 and reproduced with permission from the *Proceedings of The Royal Institution of Great Britain*, vol. 46 (1973).

of the poor by the Government, the Church and his own profession, and equally fired by Kant's critical philosophy, the French Revolution, and advanced and irregular ideas in education; he was a natural catalyst for the young. Had he not been dismissed from the chair of Chemistry in Oxford because of a long, dangerous satirical poem? He brought together in his library and laboratory men of lively imaginations like his own, radical, literary, philosophical and scientifically inquisitive.[1]

When Davy and Coleridge met in 1799, Davy was twenty, Coleridge nearly twenty-seven. They were in some respects not unlike – two impulsive idealistic young men. Neither was professionally trained. Coleridge, after a spasmodic career at Cambridge, had left without a degree, and Davy never attended a university. Both were precocious dreaming youths, interested in philosophy and poetry and the beauty of the natural world. Lamb remembered Coleridge at Christ's Hospital as a schoolboy spouting Plotinus and Homer,[2] and Maria Edgeworth early complained that Davy got into what she called 'the depths of metaphysics' in the middle of Bond Street.[3] Both had written a good deal of verse; Coleridge had already two volumes published over his own name and *The Rime of the Ancient Mariner* and some other poems anonymously in the *Lyrical Ballads*. When they met, Davy's heroes were, I suppose, Newton and Lavoisier, Coleridge's, to select but two of an army, Plato and Wordsworth.

Their questions to each other and their shared enthusiasms promised to set the world on fire. It is not altogether surprising that their plans for their own education show a remarkable resemblance. Davy at sixteen made his list of subjects:

1. Theology.
    Or Religion,   ⎫   ⎧ taught by Nature.
    Ethics, or moral virtues ⎭   ⎩ by Revelation.
2. Geography.
3. My Profession.   5. Language.
    1. Botany.   1. English.
    2. Pharmacy.   2. French.
    3. Nosology.   3. Latin.
    4. Anatomy.   4. Greek.
    5. Surgery.   5. Italian.
    6. Chemistry.   6. Spanish.
4. Logic.   7. Hebrew.

6. Physics.
   1. The doctrines and properties of natural bodies.
   2. Of the operations of nature.
   3. Of the doctrines of fluids.
   4. Of the properties of organised matter.
   5. Of the organisation of matter.
   6. Simple Astronomy.
7. Mechanics.   9. History and Chronology.
8. Rhetoric and Oratory.   10. Mathematics.[4]

Coleridge's plans for himself in 1796 in a letter to his friend
Thomas Poole are of a similar magnitude:

1. To learn German in order to translate all of Schiller (he
   already knew Latin, Greek and some French & Hebrew).
2. To study Chemistry & anatomy in Germany.
3. To bring home a load of German theologians, and Kant.[5]

To prepare himself for writing an epic poem he said:

> ... I would be a tolerable Mathematician, I would thoroughly
> know Mechanics, Hydrostatics, Optics, and Astronomy,
> Botany, Metallurgy, Fossilism, Chemistry, Geology, Anatomy,
> Medicine – then the *mind of man* then the *minds of men* – in
> all Travels, Voyages, and Histories. . . .   (CL I 320–1)

These ambitious young polymaths, their childhoods rooted
in the late eighteenth century, found common ground in a
passionate desire to carry further the Newtonian picture of the
grand design of nature and also in the conviction that, by the
grace of God, and the new revolutionary humanitarianism blow-
ing over from France, and by the critical philosophy from
Germany, and by the literary and moral purgation going on in
the return to naturalness in English poetry, men's lives were
going to be transformed.

Davy and Coleridge both contributed to Southey's so-called
Annual Anthology of poetry. It is of some interest to notice
their choices of subject. In the volume for 1799, in which many
of the contributions (by Charles Lamb, George Dyer, Charles
Lloyd, Robert Lovell, the two Cottles, and many by Southey
himself) showed considerable lightness of heart, or at least some
fun here and there, Davy's first poem, grandly entitled 'The

Sons of Genius', was rather solemn in the rhetorical late eighteenth-century style; his sons of genius were pretty clearly scientists.

Coleridge's contributions to the next volume tended to be either angry-young-man poems, like 'The British Stripling's War-Song' or 'Fire, Famine, and Slaughter' or delicate little bits of sentiment like 'Home-sick, Written in Germany', or 'Something Childish, but very Natural'. His most memorable poem in the volume was one of his finest, 'This Lime-Tree Bower my Prison'. Coleridge's poems in these early volumes have a freshness, a freedom and a modesty about them; Davy's are a bit shrill, strained and conventional. On the whole these two decided their careers wisely, Davy for chemistry and Coleridge for poetry and the written word. But they both had a real zest for poetry, and a seriousness about their mental preoccupations that must have brought them together.

Through Beddoes, Davy and Coleridge also met a more conservative character, Dr Erasmus Darwin, grandfather of the more famous Charles Darwin, another physician-scientist-cum-poet, then in his seventies, who strongly influenced both of them. He managed to unite chemistry and versification, for example, in 200 octavo pages of *The Botanic Garden*, where the learned and speculative notes on physical, chemical and electrical topics interested Coleridge more than the poetry, notes on such topics as 'Nymphs of Fire' which nymphs turn out to be gases expanding under heat! There are long notes on Herschel's discoveries, Cavendish and Lavoisier on hydrogen, the gymnotus or electrical eel, caloric and electricity, and others of the same kidney. Dr Darwin was the poet as practical man. In my view his most charming and perhaps most practical work – I speak here as a dabbler myself in the primitive art and science of farming – is a poem printed in a large prose work entitled *Phytologia; or the Philosophy of Agriculture and Gardening, with the theory of draining morasses, and with an improved construction of the drill plough*. The poem entitled 'The Cultivation of Broccoli' is full of good advice, *still sound*, all in heroic couplets.[6] In fact the whole work, as they used to say, 'should be had in all families'. Not to digress further than even a Coleridgian should, the point of mentioning Erasmus Darwin is that although Davy quickly left him far behind as a scientist, and

Coleridge as poet and philosopher, both of them were drawn to him as a practising scientist and poet, a mind of considerable originality that supported their desire to believe in and understand the necessary links between all aspects of the cosmos and the human mind.

A stimulating intellectual life was flowing around the young men in Bristol.

There are various amusing stories about the Pneumatic Institution there and Davy's experiments with nitrous oxide in which all his friends, including Coleridge, joined, but there is one told by Davy's biographer, John Ayrton Paris, that involved a moment of eye-catching between Davy and Coleridge.[7] A paralysed patient had been encouraged to believe in the success of Davy's nitrous oxide treatment. Coleridge was present when Davy, as part of the examination, put a thermometer under the man's tongue. Thinking that treatment had begun, the man enthusiastically acclaimed the good effects all over his body. Davy, throwing a meaning glance at Coleridge, told the chap to return tomorrow. After about a fortnight's treatment of thermometer-under-tongue the patient was dismissed cured. Now Coleridge was always interested in what we should now call psychosomatic illnesses, in delusion of all kinds, as phenomena. Indeed, coining the word, he said there should be a science of psycho-somatology.[8] Was this not a bond between him and Davy – as for instance it would not be between either of them and Southey? At least Davy appears to have counted on Coleridge's making no blundering remark where a tactful silence was needed.

It was Coleridge who in London in January 1800, while Davy was still in Bristol, negotiated with Longman for the publication of Davy's first book, *Researches chemical and philosophical chiefly concerning nitrous oxide.* He wrote to Davy about the business details and then went on:

> Godwin talks evermore of you with lively affection. – 'What a pity that such a Man should degrade his vast Talents to Chemistry' – cried he to me. – Why, quoth I, how, Godwin! can you thus talk of a science, of which neither you nor I understand an iota? &c &c – & I defended Chemistry as knowingly at least as Godwin attacked it – affirmed that it united

the opposite advantages of immaterializing [the] mind without destroying the definiteness of [the] Ideas – nay even while
it gave clearness to them – And eke that being necessarily
[per]formed with the passion of Hope, it was p[oetica]l – &
we both agreed (for G. as we[ll as I] thinks himself a Poet)
that *the Poet* is the Greatest possible character – &c &c.
Modest Creatures! – Hurra, my dear Southey – You [& I,] &
Godwin, & Shakespeare, & Milton, with what an athanasiophagous Grin we shall march together – *we poets*: Down with
all the rest of the World! – By the word athanasiophagous I
mean devouring Immortality by anticipation – 'Tis a sweet
Word! –

God bless you, my dear Davy! Take my nonsense like a
pinch of snuff – sneeze it off, it clears the head – & to Sense &
yourself again – With most affectionate esteem

Your's ever

S. T. Coleridge   (CL I 557)

I read this characteristic bit of Coleridgian boisterousness as an
indication of the spirit in which the non-warfare between science
and poetry was conducted by these two brilliant young men.

A negative attitude towards chemistry and science generally
has been sometimes attributed to Coleridge. He has been said
to hold that the scientific intellect is merely 'passive' and that
science is 'dead and spiritless'.[9] This interpretation, every way
false to Coleridge's position, comes partly from lumping Coleridge with Wordsworth, partly from a mistaken view of what
Coleridge meant by the Kantian 'understanding' (which though
second fiddle to reason and imagination was for him neither
passive nor superficial), and in part from misconstruing a certain
letter he wrote to Davy in 1801, as follows:

... If you write to me, pray in a couple of sentences tell me
whether Herschel's Thermometric *Spectrum* (in the Philos.
Trans.) will lead to any Revolution in the chemical Philosophy.
– As far as *words* go, I have become a formidable chemist –
having got by heart a prodigious quantity of terms &c to
which I attach *some* ideas – very scanty in number, I assure
you, & right meagre in their individual persons. That which
most discourages me in it is that I find all *power* & vital
attributes to depend on modes of *arrangement* – and that

Chemistry throws not even a distant rush-light glimmer upon this subject. The *reasoning* likewise is always unsatisfactory to me – I am perpetually saying – probably, there are many agents hitherto undiscovered. This cannot be *reasoning*; for in all conclusive reasoning we must have a deep conviction that all the *terms* have been exhausted. This is saying no more than that (with Dr Beddoes's leave) chemistry can never possess the same kind of certainty with mathematics – in truth, it is saying nothing. I grow however exceedingly interested in the subject. – ...   (CL II 72)

This is hardly a letter hostile to chemistry, though Coleridge is having intellectual problems with it, but one admittedly awkward sentence in it has been distorted in quotation. Coleridge wrote:

This is saying no more than that chemistry can never possess the same kind of certainty with mathematics – in truth, it is saying nothing.

This by elisions was made by at least two eminent Davy scholars[10] to read:

Chemistry is saying nothing.

The impersonal pronoun *it* is the culprit, but Coleridge's intention appears clearly to be – in paraphrase –

To say [as some persons do] that chemistry cannot possess the same kind of certainty with mathematics is, [in effect,] to say nothing at all.

No, Coleridge's excitement about the rapidly developing chemistry of his day was intense. 'Every subject in Davy's mind has the principle of vitality. Living thoughts spring up like turf under his feet,'[11] he said to Cottle. For the extent of his involvement in Davy's work and chemical problems there is plentiful evidence. For example: Davy in his first Bakerian lecture in 1806 on 'The Chemical Agencies of Electricity' speculated that chemical affinity, or 'combination', might 'depend upon the balance of the natural electrical energies of bodies'.[12] In a marginal note about 1812 or later, on a pamphlet of Schelling (1806), Coleridge remarked that it would be well if, as Schelling

had argued, compounds were in fact bits of matter bound together by a living copula, but it was not proved. He went on to
say:

> So I hoped it would have been when Sir H. Davy adopted my
> suggestion that all Composition consisted in the Balance of
> opposing Energies. But alas! this still doubtful Copula of the
> neg. and pos. Electricities is a mere plausible Datum for Hope
> as to the union of two or more in a third. . . .[13]

Coleridge's memorandum was made only to himself and one
would not wish to make foolish claims, but one may I think
legitimately argue that at the very least the new chemistry and
its use of electrical polarities excited Coleridge's lively interest
and participation. The suggestion he says he had made to Davy
is central in his thinking.

By March 1801 Davy was established and lecturing at the
Royal Institution. By a truly Coleridgian circumnavigation we
come back, then, to Davy's course of public chemistry lectures
from January to March 1802 which Coleridge rushed up to
London to attend. Forsaking his hosts and the Christmas parties
in Somerset, he made the journey (thirteen changes of carriage)
to sit at Davy's feet, a new pocket notebook in his hands, now
called Notebook 8. He said he went to Davy's lectures to increase
his stock of metaphors.[14] I wonder – without underrating the
importance of metaphor to Coleridge – if this was not a jesting
bit of one-upmanship in their friendly rivalry? The quips of
young men should not necessarily be taken so seriously as they
sometimes are in academia, and at a distance in time. In any case,
it is clear that in this lecture auditorium in 1802 the irrepressible
inquirer in Coleridge was clearly fascinated by a chemist's way
of presenting concepts through the visual experience of the
experiments. And by a chemist's way of thinking about matter.
He took no notes on Davy's magnificent Introductory Discourse
on the general relation of chemistry to other sciences and
the arts. He was waiting for the factual chemistry of the laboratory. It is something of a shock however, even to a hardened
Coleridgian, to open Notebook 8 and find in Coleridge's auto-
graph such specific chemistry as this:

> Zinc filings acted on by a diluted sulphuric acid evolves
> hydrogen gas. Borax with a porcelain clay good Lute for high

degrees of heat – for lower degrees Lime with white of Eggs, but this must be applied fresh. Oxygen Gas discovered by Priestly – easiest procured by the action of black Oxyd of Manganese – & Sulphuric Acid – mix equal quantities in a retort thro' a funnel (to prevent the neck of the Retort being dirtied) – take out the funnel & put the glass stopper in the place – & put it over the Lamp, the end of the Retort in the water Trough—   (CN I 1098)

So, using his skill as one of the best newspaper reporters of his day, Coleridge rapidly wrote his detailed notes as he watched Davy go through demonstrations of the properties of oxygen, hydrogen and nitrogen, of phosphorus, sulphur and carbon, and what were called 'fixed alkalis'.

During some of Davy's lecture experiments involving carbon, Coleridge found at least one metaphor he was looking for. To quote his notes:

Carbon pure in Diamond – Diamond pure chrystallized Carbon/ – The Carbon in charcoal & common Coal burns with much less degrees of Heat than the Diamond/Charcoal contains Carbon in proportion to its weight & density—
(Ibid. f12)

Then, after a few more jottings,

Diamond $+ \times$ Oxygen $=$ Charcoal. N.B. Cottle's Psalms.
(Ibid. f28v)

Joseph Cottle, to whom William Wordsworth and Coleridge and the rest of us owe the publication of the *Lyrical Ballads*, was the butt of many good-natured jokes because of his uncontrollable vanity about his own feeble poems and translations. The jests tended to outlive the poems. About twenty years later Coleridge in another notebook paraphrased his lecture note:

Cottle's Psalms with morals of his own added to each. – Diamond + Oxygen = Charcoal. Even so on the fire-spark of his Zeal did Cottle place the King David Diamond (worth a hundred Pitt, or even Great Mogul Diamonds) and caused to pass over it ⟨the oxygenous⟩ *blast* of his own Inspiration . . . – – & lo! the Diamond becomes a bit of Charcoal. N.B. – Oxygene, just as Homogene, Heterogene &c – i.e. of

the Ox genus: on which Jo. ought to congratulate himself, as
it follows perforce, that he is so far secure from blundering
that he will never make a *Bull*.   (N 24 f59v)

Coleridge as punster is admittedly more in evidence here than
Coleridge as chemist, or poet either, yet chemistry supplied the
ammunition and the critic of poetry the aim for a pretty accurate
hit. Again in the 1802 lecture, he forgot gravity and jotted down
in his notebook, a few minutes after experiments with chlorine
and nitrogen peroxide:

If all aristocrats here, how easily Davy might poison them
all—   (CN I 1098 f31)

Yet it is clear from his sixty pages of full notes that metaphors
and puns and jokes, irresistible though they were, were secondary to his attempts to learn some chemistry, especially its mode
of thought, as well as its results.

His early reading of Newton, and Priestley, and later his
reading of the Germans, all show an untiring interest in theories
of colour and light, but his notes in this lecture room show also
the sensuous delight he took in the actual colours released in
Davy's experiments:

... *Exper.* Ether in the same manner, burns bright indeed in
the atmosphere, but o! how brightly whitely vividly beautiful
in Oxygen gas. ...   (Ibid. f5)

There followed another experiment in an eudiometer to
examine the purity of Oxygen. 'Hydrogen Gas', Coleridge then
notes, was 'discovered truly by Cavendish'.

'Sulphur', Coleridge observed, 'heated, burns blue, in higher
heat white, in Oxygen gas a most beautiful purple,'[15] and in the
next lecture, on the combustion of metals by Oxygen, he follows
Davy through his flaming demonstrations with zinc, tin, lead,
copper, iron, steel, gold, silver and platina – and then with
various earths – where of 'Alumine, or earth of clay' Coleridge
made a note that it is 'insoluble in water, but easily diffused thro'
it – combinable with all the acids – contracts in volume in proportion to its heat – hence Wedgewood's pyrometer, Alumine
forms the basis of Porcelain & pottery – combined with flint,
magnesia, & other earths'.[16] Just as he had been interested earlier

in the chemistry of Thomas Poole's tanyard, so he is personally involved here in the chemistry of Wedgwood china. Chemistry had meaning for him in daily experience, simply because he asked questions about cause and effect everywhere.

Part of what most attracted him to chemistry, and what was to propel him towards reading English and German chemists for the rest of his life, was his awareness that what Davy in this room was releasing from combinations of matter was energy. Flames, detonations, smells, changes of weight and colour, gases expanding and contracting, metals fusing, minerals making water boil, and so on. It is a philosophical interest rather than a purely scientific one; the scoffers may say that it arose out of a desire to see matter proved to be non-material. Perhaps it did. It came also from a desire to understand the links between the perceiver and the perceived, still a major problem in philosophy. Coleridge spent his life searching for the laws within the impalpable, within poems, within persons, within social systems, and for the relation of these to things without us. Davy was searching out laws of substances hitherto unknown by revealing that beneath the static appearance of the stone, or the powder, or the liquid, there may be the flame, the loud bang, the explosive energy. They were both enraptured by the revelation of unsuspected relationships in the vast diversities of things, inanimate as well as animate. Was there then a vital principle behind everything, even matter?

Coleridge has often been accused of being so interested in generalities as to be vague and superficial, or worse. In fact his observations and curiosity were remarkably specific, and his interest often very practical. For instance, on board ship he made a note to ask Davy about the chemistry of bilge water, prompted by the colour and the stench, and similarly he wanted to know about 'the large and small pieces of Kennel Coal found frequently mixed with Sea-coal in my fireplace in the Courier office in the Strand'.[17] In Germany, finding sugar made out of beets, he brought back in his notebook a detailed account of the process, possibly for Davy and the Board of Agriculture; in 1799 in the wartime sugar shortage, it would be not only useful, but a weapon against the sugar and slave-trade.[18] Again, irritated by the poor paper of many German books, so highly absorbent that he could not write his marginal jottings in ink, he bursts out, about 125 years before the ball-point pen was invented, 'what we need is a dry ink'.[19]

It is hoped that one of the merits of publishing his works *in toto* will be that this concreteness will be displayed; otherwise we tend to fall back on generalities (our own and his) and create the impression of a vague theoriser. What his works fully published will show is that Coleridge mostly knew what he was talking about from knowing it on the skin, from experience, from strenuous thought and hard work. No one of the sciences was his central concern; all were involved in his attempts to order his intellectual world, but chemistry in a primary way. If I cannot adequately represent here the range of his scientific knowledge (nor am I equal to that task) I can perhaps illustrate from an unpublished notebook entry written some time in the 1820s how real and permeative were its relations in his mind.

He has drawn six or seven pages of diagrams representing a 'Genesis and ascending scale of physical Powers', and then says:

... The object, which I proposed to myself in the fore-going Scale, is simply that of awakening and exercising in the Beginner's Mind the faculty of recognizing the same Idea or radical Thought in a number of Things and Terms which he had ⟨never⟩ previously considered as having any affinity or connection; which he had taken, each by itself and insulated, or if he ever had thought of two of them at the same time, had brought them together by the conjunction disjunctive of Contrast or Contrariety: Thus the common men would either never think of the Gas Lights in the London Shops, and of Water in any relation to each other, or only as Contraries, Fire and Water – and such compleat Contraries, that he sports at their conjunction as an instance of difficulty that is humanly an impossibility. – 'He will never set the Thames on Fire' – i.e. He is no Conjuror: He will not work *miracles* –. Who ever attended a first course of Chemical Lectures, or read for the first time a compendium of modern Chemistry (Lavoisier, Parkinson, Thomson, or Brande) without experiencing, even as a *sensation*, a sudden *enlargement* & *emancipation* of his Intellect, when the conviction first flashed upon him that the Flame of the Gas Light, and the River-Water were the same things (=elements) and different only as A *uniting* with B, and AB united? or AB balanc*ing* and AB balanc*ed*? 'Thus, as the Lunatic, the Lover, and the Poet' suggest each other to (*Shakespear's*) Theseus, as soon as his mind presents to him the *one Form*, of which they are but Varieties; so Water and Flame, the Diamond, the Charcoal, and the mantling Champagne with its ebullient sparkles, are convoked and fraternized by the Theory of the Chemist.— (*Turn to the Friend, Vol. III. P. 174*)   (N 23 ff 31–2)

When we turn as instructed to the *Friend* III 174, we find references to the law

> which, as the root of all these powers, the chemical philosopher, whatever his theory may be, is instinctively labouring to extract. This instinct, again, is itself but the form, in which the idea, the mental Correlative of the law, first announces its incipient germination in his own mind: and hence proceeds the striving after unity of principle through all the diversity of forms.... This is, in truth, the first charm of chemistry, and the secret of the almost universal interest excited by its discoveries.... It is the sense of a principle of connection given by the mind, and sanctioned by the correspondency of nature. Hence the strong hold which in all ages chemistry has had on the imagination. If in SHAKESPEARE we find nature idealized into poetry, through the creative power of a profound yet observant meditation, so through the meditative observation of a DAVY, a WOOLLASTON, or a HATCHETT;... we find poetry, as it were, substantiated and realized in nature: yea, nature itself disclosed to us, GEMINAM *istam naturam, quae fit et facit, et creat et creatur,* [the dual nature, which is made and makes, both creates and is created] as at once the poet and the poem!   (Friend I 471)

So Humphry Davy and Shakespeare are yoked together.

From Davy's 1802 lectures until the Bakerian lecture in 1807 in which he announced the decomposition of the caustic alkalis, relations with Coleridge were close and cordial. Letters exchanged in 1804 just as Coleridge left for Malta are moving in their confident and intimate candour. In that period Davy went from strength to strength, Coleridge from unhappiness to prolonged despondency, from rheumatic and respiratory illnesses to addiction to opium, from an acute sense of personal defeat to suicidal despair. Late in 1807 Davy, as Professor of Chemistry, bullied and cajoled Coleridge and arranged with the managers of the Royal Institution for him to give here a course of lectures on the 'Principles of Poetry'.

We know a little about these lectures but no full reports have been found. And some of the details are as well passed over. There were lectures cancelled because some days Coleridge was undoubtedly stricken and confined to bed. Only his close friends knew how suddenly this could happen, and how equally sudden might be the startling recovery. There was in fact a good deal of social lionising in the weeks from mid-January to mid-June 1808 when he gave some eighteen lectures. But the unannounced cancellations and the dramatic returns to health, the apologies, the ill-prepared lectures, were naturally looked upon with suspicion in high quarters. And there was sometimes lack of tact, to put it mildly.

For instance, in one lecture on education, though Crabb Robinson – not an easy judge – called it 'most excellent', Coleridge fell into the nightmarish trap of the script-free lecturer, hobby-horse riding. His hobby-horse of that moment in the spring of 1808 was the New System of Education being introduced into England by Dr Andrew Bell. This had been controverted, sometimes acrimoniously, by the supporters of Joseph Lancaster with a similar rival scheme. Both men were very advanced in advocating the education of the child (rather than the teaching of subjects), both used student assistants, both encouraged the individual incentive of the pupil. But Coleridge, rightly or wrongly, got it into his head that the Lancastrian system among its other mistakes was guilty of punishing children by ridicule and other cruelties in the classroom. This was enough to distract him from Shakespeare and poetry and all fine arts whatever into a vitriolic attack on Lancaster and a fulsome eulogy of Dr Bell, that according to Crabb Robinson 'kept his audience on the rack of pleasure and offence two whole hours and ten minutes'.[20]

Yet the lectures on the whole, in spite of the occasional sudden failures of power, show in the fragments of notes that remain the true Coleridgian quality, and the essence of later views. But for a few digressions, they dealt in one way or another with the

'Principles of Poetry', sometimes broadly interpreted as principles of creativity in general. He went back to Grecian mythology and its symbolism, discussed the rise of tragedy and comedy and the relation in primitive times of literature to religion, and treated the arts as developing out of man's need to idealise, to find the universal and permanent elements in human nature.

Crabb Robinson said of these first public lectures of Coleridge on poetry, in a letter to Mrs Clarkson, 'I find from my notes that Coleridge was not very methodical. You will excuse my not being more so.'[21] I feel in need of the same excuse, and yet if we try to summarise Coleridge's poetics, with particular attention to his treatment of Shakespeare, we can readily understand why the father of the new chemistry and the father of the new criticism found much in common. Looking at Davy's *Elements of Chemical Philosophy*, published in 1812, and Coleridge's lectures and notes up to that time, we can see that the relationship was mutually productive. For instance, there is, I think, not a chemist, ancient or modern, referred to by Davy in his Introduction to that work (and he refers to a great many of them, tracing the history of the subject back to classical times), not one, that Coleridge did not refer to, knowledgeably. He read the new manuals of chemistry as they appeared, such as Thompson's, and Brande's and (whether Davy did or not is a question) he read the German chemists also. But the significant point seems worth repeating, that in the relatively chaotic condition of chemistry in the first decades of the nineteenth century, Davy began searching for its laws as Coleridge searched for the laws of poetry, drama and the fine arts. They both look for the general principles, as well as at the mass of particulars; they both distinguish between the accidental and the constant, the apparent and the real; in early days as dynamists they both believed in a dynamic fundamental principle.

Coleridge's description in *Biographia Literaria* of the imagination[22] derives at least some of its vitality and power from the fact that although he is talking about the nature of poetry, he might in places equally be talking about Davy's chemistry, which, in respect of some of the mental processes involved, he saw as a kind of poetry of the natural world.

Compare Davy and Coleridge on the scientist and the poet respectively:

'Chemistry', Davy says, is 'valuable in its *connexions* with the sciences, some of which are speculative and *remote from our habitual passions and desires*' yet it also 'applies to most of the processes and operations of *common life*.'[23] As one of the promises of *poetic* genius, Coleridge cites a similar potential for making *connexions* by 'the power [in poetry], of reducing multitude into unity', and secondly, a similar 'choice of subjects very remote from the private interests and circumstances of the writer himself'.[24]

And yet, at the same time, Davy argues for the necessity of an emotional element in scientific research:

> The study of nature ... is eminently qualified to keep alive the most powerful passions and ambitions of the soul, which ... is never satisfied with knowledge, and which is nourished by futurity, and rendered strong by hope.[25]

As to poems, Coleridge says, 'Images ... become proofs of original genius only as far as they are modified by a predominant passion; or by associated thoughts or images awakened by that passion ... or lastly, when a human and intellectual life is transferred to them from the poet's own spirit.'[26]

For Davy, chemistry passionately pursued reconciles the abstract speculative views of physical nature with the practical operations of daily life. For Coleridge, the prime function of poetry is also a *reconciliation* of personal and impersonal, internal and external, in a (musical) form that unites images and feelings in just proportion, with that interpenetration of the universal and the particular that constitutes truth – chemical truth or poetic.

There are no 'rules from without' for the poem, or for the chemical reaction. They take place. The only rules, Coleridge said, thinking analogically as poets (and Davy said some chemists) do, are the rules of growth and production, of the stuff itself.[27] For the poet this means an obligation towards the medium itself – language – towards the 'logic' of the poem, and the obligation towards the truth to human feeling and experience – to psychology, he said. The laws of the entity, poem, are as much within the poem itself as the laws of oxygen and hydrogen are within the fact of water. The laws of the poem are somewhat more difficult to find, to be sure, the facts less and more than palpable, and the strict relevancies subtle and fugitive. But Coleridge himself demonstrated that an imaginative literary chemist can separate the dross from the ore.

Controversy has sometimes raged over his criticism of Shakespeare, but somehow it survives all his commentators, not only undimmed by time but growing in its twentieth-century development as we begin to catch up with his meaning. Shakespeare, Coleridge held, could not be adequately judged and understood by any *a priori* canons of criticism. His plays have the single unity of the operation of an idea, of forces in conflict, of character or of some other inexorable process of human situations. Their unity is not mechanical, and does not depend on the externals, say of a physical place or one short span of time appropriate to the Greeks or the French theatre. The unity of a Shakespeare play lies elsewhere. Enriched by and not sacrificed to its diversity, its unity lies in the imaginative vision behind it and in the mind of the perceptive spectator, a concept so obvious to us now that we forget that it was Coleridge who made it so. (Indeed some recent producers of Shakespeare have hardly grasped it.) By contrast, he says,

> The plays of B[eaumont] and F[letcher] are mere aggregations without unity; in the Shaksperian drama there is a vitality which grows and evolves itself from within – a keynote which guides and controls the harmonies throughout.
>
> (Misc C 44n.)

With all this unification, Shakespeare still 'preserved the *individuality* of his characters', reconciling as inseparables, their 'morality and passion'. It was Shakespeare's particular gift, Coleridge thought, to project his imagination into lives and concerns utterly remote from his own, achieving a great impersonality in probing a character while still feeling intensely the agony or the ecstasy in every fibre of it. This gift of distance without detachment (or with involvement) he said was genius. Davy made a similar claim for science.

Davy was seeking to extend knowledge of external facts; he is credited with the discovery of many of the chemical elements, and in fact I believe more of the elements discovered in the nineteenth century were discovered in this place than in any other. Coleridge was seeking to extend conscious awareness of experience, the experiences of art and of life. Both were convinced of the vast total implications of their subjects, the primary nature of their elements. The principles of poetry in its essential decompounded elements was what Coleridge wished to articulate, because to understand them meant grasping the fundamental principles of creativity itself.

Most basic of all for Coleridge was the dynamism of poetry, the energy and pleasurable excitement achieved by the free activity of the spontaneous impulse controlled only by the need for form. Davy also was a dynamist – till about 1812 when he retracted earlier statements and accepted Dalton's atomistic theories. 'Alas!' Coleridge wrote in the margins of Law's *Behmen*, 'Humphry Davy has become Sir Humphry Davy and an Atomist!!'[28] The shock was severe. Coleridge hardly knew which was worse. Mechanist explanations, early rejected by him, left no place, he thought, for mental initiative. Davy's earlier identification of chemical affinity with electrical attraction had seemed to Coleridge a great portent for vitalist views everywhere, in the arts as well as in the sciences. Behind matter was there not an energising power, as galvanism, magnetism and electricity seemed to hint? The whole conception of poetry and Shakespearean power seemed to be related, at least analogically, to it.

To Coleridge the poem must always be a living organism, a two-way dynamo of reconciliation of all imaginable and as yet unimagined things. The words inked on the page might be subjected to analysis by chemistry; the poem itself was made of *living words*,[29] an activity in the mind, in the culture, that would be variously understood, as variously as other living things, but would nevertheless have its own forceful unity with which interpreters must come to terms. As they must come to terms with the fact of Shakespeare.

Davy and Coleridge did not quarrel over the greatness of Shakespeare, but they certainly differed about the nature of genius, and directly and indirectly were always attacking each other on the subject. Davy thought of himself as a genius, as we all know, and only slowly inquired his way towards an ultimate humility. Coleridge, alas, was sure he himself was not a genius. He had 'power without strength', he wrote to Davy, abjectly.[30] But then he would thunder out against the overweening pride of the scientists of the world. 'The souls of 500 Sir Isaac Newtons would go to the making up of a Shakespeare or a Milton.'[31] In later years he became embittered about Davy as they grew apart, regarding Davy as a worldling, his true creative genius submerged in the social lion, the fashionable time-server. Coleridge was more deeply a participant in the world's moral problems, a writer of pamphlets attacking child labour, advocating the Bible as the best guide for politicians, urging a reconsideration of the relations between Church and State. Coleridge was a poet and an educator, Davy an ingenious discoverer, and inventor, and then a populariser.

But for all their growing differences and irritations in middle age, temperamental as well as intellectual, in 1812 we find Davy writing as the conclusion of his Introduction to his *Elements of Chemical Philosophy* words Coleridge must have applauded:

> ... It is contrary to the usual order of things, that events so harmonious as those of the system of the earth, should depend, on such diversified agents, as are supposed to exist in our artificial arrangements; and there is reason to anticipate a great reduction in the number of undecompounded bodies, and to expect that the analogies of nature will be found conformable to the refined operations of art. The more the phaenomena of the universe are studied, the more distinct their connection appears, the more simple their causes, the more magnificent their design, and the more wonderful the wisdom and power of their Author. (DW IV 42)

So while Davy is trying to see nature as an art, Coleridge sees in the works of the artist an analogy with the spirit that moved upon the face of the waters in Genesis 1. Shakespeare's creations Coleridge described in the very terms of the natural elements – in line with his description of the imagination as 'a repetition in the finite mind' of the eternal act of creation. He asks, in a lecture of 1818,

> What is Lear? – It is storm and tempest – the thunder at first grumbling in the far horizon, then gathering around us, and at length bursting in fury over our heads, – succeeded by a breaking of the clouds for a while, a last flash of lightning, the closing in of night, and the single hope of darkness! And

Romeo and Juliet? – It is a spring day, gusty and beautiful in
the morn, and closing like an April evening with the song of
the nightingale; – whilst Macbeth is deep and earthy, – composed to the subterranean music of a troubled conscience,
which converts everything into the wild and fearful! –

(Misc C 45)

Poets, Coleridge said, are gods of love that tame the chaos,[32]
and as such a part of the continuing animating principle of the
universe. At their creative best the Davys of the world belonged
in this company.

Yet in one important respect – and it is bold to say it from
this podium – Coleridge went beyond Davy in his view of both
poetry and science. He was more concerned about the moral
responsibilities of science, and of poetry. He had no use for
didacticism in any form. Exploration, inquiry, imagination,
creativity, these in whatever field are essential to the ongoing
process of life, affect the way all think about it, and the way we
live it. But Coleridge was more deeply conscious of values from
the Hebraic-Christian moral tradition – perhaps I have missed
the evidence for them in Davy. With imagination must be
coupled the moral will. Coleridge in his generation was almost
uniquely aware of the necessity of reconciling the moral impera-
tive and the imagination; and no one had more personal knowledge of the psychological difficulties in this operation. He
would have agreed with that great scientist and great human
being, the late Aharon Katzir,* in his plea for the necessary
'humility of science which is the result of the recognition of
man's limitations in time and space'.[33] For Coleridge, imagination and a self-conscious moral will provide the only context in
which he felt art and science, and all other human endeavours,
must function.

---

* The distinguished biophysicist of the Weizmann Institute of
Science, killed in the Lod Airport disaster of 1972.

5

Coleridge and the Romantic Vision of the World*

M. H. Abrams

His last name, the poet enjoins us, is to be pronounced as three syllables, with the 'o' long. 'For it is one of the vilest Belze-bubberies of Detraction to pronounce it Col-ridge, Cŏllĕridge, or even Cōle-ridge. It is & must be to all honest and honorable men, a trisyllabic Amphimacer, – ∪ –!'¹ And upon his first name Coleridge projected his self-distrust and the contempt he felt for his lack of decisiveness – attitudes which all his life made him heavily reliant on the good opinion of others to buttress his self-esteem. 'From my earliest years,' he wrote, 'I have had a feeling of Dislike & Disgust' for the name Samuel: 'such a vile short plumpness, such a dull abortive smartness, in [the] first Syllable . . . the wabble it makes, & staggering between a diss- & a tri-syllable . . . altogether it is perhaps the worst combination, of which vowels & consonants are susceptible.'²

Samuel Taylor Coleridge – S.T.C., as he preferred to call his ideal image of himself – entered into residence at this college in October 1791, just as he was turning nineteen. In his *Biographia Literaria* he recalled with nostalgia 'the friendly cloysters, and the happy grove of quiet, ever honored Jesus College, Cambridge'.³ In fact, however, the quiet grove had in his student days been the storm-centre at Cambridge of the excitement and controversy evoked by the early phase of the French Revolution. Coleridge became a follower in religion and a fervent partisan in politics of William Frend, Fellow of Jesus, who was a Unitarian and a radical supporter of the Revolution; in the spring of 1793, Frend was tried before the Vice-Chancellor's court on charges

---

* Bicentenary lecture given at Jesus College, Cambridge.

of sedition and defamation of the Church, refused to retract his
'errors' and was banished from the University. Nor were the
cloisters and the grove unalloyedly happy for Coleridge. After
a flurry of inordinate zeal in his studies, he succumbed to the
undergraduate temptations of talk instead of work and of mild
dissipation in drink and sex. Overwhelmed by debt, a bad conscience and an unrequited love for Mary Evans, he fled to
London and enlisted in the 15th Light Dragoons, retaining a
remnant of his identity in the initials of his pseudonym, Silas
Tomkyn Comberbache.

Coleridge was doubtless the most maladroit cavalryman in the
long history of the Dragoons; not the least of his deficiencies
was that he could not stay mounted on a horse, an animal which
he profoundly distrusted. He was discovered and ransomed by
his family and returned, ignominiously, to his college. He left
the university for good during the October term of 1794 without taking a degree, to pursue the abortive scheme of a Utopian
Pantisocracy and to enter into his ill-starred marriage to Sarah
Fricker. It is pleasant to know that Coleridge returned to Cambridge for a happy visit in June 1833, just a year before his
death. He reported to Henry Nelson Coleridge, who was both
his nephew and son-in-law:

> My emotions at revisiting the university were at first over-
> whelming. I could not speak for an hour. . . . I have not
> passed, of late years at least, three days of such great enjoy-
> ment and healthful excitement of mind and body. The bed
> on which I slept – and slept soundly too – was, as near as I
> can describe it, a couple of sacks full of potatoes tied
> together. . . . Truly I lay down at night a man, and arose in
> the morning a bruise.   (CL VI 953n)

My subject, however, is not the comedy and tragedy of the
life of Coleridge, that self-defeating, gentle, maddening, beguil-
ing genius, but his vision of the world at the time he reached
his philosophical maturity; and for Coleridge's intellectual stance
in this middle period the best introduction is his *Biographia
Literaria*, which he published in the summer of 1817, when he
was forty-four years old.

I want to stress two features of Coleridge's book. The first is
the significance of its elected genre. Undertaking a work that was

to set forth 'my principles in Politics, Religion, and Philosophy', as well as in poetry and criticism,* Coleridge cast his statement in the form of a literary autobiography. In this procedure he shared a salient tendency of his age to reshape a variety of earlier literary types into the biographical or autobiographical mode, and thereby to transform fixed intellectual positions into moments in an evolving education, in which each stage is a product of what has gone before and the portent of what is to come. In the 1790s Goethe and other German writers had developed the *Bildungsroman*, the novel about the education of the hero in life; in England the major achievement in this type is Carlyle's *Sartor Resartus*. At the same time many of the major German philosophers, including Lessing, Herder, Schiller, Kant, wrote examples of what they called 'Universal History' – the account of all human thought and culture, represented as the progressive education of a single protagonist named 'Man', 'Mankind', or 'Humanity'. The most extraordinary achievement in this mode is Hegel's *Phenomenology of the Spirit*, which narrates the total history of the evolving human consciousness as the adventures and misadventures of a single *dramatis persona* whom he calls 'spirit', or 'the general individual', as it continuously repossesses its own persistently alienated selves in a progressive educational process, to the point at which the expanding consciousness recognises its own all-inclusive identity in the final stage of 'absolute knowledge' – that is, in the *Wissenschaft* that is Hegel's own systematic philosophy of man and the world. The biographical form is no less prominent in Romantic narrative and lyric poetry. To Wordsworth, for example, it seemed 'a reasonable thing' that, before he undertook his great work, *The Recluse*, he should 'take a review of his own mind' and 'record, in verse, the origin and progress of his own powers'. The resulting work Wordsworth referred to as 'the poem on the growth of my own mind' and his wife later named *The Prelude*; it turned out to be the masterpiece to which he intended it to serve merely as a 'preparatory poem'.[4]

The *Biographia Literaria*, then, is in Coleridge's stated

---

* BL I 1. As early as 1803 Coleridge had jotted in his notebook: 'Seem to have made up my mind to write my metaphysical works, as *my Life*, & *in* my Life – intermixed with all the other events/or history of the mind & fortunes of S. T. Coleridge.' CN I 1515.

intention a romantic *Bildungsgeschichte*, representing the growth
of the poet-philosopher-critic's mind. A second, and neglected,
feature of this book is that, like many of the contemporary
works to which it is allied, its design is that of a crisis-autobio-
graphy. That is, the evolving educational process is broken by
a stage of extreme doubt, apathy and despair, from which the
protagonist emerges as a new man, assured of his identity and
role in life, who, when he looks about him, sees a new world.

In the tenth chapter of the *Biographia*, Coleridge summarises
his intellectual and spiritual condition when he was in his
middle twenties. He had absorbed the English empirical philosophy in the tradition of John Locke and adopted the radical
mechanistic views of the mind of David Hartley – an earlier
Jesus College man who in his *Observations on Man* (1749) had
undertaken to extend the principles of Newtonian physics to
perception and all the processes of mind.* As Coleridge had said
in 1794: 'I am a compleat Necessitarian – and understand the
subject as well almost as Hartley himself – but I go farther than
Hartley and believe the corporeality of *thought* – namely, that
it is motion.'† In religion he had taken over the views of William
Frend and Joseph Priestley and become 'a zealous Unitarian'.⁵
He also shared his mentors' enthusiasm for the French Revolution, and the belief of Priestley and other radical Dissenters that
the Revolution portended the imminence of the millennium
foretold in the Book of Revelation. Coleridge ironically recalls
how, while soliciting subscribers to his periodical *The Watch-
man* in 1796:

> I argued, I described, I promised, I prophesied; and beginning
> with the captivity of nations I ended with the near approach
> of the millennium, finishing the whole with some of my own
> verses describing that glorious state out of *the Religious
> Musings*. . . .   (BL I 116)

* On Hartley's adaptation of Newton's theories into his own views
of the mechanistic bases of sensation and of the association of ideas,
see H. Guerlac, 'An Augustan Monument: *The Opticks*', in *The
Varied Pattern: Studies in the 18th Century*, ed. P. Hughes and D.
Williams (Toronto, 1971) pp. 145–6, 160–1.
† 11 Dec 1794, in CL I 137. Cf. BL ch. x: '. . . so profound was my
admiration at this time of Hartley's Essay on Man, that I gave his
name to my first-born' (in 1796).

The occasion for such prophecy is laconically summarised in Coleridge's prose 'Argument' to 'Religious Musings', a long poem he published that same year: 'The present State of Society. The French Revolution. Millennium. Universal Redemption. Conclusion.'

Coleridge then describes in the *Biographia* his disillusion with the promise of the French Revolution until, after the French invasion of Switzerland, he became, in a drastic turn-about, a 'vehement anti-gallican, and still more intensely an anti-jacobin'.[6] He had experienced 'the very hey-day of hope', but now 'my mind sank into a state of thorough disgust and despondency'. Coleridge cites his poem, 'France, *a Palinodia*' (1798), which expressed his revulsion from his commitment to revolutionary France, and goes on:

> I retired to a cottage in Somersetshire at the foot of Quantock [in 1797] and devoted my thoughts and studies to the foundations of religion and morals. Here I found myself all afloat. Doubts rushed in; broke upon me '*from the fountains of the great deep*,' and fell '*from the windows of heaven*.' The fontal truths of natural religion and the books of Revelation alike contributed to the flood; and it was long ere my ark touched on an Ararat, and rested.   (BL I 132–3)

Elsewhere in the *Biographia* Coleridge shifts the biblical parallel for his condition at this time from Noah's flood to the Exodus, referring to the religious 'mystics' as 'always a pillar of fire throughout the night, during my wandering through the wilderness of doubt', enabling him 'to skirt, without crossing, the sandy deserts of utter unbelief'.[7]

We may note about Coleridge's account of his crisis, first, that, as in other spiritual autobiographies of the age, the precipitating cause is the failure of the inordinate hopes he had invested in the French Revolution. Hegel, for example, in his *Phenomenology of the Spirit* represented the Revolution and the Reign of Terror as the ultimate crisis of consciousness in Western man, in which 'spirit in the form of absolute freedom' turns upon itself in 'the fury of annihilation', in a self-negation which 'is meaningless death, the sheer horror of the negative'.* In Wordsworth's

* G. W. F. Hegel, *Phänomenologie des Geistes*, ed. Johannes Hoffmeister (Hamburg, 1952) pp. 415–21. For Hegel's description of the

Prelude the 'disastrous issues' of the times, marking the collapse of his hopes in the Revolution, led finally to 'utter loss of hope itself,/And things to hope for,' in the stage he describes as the dark night of his soul: 'I was benighted heart and mind.'[8]

It is clear from the *Biographia*, however, that Coleridge's crisis involved not only politics, but the overall forms of thinking he had derived from the eighteenth century – the empiricism, mechanism and scepticism in philosophy, together with the Unitarianism in religion which he associated with the rationale that led to the French Revolution and with the radicalism of the English Dissenters who were its zealous supporters. And when, for comfort and sanction, he turned his studies to 'the foundations of religion and morals', both his philosophy and theology proved inadequate to the task and merely added to the flood of doubt. In a parallel way Wordsworth tells us in *The Prelude* that, in a desperate effort to re-establish his hope in human possibility, he had turned to the philosophical speculations of William Godwin and other philosophers of the Enlightenment, but that the result was only to complete the disaster. 'Sick, wearied out with contrarieties,' he said, 'I

> Yielded up moral questions in despair.
> This was the crisis of that strong disease,
> This the soul's last and lowest ebb. . . .'
>
> (W Prel (1850) xi 279–307)

Coleridge's crisis, then, was a total one, involving his religion, philosophy, politics and theory of poetry, and like the spiritual histories of his romantic contemporaries, his narrative conforms to the plot of that prototype of all spiritual autobiographies, Augustine's *Confessions*, written at the close of the fourth century. Ever since Augustine's circumstantial account of his doubts, anguished self-conflict and despair – resolved under a fig-tree in a garden at Milan, in the experience of 'dying unto death and living unto life'[9] – we have all known how to undergo a spiritual crisis, whether we call it by the religious term 'conversion' or by a secular term such as 'identity crisis'. Augustine's

---

widespread sense of millennial expectation evoked by the early period of the Revolution, see *Vorlesungen über die Philosophie der Weltgeschichte*, ed. G. Lasson (Leipzig, 1919) II 926.

laborious pilgrimage towards the experience of being born into a new life had been not less intellectual than it was religious, and in his *Confessions* the reading of pagan philosophers is hardly less prominent than his poring over the writings of St Paul and the rest of the Scriptures. In the *Biographia* Coleridge commented that, before he could achieve his 'final re-conversion to the whole truth in Christ', a 'more thorough revolution in my philosophic principles, and a deeper insight into my own heart, were yet wanting'; and he explicitly compared his conversion, in its double aspect as philosophy and faith, to that of Augustine, according to whose 'own confession', Coleridge said, 'the books of certain Platonic philosophers . . . commenced the rescue of [his] faith from the same error . . .'.[10]

Like other authors of spiritual autobiography, Coleridge wrote his *Biographia Literaria* after he had escaped from the flood of doubt and the wilderness of despair, in the persona of a new creature who sees the world with new eyes; and it will help us to read not only the *Biographia*, but the other writings of Coleridge's middle and later life, if we recognise that, like other converts, religious or philosophical, Coleridge looked upon the intellectual landscape with a radically simplifying bipolar vision. On the one side he puts the thought and products of the eighteenth century, English and French – 'the Epoch of the Understanding and the Senses', as he calls it, with its 'modes of reasoning grounded on the atomic, Corpuscular and mechanic Philosophy'.[11] This was the way of seeing and thinking to which the old Coleridge had in large part succumbed, and on which he now blames not only the disaster of the French Revolution but also the general vitiation of thought, values and the form of life; it has affected, he says, 'the Taste and Character, the whole tone of Manners and Feeling, and above all the Religious (at least the Theological) and the Political tendencies of the public mind'.* On the other side he puts all the influences which had gone into the formation of the new Coleridge – first, the Bible and Christian theologians; then Plato and the Neoplatonists,

---

* CL IV 758–9. See *Friend* I 446–7 on the pervasive effects of the 'Mechanical Philosophy', which include its being 'hailed as a kindred revolution in philosophy, and espoused, as a common cause, by the partizans of the revolution in the state'. Also, *The Statesman's Manual* (LS 11–17).

together with Jacob Boehme and the other 'mystics' who had helped sustain in him the saving vision; and finally, and decisively, the recent or contemporary German philosophers, especially Kant and Schelling, who provided him with the conceptual grounds for articulating an alternative vision of the universe. And for his new world-view the latter Coleridge speaks as a fervent evangelist, with results, as John Stuart Mill early recognised in his essay on 'Coleridge', that did much to alter the intellectual climate in England, and as we now recognise, in America as well.

I. CONVERSION, REVOLUTION AND VISION IN PHILOSOPHY

More than one historian of philosophy has noted the intense excitement, the extravagant claims and the breathtaking velocity of the development of German Idealism in the two or three decades after Kant's *Critique of Pure Reason* in 1781. The movement has the aspect of an epidemic conversion-experience in philosophy. Its character, Richard Kroner has said, is 'explosive'; 'there passed through the epoch something of the breath of the eschatological hopes of the era of emergent Christianity; now or never must dawn the day of truth, it is near, we are called to bring it into being'. The participants are convinced 'that a new evangel has appeared in the world'.[12] Sober-minded though he was, Kant remarked that 'philosophy too can have its chiliasm . . . which is nothing less than visionary'.[13] In his second Preface of 1787 he described his *Critique* as the attempt 'to introduce a complete revolution in the procedure of metaphysics', equivalent to the revolution inaugurated by Copernicus, who reversed the assumption 'that all the heavenly bodies revolved round the spectator' by assuming 'that the spectator revolved, while the stars remained at rest'. In place of the philosophical assumption hitherto 'that our cognition must conform to the objects', Kant proposes 'that the objects must conform to our cognition' − that is, that in all experience the unknowable 'things in themselves' are inescapably structured by the mind's own forms of space, time and the categories.

In the 1790s other German philosophers exploited Kant's metaphor of a philosophical revolution. They shifted the reference, however, from the Copernican revolution in science to the dominant conceptual model of the Romantic age; that is, the violent destruction of existing conditions, the establishment of a totally new order of things, and the explosive enlargement of human expectations represented by the political revolution in France. In 1790, soon after the fall of the Bastille, C. L. Reinhold, writing on Kant's philosophy, described the philosophical era as an unexampled 'convulsion of all hitherto known systems, theories, and modes of conception' – a 'revolution' paralleling the political revolutions of the age and ascribable to 'one and the same cause' in 'the spirit of our age', although it manifests itself as 'a phenomenon of spirit' and 'in the arena of knowledge' rather than of external political struggle.[14] Five years later Fichte said that 'the first hints and presentiments' of his philosophical system came to him while he was writing in defence of the French Revolution; his system, in fact, is a revolution that completes Kant's philosophical revolution, in that it frees the mind of man even from the limiting conditions imposed on it by Kant's postulate of unknowable things-in-themselves:

> My system is the first system of freedom; just as [the French] are tearing man loose from his outer chains, so my system tears him loose from the fetters of the *Ding an sich*, from any external influence, and establishes him in his first principle as an autonomous being.[15]

And that same year, 1795, the young Schelling declared that his philosophy, in its turn, aims 'not merely at a reform of knowledge, but at a total reversal of its principles; that is to say, it aims at a revolution of knowledge' – a cognitive revolution, the dawning of a 'more beautiful day of knowledge' which, by changing man's concept of his mind and powers, will transform the conditions and possibilities of his life in the world.*

In his *Phenomenology of the Spirit* (1804) Hegel narrates how the spirit – the vanguard of the collective human consciousness – has recovered from the self-destructiveness represented by the

---

* F. Schelling, *Sämmtliche Werke* (Stuttgart, 1856–61) Pt. I vol. I 156–9. Cf. Pt. I vol. III 329: His system 'entirely alters, even inverts the ruling views not only in ordinary life, but in the greater part of systematic philosophy'. On the 'true revolution' in philosophy that will bring on a non-political 'golden age', see Pt. I vol. VI 562–4.

convulsions of the French Revolution, to reach the culminating stage of Hegel's own philosophical *Wissenschaft*. In this stage, he says, the spirit's 'former being' has been both annulled and transcended, so that 'new-born out of knowledge' it is a 'new being, a new world and form of the spirit'.[16] He describes this latest form of the spirit as 'the product of a far-reaching revolution in ever so many forms of culture and education' which will achieve the new heaven and earth sought vainly by the political revolutionists:

> The spirit has broken with what was hitherto the world of its existence and imagination.... The spirit that educates itself matures slowly and quietly toward the new form, dissolving one particle of the edifice of its previous world after another.... This gradual crumbling ... is interrupted by the break of day that, like lightning, all at once reveals the edifice of the new world.[17]

It is clear that human consciousness, in breaking through to Hegel's system of knowledge, has been reborn and looks out upon a new world. But this new world is no other than the old world, which has been transformed by a 'revolution' in philosophical vision.

Coleridge repeatedly employs metaphors that posit a triple parallel between religious and moral conversion, political revolution and a radical change in the premises of philosophy. He characterises the soul's 'efforts at self-condemnation and self-reformation' as an attempt at 'spiritual Revolution', and classes together 'those great Men, who in states or in the mind of man had produced great revolutions'.* I have already cited his statement that a prerequisite to his 'final re-conversion' in religion was 'a more thorough revolution in my philosophic principles'.[18] He later described his projected *Magnum Opus* as 'a revolution of all that has been called *Philosophy* or Metaphysics in England and France' since the predominance of 'the mechanical system at the Restoration of our second Charles'. In addition, Coleridge proposed in the *Biographia* that the radical ground of a philo-

---

* CN II 2541: CL III 314. In the *Friend* (I 368) Coleridge alluded to Wordsworth's *Prelude*, with its double aspect of mental growth and mental crisis-and-conversion, as Wordsworth's 'Poem on the Growth and Revolutions of an Individual Mind'.

sophy consists in a primal way of seeing which he called 'the ascertaining vision' by 'the philosophic imagination' – a vision that is systematically primitive, in the sense that it is a ground that cannot itself be grounded, except as it confirms its own validity by the consequences in experience when it is achieved by each philosopher for himself.*

In the fourth chapter of the *Biographia* Coleridge describes his actual experience of a radical alteration in vision that shatters habitual categories, and so makes the old world new. The occasion is his first hearing Wordsworth read a long poem aloud in 1796, but Coleridge explicitly says that such renovation is also effected by the achievements of 'genius' in 'philosophic disquisitions':

> To contemplate the ANCIENT of days and all his works with feelings as fresh, as if all had then sprang forth at the first creative fiat.... To combine the child's sense of wonder and novelty with the appearances, which every day for perhaps forty years had rendered familiar ... this is the character and privilege of genius.... And therefore is it the prime merit of genius and its most unequivocal mode of manifestation, so to represent familiar objects as to awaken in the minds of others ... freshness of sensation....†

In a central passage in his periodical, *The Friend*, composed at about the same time as the *Biographia*, Coleridge asserts that the primitive element of a philosophy, its founding intuition, must be adopted, not by force of evidence, but an act of 'the will'. He then opposes two kinds of philosophical vision, which yield two diverse worlds. One of these is

---

* CL (30 Mar 1820) v 28; BL 1 166–7, see also 1 199. In LS 14–15 Coleridge asserts that 'all the *epoch-forming* Revolutions of the Christian World', in all areas of life and thought, 'have coincided with the rise and fall of metaphysical systems'.

† BL 1 59–60; the passage, with some differences, occurs also in the *Friend*, 14 Sept 1809 (II 73–4). In *The Prelude*, Wordsworth described his crisis as marked by a 'tyranny' of the eye, a slavery to customary ways of seeing which yielded the perception of 'a universe of death', and described his recovery from this crisis as the breakthrough to an alternative vision of the world – a world 'which moves with light and life informed,/Actual, divine, and true.' W Prel (1850) XI 127–139; XIV 157–62.

that intuition of things ... which presents itself when trans-
ferring reality to ... the ever-varying framework of the
uniform life, we think of ourselves as separated beings, and
place nature in antithesis to the mind, as object to subject,
thing to thought, death to life. This is abstract knowledge, or
the science of the mere understanding.

This world-view is that of the preceding century, the epoch of the
senses and the understanding from which he had himself
escaped. The second and opposed intuition, and its concordant
world, is that which he has now achieved. It is, he writes,

the contemplation of reason, namely, that intuition of things
which arises when we possess ourselves, as one with the whole,
which is substantial knowledge.... [By this] we know that
existence is its own predicate, self affirmation.... It is an
eternal and infinite self-rejoicing, self-loving, with a joy unfathomable, with a love all comprehensive.*

I shall sketch the salient features of the conceptual scheme
by which Coleridge undertakes to provide a coherent and inclusive structure for this founding philosophical intuition or vision,
and then discuss a striking example of the way the scheme
informed Coleridge's actual experience of the world. In doing
so, I am not merely exploiting a romantic conceit that the
undemonstrable ground for a philosophy is a way of envisioning
reality, and that a change of ground is a philosophical conversion which effects a revolution in experience; for we find that
philosophers of diverse persuasions have described a radical shift
in their premises in similar metaphoric terms of inner transformation, of escape from imprisonment to freedom, and of a
revolution in vision that yields a new world.

One instance is the testimony of a recent philosopher associated with Cambridge. In an autobiographical essay, Bertrand
Russell describes how the influences of McTaggart and of F. H.

---

* *Friend* I 519–21. Coleridge remarked, with respect to demon-
strating 'the absurdity of the corpuscularian or mechanic system':
'But we cannot force any man into an insight or intuitive possession
of the true philosophy, because we cannot give him abstraction,
intellectual intuition, or constructive imagination....' TL 57–8. For
Schelling on the founding intuition of a philosophy, see *Sämmtliche
Werke*, Pt. I vol. II 12, 46, 343; IV 77; V 275.

Bradley's *Appearance and Reality* 'caused me to become a Hegelian'. The crucial turn to this world-view occurred in a flash of insight:

> I remember the precise moment, one day in 1894, as I was walking along Trinity Lane, when I saw in a flash (or thought I saw) that the ontological argument is valid. I had gone out to buy a tin of tobacco; on my way back, I suddenly threw it it up in the air, and exclaimed as I caught it: 'Great Scott, the ontological argument is sound.'

During the several years following he planned, he tells us, a series of comprehensive books that 'would achieve a Hegelian synthesis in an encyclopaedic work dealing equally with theory and practice'. But during 1898 various causes led him to abandon this outlook, and especially the influence of his younger friend, G. E. Moore, who 'also had had a Hegelian period', but now reverted 'to the opposite extreme . . . that *everything* is real that common sense . . . supposes real'. As Russell describes his second philosophical conversion and its consequences in experience:

> [Moore] took the lead in rebellion, and I followed, with a sense of emancipation. . . . With a sense of escaping from prison, we allowed ourselves to think that grass is green, that the sun and stars would exist if no one was aware of them, and also that there is a pluralistic timeless world of Platonic ideas. The world, which had been thin and logical, suddenly became rich and varied and solid.[19]

Another Cambridge philosopher, Ludwig Wittgenstein, put forward two distinct philosophies. The first is that of the *Tractatus*, published in 1921. The second, which he developed in a sudden burst of philosophical activity after a ten-year hiatus, is represented by his *Philosophical Investigations*, published in 1953; the book addresses itself specifically to counter what he called 'my old way of thinking' in the *Tractatus*. In the *Investigations*, Wittgenstein says that 'philosophy may in no way interfere with the actual use of language', and that philosophy 'leaves everything as it is'. That may be; but Wittgenstein's writings show that philosophising has profoundly changed the philosopher himself, who, by developing a new language for doing philosophy, has in his phrase discovered 'a new way of looking at things' and thereby has changed everything.*

Coleridge began to study Kant at the turn of the nineteenth century when, as he said in the *Biographia*, the writings of that philosopher 'took possession of me as with a giant's hand'.† For a short while Coleridge exhibited a philosophical chiliasm, a sense that he was on the verge of a consummation of all metaphysics hitherto, similar to that of his post-Kantian contemporaries in Germany. In a quick succession of letters early in 1801 Coleridge wrote: 'I feel, that I have power within me.' 'My heart within me *burns*' to write a book on 'the affinities of the Feelings with Words & Ideas' which will 'supersede all the Books of Metaphysics hitherto written and all the Books of Morals too'. 'I have not only completely extricated the notions of Time, and Space; but have overthrown the doctrine of Association, as taught by Hartley, and with it ... the doctrine of Necessity,' and he is about to go on 'to solve the process of Life & Consciousness'. All this in an 'intensity of thought', and of 'minute experiments with Light & Figure' which have made him 'nervous & feverish', when 'Truths so important ... came to me almost as a Revelation'.‡ But this brief afflatus led to no extensive philosophical achievement, and it was followed by the decade

* L. Wittgenstein, *Philosophical Investigations*, tr. G. E. M. Anscombe (Oxford, 1953), Foreword, p. X, Sections 124, 400–1; see also 122. Commentators on the *Philosophical Investigations* have noted its likeness in procedure to Augustine's *Confessions*, in that the radically altered Wittgenstein harshly criticises his former self, conducts a dialogue in which he combats the persistent temptations to fall back into former errors, and attempts to help his readers to achieve a similar philosophical conversion. See Stanley Cavell, 'The Availability of Wittgenstein's Later Philosophy' (1962), reprinted in Cavell's *Must We Mean What We Say?* (New York, 1969), pp. 70–72; K. T. Fann, *Wittgenstein's Conception of Philosophy* (Berkeley and Los Angeles, 1971) pp. 106–8.

† BL I 99. On the same page Coleridge speaks of his 'fifteen years' familiarity' with Kant's major works. On the dating of Coleridge's reading of Kant see G. N. G. Orsini, *Coleridge and German Idealism*, (Carbondale, Ill., 1969) pp. 47 ff.

‡ CL II 669, 671, 706–7. In the last letter of 16 Mar 1801, Coleridge goes on to say that he is planning a book on 'Locke, Hobbes, & Hume' which will manifest his 'attentive Perusal' of his philosophical predecessors 'from Aristotle to Kant' (p. 707).

that W. J. Bate has called 'the dark years', the nadir of Coleridge's life-crisis.

Coleridge's letters and notebooks of the next decade and a half make very painful reading. He is racked by pain, recurrent illness and nightmares; his marriage shattered, he suffers a hopeless love for Sara Hutchinson; in the medical ignorance of the time, he becomes addicted to opium – that 'dirty business of Laudanum', he called it, that '*free-agency-annihilating* poison';[20] he is alienated from Wordsworth; he is guilt-ridden, experiences a paralysis of his intellectual and poetic powers, seems recurrently close to death and longs for it as a release;[21] and at one point wants 'to place myself in a private madhouse' since 'my Case is a species of madness, only that it is a derangement, an utter impotence of the *Volition*, & not of the Intellectual Faculties'.[22]

In the latter part of this dark time (beginning about 1810) Coleridge took up the close study of Friedrich Schelling. To this brilliant young philosopher, Coleridge says in the *Biographia*, he at once felt a special affinity, 'a genial coincidence with much that I had toiled out for myself, and a powerful assistance in what I had yet to do'.* In a sudden burst of activity during a four-year span beginning in 1815, Coleridge composed the bulk of the works on which his intellectual reputation depends: the *Biographia Literaria*, the *Theory of Life*, the two *Lay Sermons*, the 'Treatise on Method' the radically revised version of his earlier periodical the *Friend*, two sets of lectures on Shakespeare and other English and European poets and dramatists, a series of lectures on the history of philosophy, as well as a number of important philosophical letters and a mass of manuscript materials which are only now being published in full. The years 1815–19 are for Coleridge as metaphysician and critic what the years 1796–98 – the time of *The Ancient Mariner*, *Christabel* and *Kubla Khan*, as well as his hardly less innovative 'conversation poems' – are for Coleridge as a bard. The range and quality of his achievement in these latter years would for any man be remarkable; for Coleridge, given the circumstances of his life, it must count as a feat of massive spiritual heroism.

* BL 1 102. In an annotation to a work by Schelling, Coleridge described it as 'a book I value, I reason and quarrel with *as* with myself when I am reasoning'. Quoted Orsini, *Coleridge and German Idealism*, p. 50.

In these middle years of Coleridge, it is Schelling who is the dominating philosophical influence – the Schelling who, Coleridge asserted in his *Biographia*, 'as the *founder* of the PHILOSOPHY OF NATURE, and as the most successful *improver* of the Dynamic System', completed the 'revolution in philosophy' begun by Kant.* And it is in Coleridge's special adaptation of this revolution in philosophy – based on Schelling's *Naturphilosophie* and to some extent on the speculations of Schelling's followers, especially Henrik Steffens – that we find the conceptual structure which Coleridge developed to articulate, to support and to render all-comprehensive his founding vision of the natural world and of man's place in it.

II. THE METASCIENCE OF NATURE

Coleridge's nature-philosophy is a strange and daunting area of his thought. Until recently scholars have either discreetly passed it over or else – assessing it as an attempt to achieve by fantasy what scientists discover by patient experiment – have rejected it (in the terms of Joseph Warren Beach) as 'mere abracadabra', 'highly fantastic', 'a bizarre farrago of pretentious nonsense'; it is, Norman Fruman has charged, Coleridge's commitment 'to the most anti-scientific movement of his day'.[23] Such judgements are inevitable if we simply apply to Coleridge's scheme of nature the criteria of philosophical positivism that Coleridge's philosophy was specifically intended to dispossess. If our aim, on the other hand, is to understand an important development in nineteenth-century intellectual history, we need to follow Coleridge's own procedure, which John Stuart Mill identified, and to which he attributed his own liberation from dogmatism. Mill pointed out that by Bentham (the great philosophical positivist of his time) men have been led to ask of an opinion, 'Is it true?' By Coleridge, they have instead been led to ask, 'What is the

* BL I 103–4. In referring to Kant as putting forward the 'germs' of the 'Dynamic System' which was developed by Schelling (I 103–4 and n.), Coleridge has in mind especially Kant's essay 'Metaphysische Anfangsgründe der Naturwissenschaft' (1796), which proposed a 'metaphysical' analysis of 'matter' as a product of the elemental 'powers' of attraction and repulsion. In I 99, Coleridge lists this essay as one of the four works of Kant that 'took possession of me as with a giant's hand'.

meaning of it?' and to answer by looking at the opinion 'from within'.

> The long duration of a belief, [Coleridge] thought, is at least proof of an adaptation in it to some portion or other of the human mind . . . some natural want or requirement of human nature which the doctrine in question is fitted to satisfy. . . .[24]

Let us try to look at Coleridge's nature-philosophy, according to his own formula, from within, to see what it undertook to do and what natural want it served to satisfy.

The first thing to note is that Coleridge's intention was not to discredit or to replace the findings of experimental science. Instead he undertook to accommodate valid scientific discoveries within a counter-metaphysic to the metaphysical foundations of contemporary science; his nature-philosophy, in short, was not science, nor was it anti-science, but metascience. In this area Coleridge set up as his chief opponent Sir Isaac Newton, and especially what he called the 'monstrous fictions' in Newton's *Opticks*. He did not mean to call into question Newton as an experimental physicist, whom he called 'the immortal Newton', and to whose procedures and discoveries he paid frequent tribute.* Coleridge's objection was to Newton as a speculative thinker whose immense prestige as a physicist had given impetus to a metaphysical world-view, the 'Corpuscular and mechanic Philosophy', that had reigned for the preceding century. For despite his reluctance to frame hypotheses, Newton had put forward, in the 'Queries' he added to his *Opticks*, the stark image of a machine-universe whose ultimate elements are in-divisible particles of matter capable of being set in motion. There Newton wrote:

---

* CL IV 750; *The Statesman's Manual*, LS 85. So early as 23 March 1801, when he began to study the *Opticks*, Coleridge discriminated between the experimental and theoretical elements in Newton's work. He was, Coleridge said, 'exceedingly delighted' with Newton's 'experiments & with the accuracy of his *immediate* Deductions from them'; but the opinions which Newton 'founded on these Deductions, and indeed his whole Theory' are so superficial as 'to be deemed false' (CL II 709). For Coleridge's lifelong interest in experimental science, and his varied judgements on Newton, see the anthology, *Coleridge on the Seventeenth Century*, ed. R. F. Brinkley (Durham, N.C., 1955) pp. 393–408.

It seems probable to me, that God in the Beginning form'd Matter in solid, massy, hard, impenetrable, moveable Particles, of such Sizes and Figures, and with such other Properties, and in such Proportion to Space, as most conduced to the End for which he form'd them.

Newton also proposed a hypothetical 'aether', a very 'rare and subtile' but none the less material medium, that pervades both space and bodies, and serves to explain the phenomena of gravity and light, as well as the conduction of both light and sound from the eye and ear through the nerves into the mental 'place of Sensation', where they are converted into the images of sight and hearing.[25]

Worse still, as Coleridge saw it, was that, having reduced ultimate reality to masses and motion, Newton reconstrued the Creator of reality to accord with this picture of his creation. That is, Newton represented God as the omnipresent mover of all particles 'within his boundless uniform Sensorium', and also as the seer of the particles as such, 'wholly by their immediate presence to himself', which human beings perceive only after they have been altered by the intermediation of the senses. As Newton put it, we are capable of perceiving 'the Images only' which, transmitted 'through the Organs of Sense . . . are there seen and beheld by that which in us perceives and thinks'.[26]

Newton's move, in Coleridge's view, was an immense extrapolation of the working model of physical science – the masses and motion which are the only things that the specialised techniques of the physicist can manage mathematically – into a picture of the actual make-up of the universe. As Coleridge puts the matter, in discussing the grounds of the 'Mechanico-corpuscular Philosophy': 'In order to submit the various phænomena of moving bodies to geometrical construction, we are under the necessity of abstracting from corporeal substance all its *positive* properties', leaving it only 'figure and mobility'. 'And as a *Fiction of Science*,' he says, 'it would be difficult to overvalue this invention.' But Descartes and later thinkers 'propounded it as *truth of fact*: and instead of a World *created* and filled with productive forces by the Almighty Fiat, left a lifeless Machine whirled about by the dust of its own Grinding. . . '.[27]

To Coleridge this picture of the elemental structure of reality was both incompatible with human experience and intolerable to human needs. As no more than a drastic subtraction from the rich diversity of sense-phenomena, it remains itself thinly phenomenal, the product of what Coleridge repeatedly described as a 'slavery' to the senses, and especially to the eye. And against this world-picture, in the literal sense of 'picture' as something that can be visualised, Coleridge again and again brings the charge that it is, precisely speaking, lethal; it 'strikes death through all things visible and invisible'. It has killed the living, habitable and companionable world of ordinary experience. It has also killed the metaphysical world of the pre-Cartesian and pre-Newtonian past, in which the mind of man had recognised an outer analogue to itself and to its life, purposes, values and needs; a world, therefore, of which man was an integral part, with which he was a participant, and in which he could feel thoroughly at home. By translating what he called the 'scientific calculus' from a useful working fiction into an ontology, Coleridge claimed in 1817, man has lost 'all communion with life and the spirit of Nature', and is left isolated and alien, his mind the passive recipient of the impact of particles which it converts into images of sensation.[28]

Against this 'philosophy of death', which posits only the 'relations of unproductive particles to each other', Coleridge posed his own philosophy of life, in which, he says, 'two component counter-powers actually interpenetrate each other, and generate a higher third, including both the former. . .'.* That is, in radical opposition to the post-Newtonian picture of the world Coleridge puts forward what, following Schelling, he calls a 'vital', or 'dynamic', or 'constructive' philosophy of nature. I shall try, very briefly, to outline this system, as Coleridge represented it in his middle years.

The primitives of Coleridge's metascience, from which he constructs the entire cosmos, mental as well as physical, are not material particles and motion, but inherent energies which he calls 'powers'. There are two primal counter-powers; these

---

* *The Statesman's Manual*, LS 89. See also BL I 197–8. In 1815 Coleridge described the 'substition of Life, and Intelligence' for 'the philosophy of mechanism which . . . strikes *Death*' as 'a general revolution' in the discipline of the mind. See CL IV 575.

polarise into positive and negative 'forces' and interact, as he puts it, according to 'the universal Law of Polarity or essential Dualism'.[29] By this Coleridge means that the generative and sustaining elements of his universe exist only relatively to each other and manifest a tension-in-unity – that is, an equal and irremissive tendency on the one hand to oppose themselves and on the other hand to reunite in a 'synthesis' of 'thesis' and 'antithesis'.

The primitive counter-powers, 'the two poles of the material Universe', Coleridge says, are 'Light and Gravitation'. These terms, of course, denote the phenomena to which Newton had devoted his great researches in the *Opticks* and the *Principia*. But in Coleridge's system, light and gravitation are not physical or phenomenal matters, but pre-phenomenal concepts; in his terms, they are not 'real' but 'ideal'. That is, the 'powers' of light and gravity are not the light we see, nor the weight, or gravitational force, we feel, but have a different and prior conceptual status; hence they cannot be pictured, but only imagined. Of these ideal powers, however, 'real' light and gravity are the kind of especially close and revealing analogues that Coleridge calls by a special term, 'exponents'.

'Under Gravity,' Coleridge writes, 'we place Attraction and Repulsion: and under Light the Powers of Contraction and Dilation. . . .' That is, each of these root-powers manifests two counter-forces: gravity involves a pull in and its opposite, a push out, while light pulses radially in all directions and at the same time contracts back to its centre. It is only by their 'living and generative interpenetration' that the pre-phenomenal powers and forces achieve the condition of matter, and so move into the phenomenal realm available to the human senses. 'Matter', as Coleridge says, is to be considered 'a Product . . . the pause, by interpenetration, of opposite energies.'*

From these two elemental powers and two pairs of contrary

---

* See Coleridge's *Theory of Life*; CL iv 760, 771, 775; and MS quoted by Owen Barfield, *What Coleridge Thought* (Middletown, Conn., 1971) p. 141. The pioneering study of Coleridge's nature-philosophy is Craig W. Miller, 'Coleridge's Concept of Nature', *Journal of the History of Ideas* xxv (1964) pp. 77–96; the fullest account of the role of such concepts in various areas of Coleridge's concern is Barfield's.

forces Coleridge 'constructs' (in the sense of renders intelligible by reference to a single genetic principle) the total universe. Driven by their inherent stresses of opposition-in-unity, and manifesting in the process diverse degrees of 'predominance' relative to each other, the powers of light and gravity evolve by a progressive synthesis of prior syntheses. Their evolution can be viewed as a great ascending spiral through the several distinctive orders of organised forms which Coleridge, following Schelling, calls 'potences'. At each potence, or level of organisation, entities are linked by correspondences – according to an equivalence in the 'predominance' of elemental light versus gravity in their make-up – to entities on all other levels; Coleridge calls the lower entity that corresponds to an entity on a higher level a 'symbol'. On the first level of organisation we get magnetism, electricity and galvanism (which to Coleridge includes chemical attraction), then comes the level of the inorganic world, then the level of the organic world of plants and animals, up to the highest stage of organic life, man; at which point, the continuing sytheses of opposing powers produce mind, or consciousness. This culminating production is a radical breakthrough in the developmental process, for consciousness is capable of a reflex act by which – in a continuing play of the law of polarity whereby it counterposes, in order to reconcile, the world, as 'object', to itself, as 'subject'[30] – consciousness re-engenders as knowledge the natural world within which it has itself been engendered, and of which it remains an integral component. Thus man's mind closes the evolutionary circle of polar generation, the human and non-human world merging at the focal point of consciousness.

What made this world-construction so compelling to Coleridge's philosophic sensibility is that it asserts the equal reality both of nature and of mind, and also confirms the diversity and distinctiveness of all existing kinds and individuals, without postulating any metaphysical jumps or divisions in the scheme of things. All differences in kinds and qualities are saved, in what Coleridge called 'distinction without division', as a 'multeity in unity'. There is no gap between the living and the lifeless, between nature and man, or between matter and mind, for all these modes of being consist of diverse and inter-correspondent levels of organisation of the same two elemental

powers and their respective polar forces. And this common component, the primitive pulsation of opposition-in-unity between
the counter-powers, Coleridge identifies as the principle of life
itself. 'What is *not* Life,' Coleridge asks, 'that really *is?*' For 'in
the identity of the two counter-powers, Life *subsists*; in their
strife it *consists*: and in their reconciliation it at once dies and
is born again into a new form. . . .' What he calls this 'universal
life' – or alternatively, 'the one Life' – of ever-resolving and
ever-renewing opposition and reconciliation pulses through all
individual forms and all ascending orders of being, beginning
with what he calls 'its utmost *latency*' in the inorganic 'life of
metals', through the progressive spires of 'individuation', up to
the human body, mind, and consciousness.[31]

It is on this level of consciousness, which culminates and
crowns the generative process of nature, that the specifically
human troubles begin. For man's consciousness involves 'self-
consciousness and self-government' – the awareness of self, the
power to reflect, the knowledge of alternatives and the need to
make moral choices. Man thus 'is referred to himself, delivered
up to his own charge'. If, as Coleridge puts it, he then turns in
'upon his little unthinking contemptible self', man falls into
conflict with himself, severs his interdependence with other
men, and cuts off his intercommunion with the outer world,[32]
in that state in which, Coleridge said, 'we think of ourselves as
separated beings, and place nature in antithesis to the mind, as
. . . death to life'. And from this condition we can only be
rescued by that redeeming contrary vision which, we recall,
Coleridge described as the integrative 'intuition of things which
arises when we possess ourselves, as one with the whole',[33] and
for which Coleridge's mature philosophic enterprise is a sustained evangel.

III.　METASCIENCE AND RELIGION: COLERIDGE'S MYTH OF CONCERN

In this sketch of Coleridge's metascience I have omitted a con-
spicuous and pervasive feature. The lack of this feature in
Schelling's *Naturphilosophie* dismayed Coleridge and underlay
his varying estimates of his predecessor and his recurrent charges
that Schelling's system was a form of 'Pantheism'. By this

Coleridge meant that Schelling absorbs a transcendent Creator of nature, without remainder, into the life and processes of nature itself, so that his nature-philosophy is at the same time a nature-religion. 'In his Theology,' Coleridge exclaimed in a marginal note, Schelling's positions are 'in their literal sense scandalous'.[34]

Coleridge's own aim, he wrote in the *Friend*, is to remove 'the opposition without confounding the distinction between philosophy and faith'.[35] His philosophy, accordingly, has an explicit theological dimension, in the conviction that his meta-science is consonant with his Christian beliefs. He claimed that he had arrived at his derivation of the universe from light and gravitation on the basis of 'the First Principle of my Philosophy', and only afterwards became aware 'of it's exact coincidence with the Mosaic Cosmogony'[36] – that is, with the account of the creation in the Book of Genesis. Coleridge's interpretation of the creation story is grounded on his view that the statements in the Bible are the 'living *educts* of the Imagination', which incorporates the ideas of 'the Reason in Images of the Sense', and therefore are not to be read literally, but as 'a system of symbols'.[37] He also regarded the first chapter of the Fourth Gospel – always for Coleridge the key Book of the Bible – as an expanded version of the account of the creation in Genesis. In the Book of Genesis, the first creative word is, 'Let there be light'. In the Gospel, John writes:

> In the beginning was the Word. . . . All things were made by him. . . . In him was life, and the life was the light of men. And the light shineth in the darkness. . . . And the Word was made flesh, and dwelt among us. . . .

By a hermeneutic process I won't attempt to analyse here, Coleridge brought this biblical cosmogony into accord with the generative principles of his 'speculative physics'. For example, he wrote in 1817:

> And God said – Let there be *Light*: and there was *Light*. And God divided the *Light* from the *Darkness* – i.e., Light from Gravitation . . . and the two Poles of the material Universe are established, viz. Light and Gravitation. . . . The Life of Nature consists in the tendency of the Poles to re-unite. . . .

God is the Sun of the Universe – it's gravitation or Being by
his Omnipresence, it's Light by his only-begotten Son, who is
the *Person* ... or *real* Image, of God – Deus alter et idem!

(CL IV 771)

And since Coleridge conceives the interrelation of God, the Son
and the Holy Spirit as itself the founding and paradigmatic
instance of a three-in-one of thesis, antithesis and synthesis, he
envisions the universe as manifesting, in the polar rhythm of
all its living processes, the being of a Christian God who is,
specifically, a Trinitarian God.

It is this theological aspect which, for many readers, dis-
credits Coleridge's metascience, even if they respond imagina-
tively to the grand architecture of his rationalised vision of the
world. To undertake, in the nineteenth century, to show the
concord between physical science and biblical revelation, and to
construct from their merger a unified philosophy of nature,
seems a hopeless anachronism. We must remember, however,
that in this enterprise Coleridge was working in the central
tradition of post-classical Western metaphysics, and that in
Coleridge's own lifetime Hegel (of whom Coleridge, by the way,
had read very little) claimed that his *Wissenschaft* – his all-
comprehensive system – supersedes, yet incorporates in conceptual form, the truths which are adumbrated in what Hegel calls
the 'picture-thinking', the mythical forms, of the biblical
narrative and the Christian creed.[38] In our endeavour to understand more fully the 'natural want ... of human nature' which
Coleridge's theologico-philosophical system of nature 'is fitted
to satisfy', we need to look at his metascientific enterprise from a
new point of vantage.

When he was thirty years old Coleridge had written, 'Believe
me, Southey! a metaphysical Solution, that does not instantly
tell for something in the Heart, is grievously to be suspected as
apocryphal'; and all his mature life he insisted that a valid
philosophy must appeal to the 'heart' no less than to the 'head',
and that 'all the products of the mere *reflective* faculty partook
of DEATH'.[39] Coleridge meant among other things that, as man
can not live by science alone – in his terms, by the evidence of
the senses ordered by the 'reflective faculty', the 'understanding'
– neither can he endure to live in a universe constructed to the

narrow requirements of Newtonian physics rather than to the large requirements of human life, with its need to make the world emotionally as well as intellectually manageable. He therefore set out to develop an alternative world-vision that would suffice to the heart as well as the head, by supplementing science with imagination; or, as he put it in terms of his faculty psychology, the sense-phenomena ordered by 'the understanding' – are to be 'impregnated' by 'the imagination', and so mediated to the requirements of the supreme and inclusive power of the mind that he called 'the reason'.[40]

Suppose we translate Coleridge's terms into an idiom of our own time. His prime endeavour was to assimilate the findings of science to the inherent demands and forms of the human imagination, in the kind of structured vision of man in the world that Northrop Frye, in a useful phrase, calls a 'myth of concern'. Coleridge's myth of concern is a myth of reintegration. That is, he undertakes to put man and his mind back into nature, from which the sophisticated and highly specialised logic of science had severed him, by replacing the causal relations of the post-Newtonian world scheme with the primitive imaginative categories of analogy, correspondence, participation and identity. These categories define what Coleridge calls the 'exponents', 'analagons', 'indexes' and 'symbols' in his cosmic system. As Coleridge wrote, the world of time 'presents itself to the understanding . . . as an infinite ascent of Causes, and . . . as an interminable progression of Effects', but when 'freed from the phenomena of Time and Space' it 'reveals itself to the pure Reason as the actual immanence of ALL in EACH'.[41] Also:

> [It is my philosophical faith that] in Nature Man beholds only . . . the integration of Products, the Differentials of which are in, and constitute, his own mind and soul – and consequently that all true science is contained in the Lore of Symbols & Correspondences.   (CL v 19)

By this procedure Coleridge re-endows a dead and meaningless universe with the inherent energies and generative powers of life and with humanly intelligible purposes and values, and so makes it a milieu of which man's mind is an integral and reciprocative part, in which he can be at home, and by which he can sanction a workable rule of life. And since the cultural myth of concern that Coleridge had inherited was the Christian one based on the Bible, and since Coleridge felt a deeper need than the great German system-builders to preserve the essentials of its creed of salvation, he undertook to ground the rational structure of his world-vision on what he regarded as the two distinct but correlative bases of 'speculative physics' and Scriptural revelation.

Such a description of Coleridge's nature-philosophy as a myth of concern translates the criterion of his system from a truth of correspondence to ultimate reality to a truth of correspondence to man's deep instincts and needs, and so no doubt would have been unacceptable to him. It has, however, at least this affinity with Coleridge's own views: as we know, he regarded the primitive of a metaphysical system, its founding vision, as undemonstrable by rational means, and therefore as a choice – a moral choice – which each individual must make for himself. In Coleridge's opinion, a man is ultimately responsible for the kind of world he sees.

IV.   COSMIC ECOLOGY: THE GROWING PLANT

It is one thing to know Coleridge's nature-philosophy as a conceptual scheme and quite another thing to know what nature looks like, when viewed through that scheme. I should like, in conclusion, to present to you a passage in which, in an imaginative moment, Coleridge communicates what it is to experience the world in accordance with his informing vision.

This text occurs in an unlikely place. In 1816 Coleridge published a short work, *The Statesman's Manual*, to encourage the study of the Bible as a repository, in symbolic form, of those ideas of reason which are the principles of all political wisdom. To the *Manual* he adds, characteristically, five appendices. Appendix C sets out to explain at length the difference between the thin intuition of the world which is filtered through the categories of the understanding, and the full intuition of the world as contemplated by the reason mediated by imagination. While Coleridge sits writing, he looks through his study window at the landscape outside and, just as in his early 'conversation poems', an aspect of the natural scene springs his imagination

free, and so transforms the *visibilia* into vision. Here is Coleridge's text, in part:

I seem to myself to behold in the quiet objects, on which
I am gazing, more than an arbitrary illustration, more
than a mere *simile*, the work of my own Fancy! I feel
an awe, as if there were before my eyes the same Power,
as that of the REASON – the same Power in a lower   5
dignity, and therefore a symbol established in the truth
of things. I feel it alike, whether I contemplate a single
tree or flower, or meditate on vegetation throughout the
world, as one of the great organs of the life of nature.
Lo! – with the rising sun it commences its outward life   10
and enters into open communion with all the elements,
at once assimilating them to itself and to each other. At
the same moment it strikes its roots and unfolds its
leaves, absorbs and respires, steams forth its cooling
vapour and finer fragrance, and breathes a repairing   15
spirit, at once the food and tone of the atmosphere, into
the atmosphere that feeds *it*. Lo! – at the touch of light
how it returns an air akin to light, and yet with the same
pulse effectuates its own secret growth, still contracting to
fix what expanding it had refined. Lo! – how upholding   20
the ceaseless plastic motion of the parts in the profoundest
rest of the whole it becomes the visible organismus of the
whole *silent* or *elementary* life of nature and, therefore,
in incorporating the one extreme becomes the symbol of
the other; the natural symbol of that higher life of   25
reason, in which the whole series (known to us in our
present state of being) is perfected, in which, therefore,
all the subordinate gradations recur, and are re-ordained
'*in more abundant honour.*' We had seen each in its own
cast, and we now recognise them all as co-existing in the 30
unity of a higher form, the Crown and Completion of the
Earthly, and the Mediator of a new and heavenly series.
Thus finally, the vegetable creation, in the simplicity
and uniformity of its *internal* structure symbolising the
unity of nature, while it represents the omniformity of   35
her delegated functions in its *external* variety and
manifoldness, becomes the record and chronicle of her

ministerial acts, and inchases the vast unfolded volume
of the earth with the hieroglyphics of her history.[42]

The passage has haunted me since Dr I. A. Richards brought
it to my attention when I was a student at Cambridge several
decades ago. In its projection of a distinctive authorial presence,
its rhythms and rhetoric, and its ever-widening orbit of reference,
its gives us, I think, some notion of Coleridge's conversation –
a marvel of the age that attracted crowds of domestic and foreign
visitors and is recorded in more than a hundred surviving
memoirs. John Lockhart described how Coleridge cheered and
delighted his audience with

> the evident kindliness of his whole spirit and intentions...
> the cordial childlike innocence of his smile, the inexpressible
> sweetness of his voice, and the rich musical flow into which
> his mere language ever threw itself.   (CT 291)

And James Fenimore Cooper narrates how, at a dinner party,
Coleridge discoursed for an uninterrupted hour about Homer.
Sir Walter Scott sat, like the other auditors, 'immovable as a
statue', occasionally muttering, 'Eloquent!' 'Wonderful!' 'Very
extraordinary!'[43] There were a few who were immune to the
enchantment, Carlyle most notably; but Coleridge had antici-
pated Carlyle by caricaturing his own talk. My 'grievous fault',
he confided to his notebook, is that

> my illustrations swallow up my thesis – I feel too intensely
> the omnipresence of all in each... [and so] go on from circle
> to circle till I break against the shore of my Hearer's patience,
> or have my Concentricals dashed to nothing by a Snore.
>
>   (CN II 2372)

In the passage I have reproduced, notice first that in his
description of the growing plant (lines 10–20) Coleridge incorporates the findings of experimental botanists, and that the
scientific data are detailed, accurate and up to date. In his *Vegetable Staticks* (1727) Stephen Hales had described the flow of sap,
under pressure, from the roots through the plant, and the transpiration of water-vapour through the surface of the leaves.
Joseph Priestley in the 1770s published his *Experiments and
Observations on Different Kinds of Air*, announcing his discovery that plants restore the purity of 'vitiated air' by

producing large quantities of the gas he called 'dephlogisticated air', thus rendering the atmosphere again fit for human and animal respiration. Not until Jan Ingenhousz published his classic *Experiments on Vegetables* (1779), however, was it made known that this process does not occur in darkness, but only under 'the influence of the light of the sun'; that the operation is performed 'only by the leaves and the green stalks' of the plants, which absorb common air, 'elaborate' it, and give out the 'dephlogisticated air'; and that after absorbing the air, plants 'separate from it those substances which are appropriate for their nourishment' and eject those which are 'harmful to them' but 'wholesome for animals'. By the time he wrote *An Essay on the Food of Plants* (1796), Ingenhousz had come to know what he called the 'new chemistry' of Lavoisier, and so was able to specify the activity of the green matter in the leaves of plants: under the influence of sunlight, it absorbs carbon dioxide from the atmosphere, decomposes it, exhales the oxygen, and by a process of chemical recomposition, changes the carbon remainder to its own substance and nourishment.*

Coleridge composed *The Statesman's Manual* at the time (1815–16) when he was developing his philosophy of nature, and his account of the absorption and transpiration of water, of the chemistry of photosynthesis, and of the process of plant growth is structured throughout by the humanistic categories and relationships predicated by that philosophy. He converts, that is, scientific data into metascientific terms of encounter, communion, kinship, participation and reciprocity, and he locates the processes of the plant within a universe of correspondences, through which beats the pulse of one shared life. For example:

* Jan Ingenhousz, *Experiments upon Vegetables*, in *Jan Ingenhousz, Plant Physiologist*, by Howard S. Reed, *Chronica Botanica* (XI, 1947–8), especially pp. 316, 329; and *An Essay on the Food of Plants*, reprinted by J. Christian Bay (1933) pp. 3–6, 10. See also J. Wiesner, *Jan Ingenhousz: Sein Leben und Sein Wirken* (Wien, 1905). Erasmus Darwin in *The Botanic Garden* refers to Hales, Priestley and Ingenhousz in discussing plant transpiration and interchanges with the atmosphere. This work was known to Coleridge, but his description of plant processes is much more precise and accurate than Darwin's. See *The Botanic Garden*, 2nd ed. (1794–5), the notes to Pt. I, Canto I, line 462 and to Canto IV, line 34; and 'Additional Notes' xxxiv and xxxvii.

Lo! – at the touch of light how it returns an air akin to light, and yet with the same pulse effectuates its own secret growth, still contracting to fix what expanding it had refined.

The 'air akin to light' is oxygen, and Coleridge's phrase is more than a metaphor, for in his intricate scheme of nature oxygen is an element that is a phenomenal 'exponent' – a physical correspondent – of the pre-phenomenal power he calls light. By the 'predominance', as Coleridge says elsewhere, of one or the other of the two primal counter-powers, 'Carbon most represents Gravity, Oxygen Light. . . .'[44] The oxygen that the plants breathes out (lines 15–17 in our passage) is 'a repairing spirit' because it revitalises what Priestley had called the 'vitiated air', in that sustained reciprocity wherein the plant feeds the atmosphere by which it has been fed. And the 'pulse' of the growing plant – the contraction by which it recomposes and assimilates, and the expansion by which it decomposes and exhales, the chemical elements of carbon dioxide – reiterates the polar forces of 'Contraction and Dilation' which, we recall, are the systole and diastole of the pre-phenomenal power of light that initiate the heartbeat of all natural and human life.

Coleridge goes on (lines 20–28) to situate the plant in his spiral scheme of evolving and correspondent nature. The evolutionary process performs a spiral because, Coleridge claims, since the generative principle is one that 'in every instant *goes out* of itself, and in the same instant retracts', 'the product' is of necessity a 'curve line'.[45] Halfway in the evolution between inorganic matter at one end and man at the other end, the plant occupies a position on the schematic spiral corresponding to that of the chemical elements below it and of the human reason above it. Thus, in the ceaseless 'plastic' (that is, 'formative') recompositions of its chemical elements within the stillness of its outer form, the growing plant incorporates, and so is an exponent of, 'the whole *silent* or *elementary* life' of inorganic nature. But the processes by which a plant grows are in turn incorporated in, and so serve as a 'symbol' of, the mental evolution of what Coleridge elsewhere calls the 'seminal' ideas at the upper extreme of natural evolution, the human reason.

'Symbol', by the way, is for Coleridge a specialised term that he applies only to objects in the Book of Scripture and the Book of Nature, as he is at pains to point out in *The Statesman's Manual*, in passages which present-day critics unwarily cite as though they applied to any literary use of 'symbols', in the broad modern sense. A symbol, Coleridge says in *The Manual*, 'always partakes of the Reality which it renders intelligible; and while it enunciates the whole, abides itself as a living part in that Unity, of which it is the representative'.[46] In Coleridge's scheme of nature the growing plant is a symbol of reason – 'a symbol established in the truth of things' (lines 4–7) – because it is 'the same Power, as that of the REASON', but 'in a lower dignity'. That is, the reason is consubstantial with the plant, since it is a product of the same primitive counter-powers, but on a level of organisation in which (lines 25–29) 'all the subordinate gradations recur, and are re-ordained "*in more abundant honour*"'. But to Coleridge's thinking, while human reason is the highest product of natural evolution, it is in its turn a symbol of – therefore participates in, 'partakes of the Reality' of – that divine Reason, the Logos, which (in his favourite quotation from John) is the life and the light of men. Hence Coleridge's assertion (lines 30–32) that the human reason, while it is 'the Crown and Completion of the Earthly', is also 'the Mediator of a new and heavenly series'. In other words, man's reason is the middle thing between the natural and the supranatural levels of being.

I shall not carry farther the explication of this text – so terse and lucid, but implicating Coleridge's total philosophy of nature – except for one last remark. ('Lastly!' Coleridge once exclaimed, 'O word of comfort!') The passage makes it evident that Coleridge's myth of concern envisions all existing things, from the inorganic through the human, as participants in a single system of cosmic ecology. Man, whatever more he may be, is consubstantial, interdependent and in communion with the nature of which he is the product. By having achieved self-consciousness, Coleridge says, man 'has the whole world in counterpoint to him, but he contains an entire world within himself. Now, for the first time at the apex of the living pyramid, it is Man and Nature, but Man himself is a syllepsis, a compendium of Nature – the Microcosm!' And again, in 1817:

The whole process is cyclical tho' progressive, and the Man

separates from Nature only that Nature may be found again
in a higher dignity in the Man.[47]

With whatever differences, this sense of a cosmic ecology of
nature, man and mind is shared by all romantic visionaries,
Christian or non-Christian, from Schelling and Coleridge to
D. H. Lawrence and Dylan Thomas. Coleridge's reasoned formulation of such a vision of the world seems to me a reputable
metaphysics which has intellectual, emotional and aesthetic
appeal and implies important rules for the conduct of life. It is
also eminently pertinent to our own time. Coleridge, we know,
claimed that an intuition of the world which is limited to the
categories of the utilitarian and merely scientific understanding,
by placing 'nature in antithesis to the mind', 'strikes death' both
to the world and to the human spirit. Our developing scientific
technology, by its frantic exploitation of nature, has turned
Coleridge's metaphoric death into a grimly literal possibility.
Scientists have recently taken the lead in trying to persuade us,
by an appeal to our understanding, of the imminence of racial
suicide. It remains to be seen whether merely understanding the
facts is enough, or whether it will take a recovery of something
like the romantic vision – and myth – of nature to give us, in
Shelley's great phrase, the power 'to imagine what we know',
and so suffice to release the emotions, the energies, the invention
and the will to salvage our world while it is still fit to live in.

Coleridge is two hundred years old today, and to commemorate
his birth I thought it appropriate to call to mind an area of his
wide-ranging thought which has been the least attended to and
the least esteemed. A commemoration, however, ought also to
leave us with a memory of the man himself. The Coleridge who
developed his philosophy of nature in 1815–19 was in his middle
forties and on the verge of his kindly, industrious, marvellously
loquacious, but lonely and defeated older age. It is better to
remember Coleridge as he himself chose to be remembered, by
an episode in an early letter. It is one of a group that he called
'Satyrane's Letters' – after the satyr's son in *The Faerie Queene*
whom Una converted to the true belief – which Coleridge revised
and used to fill out the *Biographia Literaria* in 1816. He did so,
he tells us, because 'I would fain present myself to the Reader',

not 'under the circumstances of late years', but 'as I was in the
first dawn of my literary life'.* In that episode Coleridge presents
himself to us dressed all in black and dancing; it was found by
the poet Wallace Stevens in its rather obscure place and quoted
by him as a chief exhibit in his essay, 'The Figure of the Youth
as Virile Poet'.⁴⁸ Here we find the authentic STC – downrightly
eccentric, a bit complacent about his powers, showing forth his
frailties, yet savingly self-ironic, talking, talking, and unex-
pectedly modulating into the music of his prose at its best.

It is a Sunday morning, 16 September 1798. Coleridge is
twenty-five years of age; he has very recently composed most
of his best poems, including *The Ancient Mariner* and 'Frost at
Midnight'; *Lyrical Ballads* is in the press; and he is on a packet
taking him to his momentous ten months in Germany. The
water roughens, and most of the eighteen voyagers retreat hastily
to the cabin. Coleridge is in somewhat better plight, and creeps
into a lifeboat for a nap. There he is sought out and summoned
to a drinking party by two Danes, one of whom is inordinately
vain of his fractured English. 'Vat imagination!' he cries to
Coleridge, 'Vat language! vat vast science! and vat eyes!... O
my heafen! vy, you're a Got!'

> I went [Coleridge writes], and found some excellent wines
> and a dessert of grapes with a pineapple. The Danes had
> christened me Doctor Teology, and dressed as I was all in
> black, with large shoes and black worsted stockings, I might
> certainly have passed very well for a Methodist missionary.
> However I disclaimed my title. What then may you be? A
> man of fortune? No! – A merchant? No! A merchant's
> traveller? No! – A clerk? No! – Un Philosophe, perhaps?...
> I was weary of being questioned, and rather than be nothing
> ... I submitted by a bow, even to the aspersion implied in the
> word, 'un Philosophe.' – The Dane then informed me, that all
> in the present party were philosophers likewise. Certes we
> were not of the stoic school. For we drank and talked and
> sung, till we talked and sung all together; and then we rose
> and danced on the deck a set of dances. ...

* BL II 131. For the original letter in which Coleridge described
this episode, see CL I 420ff. Coleridge first revised the letter for
inclusion in the *Friend* (1809) and then reprinted it, with slight
changes, in BL II 132ff.

6
Coleridge's Anxiety

Thomas McFarland

Much of Coleridge's existence was a death in life. His deep commitment to the Christian religion was sustained, on the one hand, by the need to feel that there must be something better than the torment in which he so mysteriously found himself, and, on the other, by the sense of his inability to cope with his manifold failings:

> I profess a deep conviction [he wrote] that Man was and is a *fallen* Creature, not by accidents of bodily constitution, or any other cause, which *human* Wisdom in a course of ages might be supposed capable of removing; but diseased in his Will.... (AR 136)

Certainly this view, central to Christian faith, corresponded exactly to the facts of life as he himself experienced them.* His intellect, noted Southey in 1815, was 'as clear and as powerful as ever was vouchsafed to man', but 'he labours under a disease of the volition'.[1] Earlier, in May 1809, Wordsworth, in a moment of intense exasperation, had informed Thomas Poole of his 'deliberate opinion' about Coleridge, that

> Neither his talents nor his genius mighty as they are nor his vast information will avail him anything; they are all frustrated by a derangement in his intellectual and moral constitution − In fact he has no voluntary power of mind whatsoever, nor is he capable of acting under any *constraint* of duty or moral obligation. (WLR (1806–11) 352)

* 'My Faith is simply this – that there is an original corruption in our nature, from which & from the consequences of which, we may be redeemed by Christ ... and this I believe − not because I *understand* it; but because I *feel*, that it is not only suitable to, but needful for, my nature ...' (CL II 807. To George Coleridge, 1 July 1802).

To these statements by outside observers, one could add repeated self-awarenesses by Coleridge himself. To cite a single instance, which by its almost trivial context may seem to show his 'disease of the volition' in all its mysteriousness, a note of January 1804 says:

> All this evening, indeed all this day ... I ought to have [been] reading & filling the Margins of Malthus – I had begun & found it pleasant/ why did I neglect it? ... – surely this is well worth a serious Analysis, that understanding I may attempt to heal/ for it is a deep & wide disease in my moral Nature.... Love of Liberty, Pleasure of Spontaneity ... these all express, not explain, the Fact. (CN I 1832)

If the unexplainable fact of a diseased volition was the most mysterious and destructive of the ills under which Coleridge laboured, it was, as we all know, by no means the only one. His dependence of almost forty years upon the specious consolations of opium (or 'laudanum', which, as he says at one point, 'I had taken in enormous doses for 32 years')[2] filled him even more with self-loathing than did his inability to discharge his duty, indeed, was at times charged with responsibility for that defect:

> What crime is there scarcely which has not been included in or followed from the one guilt of taking opium? Not to speak of ingratitude to my maker for the wasted Talents; of ingratitude to so many friends who have loved me ... of barbarous neglect of my family.... I have in this one dirty business of Laudanum an hundred times deceived, tricked, nay, actually & consciously LIED – (CL III 490)

Everywhere he found a bewildering sense of his own inadequacy. 'There is a something, an essential something wanting in me'.[3] Again, he writes of 'A sense of weakness – a haunting sense, that I was an herbaceous Plant, as large as a large Tree ... but with *pith within* the Trunk, not heart of Wood/ – that I had *power* not *strength* – an involuntary Imposter.... This ... is as fair a statement of my habitual Haunting, as I could give before the Tribunal of Heaven'.[4]

Beset as it was by such inner hauntings, Coleridge's life, in many of its most important outward manifestations, became a shambles. He failed to take his degree at Cambridge; he married the wrong woman; he was unable to capture the lasting respect of the women he did love; he managed, at great cost to his own self-esteem and their patience, continually to be supported by admirers; he became estranged from his dearest friend; he was humiliated by the abject failure of his first born, which seemed a repetition of his own disasters; he reneged on his aspirations as a poet and did not adequately realise those as a philosopher. Furthermore, he did not bear his troubles with the stoic dignity of Wordsworth; rather he lived a life of desperation made unquiet by interminable self-justifications and hypochondriac fancies, by a querulous inability to accept criticisms or anything less than uncritical affection. He plagiarised; he procrastinated; he spent a dismaying amount of effort, as Dorothy Wordsworth said, 'in deceiving himself, and seeking to deceive others'.[5] In sum, he was, as Humphry House has said, 'not a glamorous or systematic Romantic sinner who, like Byron or Baudelaire, seized on the idea of evil as a stimulus: he was a genuine sinner, who did what he believed to be wrong against his conscience and his better judgement; he was an important sinner, whose sins were meanness, hypocrisy, self-deceit . . . a tortured, tearful, weak, self-humiliating sinner'.[6] In such massive contexts of woe, it is difficult to imagine a more apposite epitaph than the one Coleridge himself supplied:

> Beneath this sod
> A poet lies, or that which once seem'd he.
> O, lift one thought in prayer for S. T. C.;
> That he who many a year with toil of breath
> Found death in life, may here find life in death!
>
> (PW I 491–2)

The sense of the cumulatively battering effect of Coleridge's voyage through this world can be experienced in the simple record of his physical presence as seen by others. An aura of exuberant vitality surrounded him in young manhood. 'You had a great loss in not seeing Coleridge', writes Dorothy Wordsworth in 1797:

He is a wonderful man. His conversation teems with soul, mind, and spirit. Then he is so benevolent, so good tempered and cheerful, and, like William, interests himself so much

about every little trifle. At first I thought him very plain,
that is, for about three minutes: he is pale and thin, has a
wide mouth, thick lips, and not very good teeth, longish
loose-growing half-curling rough black hair. But if you hear
him speak for five minutes you think no more of them.

(WLR (1787–1805) 188–9)

But by 1806, upon Coleridge's return from Malta, Dorothy
witnessed quite a different sight:

> ... never did I feel such a shock as at first sight of him. We all
> felt exactly in the same way – as if he were different from
> what we have expected to see; ... I know not what to hope
> for, or what to expect; ... his misery has made him so weak,
> and he has been so dismally irresolute in all things since his
> return to England, that I have more of fear than hope. He
> is utterly changed ...   (WLR (1806–11) 86)

By 1810 things were even worse. The man who had been described in the 1805 *Prelude* as 'The most intense of Nature's
worshippers'[7] was now almost wholly withdrawn and cast
scarcely a glance on the outer world:

> He lies in bed [wrote Dorothy], always till after 12 o'clock,
> sometimes much later; and never walks out – Even the finest
> spring day does not tempt him to seek the fresh air; and this
> beautiful valley seems a blank to him. He never leaves his
> own parlour except at dinner and tea, and sometimes supper,
> and then he always seems impatient to get back to his solitude
> – he goes the moment his food is swallowed. Sometimes he
> does not speak a word, and when he does talk it is always
> very much and upon subjects as far aloof from himself or his
> friends as possible.   (Ibid. 399)

After 1816, to be sure, when Coleridge came under the
devoted care of the physician James Gillman, his life became
more stable and, at least in comparison with the horrors of the
preceding fifteen years, more happy. But the impression he
conveyed was of a man intensely battered by existence:

> he was now getting old, towards sixty perhaps [writes Carlyle
> of the Coleridge of the Highgate years]; and gave you the idea
> of a life that had been full of sufferings; a life heavy-laden,

half-vanquished, still swimming painfully in seas of manifold physical and other bewilderment. Brow and head were round, and of massive weight, but the face was flabby and irresolute. The deep eyes, of a light hazel, were as full of sorrow as of inspiration; confused pain looked mildly from them, as in a kind of mild astonishment. . . . A heavy-laden, high-aspiring and surely much-suffering man.   (Carlyle 71)

This outer testimony to stress and bewilderment is paralleled by extensive inner witness by Coleridge himself. In his 'Dejection: an Ode', he writes in 1802 of a deep-lying malaise that he called

> A Grief without a pang, void, dark, & drear,
> A stifling, drowsy, unimpassion'd grief,
> That finds no natural Outlet, no Relief. . . .
>
> (CL II 790)

In 1804, he writes in this way:

> Sleep a pandemonium of all the shames & miseries of the past Life from early childhood all huddled together, & bronzed with one stormy Light of Terror & Self-torture
>
> (CN II 2091)

All this went on for many years. For instance, to Josiah Wade, in June 1814, Coleridge asks his correspondent to

> . . . conceive whatever is most wretched, helpless, and hopeless, and you will form as tolerable a notion of my state, as it is possible for a good man to have.   (CL III 511)

In short, Coleridge's 'Terror & Self-torture', his 'Grief without a pang, void, dark, & drear', his sense of being 'wretched, helpless, and hopeless', all are testimony to a consuming misery that continued with little abatement for most of his life. Like Cowper, he felt himself a psychic castaway, overwhelmed and drowning in an ocean of inner torment.

This torment, it seems clear, was deeper than the opium-addiction, deeper than the hypochondria, deeper than the plagiarisms, deeper than the inability to work. It was in fact the universal substructure upon which they reared their individual ruins. Indeed, it is probably true that the repeated recourses to opium, the repeated indulgences in hypochondria, the repeated indecorums of plagiarism and the repeated vices of procrastination were neurotic attempts to cope with this deeper malaise rather than unmixed evidence of the malaise itself. Certainly they all have in common the characteristic neurotic form of compulsive repetition. (Cf. Freud XVIII 18–23.)

The opium-addiction, for instance, though sometimes referred to by Coleridge as though it were the underlying cause of his unhappiness – he speaks at one point of 'the poison that has been the curse of my existence, my shame and my *negro-slave* inward humiliation and debasement'[8] – is at other times identified as merely a symptom:

> I have never loved Evil for its own sake; no! nor ever sought pleasure for its own sake, but only as the means of escaping from pains that coiled round my mental powers . . .
>
> (CN II 2368)

The pains that coiled around his mental powers were the indeterminate convulsions of his drowning psyche, or, as he calls it, 'infantine nervousness':

> most men [he notes in December, 1806] affected by belief of *reality* attached to the wild-weed spectres of infantine nervousness – but I affected by them simply, & of themselves – /but for the last years I own & mourn a more deleterious Action of *Fear* – fear of horrors in *Sleep*, driving me to dreadful remedies & stimuli . . . to purchase daily a wretched Reprieve from the torments of each night's Dæmons . . . (CN II 2944)

At one point 'intolerable Despair' is termed the underlying cause of the addiction:

> O me! now racked with pain, now fallen abroad & suffocated with a sense of intolerable Despair/& no other Refuge than Poisons that degrade the Being . . . (CN II 2860)

As with the opium-addiction, so with the bodily illness. One can scarcely doubt that Coleridge did suffer much physical pain and discomfort; but one can also not doubt that a very substantial portion of it was psychic, not organic, in origin. He spent an extraordinary amount of time worrying about his intestinal functions, and in his letters and notebooks the repeated reports on the state of his bowels can be wearisome to read. Some of his experiences were both fearsome and revolting. Thus, on ship to Malta in 1804, he writes of

> the dull quasi finger-pressure on the Liver, the endless Flatulence, the frightful constipation when the dead Filth *impales* the lower Gut – to weep & sweat & moan & scream for the parturience of an excrement with such pangs & such convulsions as a woman with an Infant . . . (CN II 2091)

For the last three decades of his life he believed that his troubles were caused by an obstruction of the bowels,* and was confident that an autopsy would prove him correct. At one point he speaks of a 'not unfrequent tragico-whimsical fancy' in which he is present at his post-mortem dissection, 'infusing . . . this and that thought into the Mind of the Anatomist. . . . Be so good as to give a cut just *there*, right across the umbilicar region – there lurks the fellow that for so many years tormented me on my first waking!'[9] But when the autopsy was actually performed, no obstruction was revealed. As Sara Coleridge wrote to her brother Hartley after Coleridge's death:

> He had made a solemn injunction on Mr Gillman that his body should be opened – which was accordingly done. . . . There was more than a pint of water in the chest, & the heart & liver were enlarged. But nothing was observed which could be ascribed to laudanum, & the internal pain & uneasiness which he has suffered from all his life, & which my mother remembers him complaining of before he ever had recourse to opium, is supposed to have been some sympathetic nervous affection . . . (CL VI 992)

Coleridge appears to have suspected that at least some aspects of his discomfort were psychic in origin (he admits at one point to being 'horribly hypochondriacal'[10]) and at times his report is explicitly psychosomatic. Thus he speaks of

> frightful Dreams with screaming – *breezes* of Terror blowing from the Stomach up thro' the Brain/ always when I am

* See, for instance, his complaint of 13 June 1809: 'Sleep or even a supine Posture does not fail to remind me that something is organically amiss in some one or other of the Contents of the Abdomen'. (CL III 212).

awakened, I find myself stifled with wind/ & the wind the manifest cause of the Dream/ frequent paralytic Feelings – sometimes approaches to Convulsion fit... (CL II 976)

And that the organic pain, psychosomatic pain, and imaginary pain all were enormously amplified by an extreme psychic stress seems still more clear from the fact that he felt them most when alone, and had innumerable turns for the better when in company.* Doubtless the fear of being alone was an important element in his fame as a conversationalist, for to talk to another was to ward off the psychic agony that erupted when he was by himself.† At any rate, numerous observers noted an almost obsessional quality in his discourse: 'he lays down his pen to make sure of an auditor', said Hazlitt 'and mortgages the admiration of posterity for the stare of an idler'.[11] Once the auditor was gone, terror could engulf Coleridge. As he writes in 1803, in 'The Pains of Sleep',

> ... yesternight I pray'd aloud
> In Anguish and in Agony,
> Awaking from the fiendish Crowd
> Of Shapes & Thoughts that tortur'd me!
>
> .   .   .   .   .
>
> For all was Horror, Guilt & Woe ...
> Life-stifling Fear, Soul-stifling Shame!
>
> (CL II 983)

The life-stifling fear, and its hypochondriac manifestations, were very hard on his friends. As Dorothy Wordsworth notes in her Grasmere Journal in 1801: '[William] went to meet Mary, and they brought 4 letters – 2 from Coleridge.... Coleridge's were melancholy letters, he had been very ill in his bowels. We were made very unhappy.' Again: 'A heart-rending letter from Coleridge – we were sad as we could be. Wm. wrote to him.' And again: '... two very affecting letters from Coleridge.... I was stopped in my writing, and made ill by the letters.'[12]

---

* Cf. Wordsworth to Thomas Poole in July 1801: 'He is apparently quite well one day, and the next the fit comes on him again with as much violence as ever.' (WLR (1787–1805) 338–9).

† 'The stimulus of Conversation suspends the terror that haunts my mind; but when I am alone, the horrors ... almost overwhelm me—.' (CL IV 630).

Although Wordsworth pronounced Dorothy's intense concern about Coleridge's health to be 'nervous blubbering',[13] he himself could become scarcely less upset. For instance, on 29 March 1804, he writes almost frantically to Coleridge: 'Your last letter but one informing us of your late attack was the severest shock to me, I think, I have ever received.'[14]

Coleridge once spoke of 'the accumulating embarrassments of procrastination'.[15] Hypochondria too accumulates its embarrassments, for when one arouses the sympathy and fears of his friends as often as Coleridge did, the only thing he can decently do is to die. When time goes on, and the heart-rending complaints are followed, not by death but simply by more complaints, the attitudes of the friends begin to harden. We can see this, in a sad but also almost ludicrously indignant letter written by Dorothy to Catherine Clarkson in 1811:

> How absurd, how uncalculating of the feelings and opinions of others, to talk to your Father and Sister of dying in a fortnight, when his dress and everything proved that his thoughts were of other matters. Such talks will never more alarm me. Poor William went off to London [i.e. in February 1808] ... in consequence of [Coleridge] having solemnly assured Mrs. Coleridge that he *could* not live three months; and, when William arrived, he ... saw no appearance of disease which could not have been cured, or at least prevented by himself.
> (WLR (1806–11) 495)

From these and other examples, it seems probable that a massive *anxiety*, rather than any more specific ailment, was the true source of Coleridge's varied miseries. Indeed, he himself suspected as much. 'My 44th Birth-day', he exclaims in 1815:

> and in *all* but the Brain I am an old man! Such ravages do anxiety & mismanagement make.   (CL IV 609)

Elsewhere, he identifies anxiety, or, as he calls it 'dread', as the common denominator of his woes:

> It is a most instructive part of my Life [he writes in 1805] ... that I have been always preyed on by some Dread, and perhaps all my faulty actions have been the consequence of some Dread or other on my mind/ ... So in my childhood & Boyhood the horror of being detected with a sorehead ... then a

short-lived Fit of Fears from sex ... then came Rob. Southey's alienation/ my marriage – constant dread in my mind respecting Mrs Coleridge's Temper ... and finally stimulants in the fear & prevention of violent Bowel-attacks from mental agitation/ then almost epileptic night-horrors in my sleep/ ... all this interwoven with its minor consequences, that fill up the interspaces – the cherry juice running in between the cherries in a cherry pie/ procrastination in dread of this – & something else in consequence of that procrast. &c/

(CN II 2398)

The multiplication of symptoms testifies to the depth and intensity of the anxiety, which runs like cherry juice through their interspaces. For as Freud has pointed out, in his treatise, *Hemmung, Symptom, und Angst,*

> symptoms are only formed in order to avoid anxiety: they bind the psychical energy which would otherwise be discharged as anxiety.[16]

It follows that 'anxiety', as Freud says, is 'the fundamental phenomenon and main problem of neurosis'.* Symptom formation is

> synonymous with substitute-formation.... The defensive process is analogous to the flight by means of which the ego removes itself from a danger that threatens it from outside.†

If we seek the origin of an anxiety so pervasive, so shattering and so neurotically persistent, as Coleridge's, we look, in this post-Freudian age, almost as a matter of course to his childhood. And even before more precise investigation, one might suspect that his position as the youngest of ten children, nine of whom were brothers, was psychologically precarious. The likelihood of fragmentation of attention and relation on the part of the

---

* Freud XX 144. Again, 'the generating of anxiety sets symptom formation going and is, indeed, a necessary prerequisite of it'. Cf. Otto Fenichel: 'the problem of anxiety is the essence of any psychology of neurotic conflicts' (*The Psychoanalytic Theory of Neurosis,* New York, 1945, p. 132). See further Freud XVI 393, 404, 411.

† Ibid., 145. 'Symptom-formation ... does in fact put an end to the danger-situation.'

parents, and of damaging aggressiveness from the jealously com-
peting brothers, would inevitably be very high in such a situation.

More specifically, the enormous extent of Coleridge's anxiety
points compellingly to two sources in his childhood: an extension
of what Freud calls a primal anxiety, arising from his relationship with his mother, and what in that same terminology is
called a castration anxiety, which in this instance would be
connected with his older brothers. (See Freud XXII 86–7.)

Now the subject of motherhood was one that for Coleridge
seemed to be charged with a special burden of morbid emotion.
To cite an example, some lines in 'The Three Graves' run as
follows:

> Beneath the foulest Mother's curse
> No child could ever thrive:
> A Mother is a Mother still;
> The holiest thing alive.*

As an equally revealing example, one might consider a letter
Coleridge wrote to his son Derwent in 1807, after having decided
to separate from his wife. The letter rather terrifyingly impresses
upon the child the need for respect for the mother:

> she gave *you* nourishment out of her own Breasts . . . and she
> brought you into the world with shocking pains. . . . So it must
> needs be a horribly wicked Thing ever to forget, or wilfully to
> vex, a Father or a Mother: especially, a Mother.　　(CL III 1–2)

Despite the piety of such admonitions, Coleridge's relations to
his own mother, as David Beres and others have noted, were
characterised by a peculiar coldness. For instance, in his remarkable series of autobiographical letters to Thomas Poole in 1797,
all he finds to say about her was that 'My Mother was an
admirable Economist, and managed exclusively'.[17] Perhaps a
more unmistakably significant datum, however, is his virtual

---

* *Friend* II 90. Cf. Coleridge to Mary Robinson in 1802: 'Your
dear Mother is more present to my eyes, than the paper on which I
am writing – which indeed swims before my sight – for I can not
think of your Mother without Tears.' 'What, dear Miss Robinson!
ought *you* to feel for yourself – & for the memory of a MOTHER – of
all names the most awful, the most venerable, next to that of God!'
(CL II 904, 905).

disregard of the fact of her death. He had always been reluctant
to return to his family home;* indeed, in 1802, although near
enough to Devonshire, he declined to make a visit that would
have entailed very little trouble.† And early in November 1809,
he wrote to Southey that

> my poor Mother is near her end, and dying in great torture,
> death eating her piecemeal . . . & she wishes to see me before
> her death – But tho' my Brother knows I am penniless, not an
> offer of a Bank note to en[able] me to set off. In truth, I know
> not what to do – for [there] is not a shilling in our whole
> House—   (CL III 261)

Even allowing for the differences of individual temperaments,
for the differences in family traditions, for the differences in
custom in various locales and eras, and allowing also for the
realness of Coleridge's poverty, this declaration, I think, sounds
strange to us all.

No less curious is the fact that Coleridge does not mention
her actual death in any form of writing, even though Dorothy
Wordsworth, to whom his mother can have meant nothing,
writes on 18 November 1809, that 'Mrs Fricker and Coleridge's
Mother are both dead'.[18] Coleridge's wife also takes note of the
event, saying that Coleridge was 'greatly distressed', but that
she and his 'Grasmere friends' had opposed his going because
of the 'effect such a scene would have upon his mind &
health'.[19] That Coleridge was greatly distressed shows what is

---

* For example, he writes to Southey on 12 Feb 1800 that 'In May
I am under a kind of engagement to go with Sara to Ottery – My
family wish me to fix there, but *that* I must decline, in the names of
public Liberty & individual Free-agency. Elder Brothers, not senior
in Intellect, & not sympathizing in main opinions, are subjects of
occasional Visits, not temptations to a Co-township' (CL I 570). More
bluntly, to Poole, he writes on 7 Sept 1801 of 'My family – I have
wholly neglected them – I do not love them – their ways are not my
ways, nor their thoughts my thoughts' (CL II 756).

† He writes to Southey on 31 Dec 1801 that 'I have not yet made
up my mind whether or no I shall move Devonward. My Relations
wish to see me, & I wish to avoid the uneasy feelings I shall have, if
I remain so near them without gratifying the wish' (CL II 778–9).
Nevertheless, he informs his wife, little more than a fortnight later,
that 'I shall not go to [Otter]y; but shall return to London' (CL II
779).

psychoanalytically predictable, that is, the existence of love for his mother; that he did not, however, go to Ottery St Mary either for her sickness or for her death, nor, again, mention the matter with his customary loquacity or even at all, shows how strong was the inhibition under which he laboured. Freud defines inhibitions as 'the expression of a _restriction of an ego-function_'; 'they are restrictions of the functions of the ego which have been either imposed as a measure of precaution or brought about as a result of an impoverishment of energy ...'.[20] The concept of inhibition as 'precaution' would of course here seem to relate directly to Coleridge's anxiety about his brothers. In any case, his lack of action in the face of being 'greatly distressed' and in view of a conception of a mother as 'the holiest thing alive' seems most unusual. A comparison of his conduct with that of Dr Johnson in the same relationship comes naturally to mind.

Such a remarkable distancing could have been achieved, I suggest, only as the result of traumatic experience. Although Coleridge at one point says that as a child 'I was my mother's darling',[21] the recollection refers explicitly to his mildly preferential treatment with regard to his brother Francis. Any further claim must surely be either fantasy or what psychoanalysts call a 'screen memory', for had he in any deep sense been his mother's darling, his self-confidence, as in our post-Freudian sophistications we all now know, would have been far greater than it was. Judging by the results, his mother's affection must have alternated with periods of neglect or coldness, which developed an extreme anxiety in the child. According to psychoanalytic theory, moreover, it developed rage and an equally great guilt in response to the rage. As the psychoanalyst David Beres suggested in 1951,[22] the Nightmare Life-in-Death of the intensely psychodramatic _Ancient Mariner_* seems to be a representation of the mother, deformed by the mixture of rage and guilt projected onto her:

> Her skin was as white as leprosy,
> The Night-mare LIFE-IN-DEATH was she,
> Who thicks man's blood with cold.   (PW I 194)

---

* Cf. Fenichel, _The Psychoanalytic Theory of Neurosis_, p. 370: 'In a symbolic way, [the] pursuit of rest and of protection at the mother's breast is expressed in the frequent yearning for the boundless ocean.' See further Freud XVI 314.

Such a threatening figure reappears in the dreams that Coleridge, so helpfully for future attempts to understand his psychic life, recorded in his notebooks:

> Friday Night, Nov. 28, 1800, or rather Saturday Morning – a most frightful Dream of a Woman whose features were blended with darkness catching hold of my right eye & attempting to pull it out – I caught hold of her arm fast – a horrid feel— (CN I 848)

In 1802 this baleful apparition is followed by another 'Spectre-Woman', as the Nightmare Life-in-Death is called:

> I was followed up & down by a frightful pale woman who, I thought, wanted to kiss me, & had the property of giving a shameful Disease by breathing in the face/
> & again I dreamt that a figure of a woman of a gigantic Height, dim & indefinite & smokelike appeared – & that I was forced to run up toward it – & then it changed to a stool – & then appeared again in another place – & again I went up in great fright . . . (CN I 1250)

We need not suppose that Coleridge's mother was in fact either a monster, or even, by her own lights and situation, particularly a bad mother. She was, however, very probably somewhat neurotic, for the existence of a neurotic son implies neurotic parents. And her neurosis seems to have expressed itself in a certain coldness of disposition; James Dykes Campbell stresses that 'she was comparatively an uneducated woman, and unemotional', while Gillman says that she was 'a very good woman. . . . over careful in many things, very ambitious for the advancement of her sons in life, but wanting perhaps that flow of heart which her husband possessed so largely'.[23] No great crime, surely, but her diminished store of warmth, further dissipated by the natural demands of caring for nine other children, could have seemed to her infant son to be total abandonment, and the anxiety thus generated would be very great indeed.

For as Freud has emphasised, the prototypal pattern of anxiety is the birth trauma of separation from the mother;[24] in the infant, accordingly, absence or neglect by the mother is the specific source of normal anxiety, and if pronounced enough, can become the source of neurotic anxiety:

Only a few of the manifestations of anxiety in children are comprehensible to us, and we must confine our attention to them. They occur, for instance, when a child is alone, or in the dark, or when it finds itself with an unknown person instead of one to whom it is used – such as its mother. These three instances can be reduced to a single condition – namely, that of missing someone who is loved and longed for. But here, I think, we have the key to an understanding of anxiety. . . . The child's mnemic image of the person longed for is no doubt intensely cathected [i.e. invested with emotion], probably in a hallucinatory way at first. But this has no effect; and now it seems as though the longing turns into anxiety.

(Freud XX 136–7)

The mother, as is indicated in Freud's description of the genesis of anxiety, must have been identified in Coleridge's unconscious mind as no less a benign than a vengeful figure: the two states expressing respectively the infant's love for the mother and the rage-guilt complex occasioned by her absence. Although the Ancient Mariner is harrowed by the Nightmare Life-in-Death, he is also, as the gloss informs us, 'By grace of the holy Mother . . . refreshed with rain.' Coleridge's love of his mother was such as any infant might feel; it was the rage and guilt that were abnormally intense. As he wrote in 1794, 'Alas! my poor Mother! What an intolerable weight of guilt is suspended over my head by a hair on one hand – and if I endure to live – the look ever downward — insult – pity – and hell – .'[25]

The anxiety produced in the infant Coleridge by his mother's coldness and inattentiveness was probably not only a source of his lifelong neurotic malaise, but also a factor in his failure to develop a strong sense of his own being. He says as an adult that 'I know, I feel, that I am weak – apt to faint away inwardly, self-deserted & bereft of the confidence in my own powers'.[26] The poignant statement is co-ordinate with Freud's formula that 'anxiety is seen to be a product of the infant's mental helplessness'.[27]

Coleridge, however, was probably bereft of the confidence in his own powers by still another psychologically damaging situation. His mother apparently was not the only cause of his woe; the Nightmare Life-in-Death had a companion with whom she cast dice for the Mariner's soul. To understand the possibility of this doubling effect, we again have recourse to Freud. 'Anxiety arises', he says, 'by a kind of fermentation, from a libidinal cathexis [emotional attachment] whose processes have been disturbed.'[28] Such interference can be provided not only by situations that separate the infant psychologically from its mother, but also by threats from a male. After pointing out that anxiety is an expression of the helplessness of the infant, 'as though in its still very undeveloped state it did not know how better to cope with its ... longing', Freud concludes that

> anxiety appears as a reaction to the felt loss of the object; and we are at once reminded of the fact that castration anxiety, too, is a fear of being separated from a highly valued object, and that the earliest anxiety of all – the 'primal anxiety' of birth – is brought about on the occasion of a separation from the mother. (Freud XX 137)

To continue with psychoanalytic theory, therefore, it seems that Coleridge developed an extreme anxiety from his relation to his brothers, and that this, as another form of the infantile sense of object loss, operated in conjunction with the more basic anxiety connected with his mother.* On his very deathbed, as Henry Crabb Robinson noted in his diary, Coleridge expressed 'his sense of the unkindness with which he had been treated by his brothers'.[29] Nor had he ever felt himself 'their Brother in any sense that gives to that title aught that is good or dear'.† 'The shipmates', says the gloss to Coleridge's great poem, '... would fain throw the whole guilt on the ancient Mariner.'[30] And it is surely not without psychological significance that his declining to visit his mother during her last days was based on

---

* In a neurotic, the replacement of one phase of anxiety by another need not take place. As Freud puts it, '... each period of the individual's life has its appropriate determinant of anxiety.... Nevertheless, all these ... determinants of anxiety can persist side by side and cause the ego to react to them with anxiety at a period later than the appropriate one; or, again, several of them can come into operation at the same time' (XX 142). Cf. XXII 88.

† CL II 757 (to Poole, 7 Sept 1801). Again: 'I have three Brothers/ that is to say, Relations by Gore ... but alas! we have neither Tastes or Feelings in common.' (CL I 528. To Poole, 16 Sept 1799).

the curious stipulation that a brother had not provided him money to do so.

Of Coleridge's numerous brothers, Francis seems to have been the most harmful to his development. He recalls to Poole that 'Frank hated me' and that 'Frank had a violent love of beating me'. The relationship was not exclusively violent. Whenever Frank's love of 'beating me' was 'superseded by any humour or circumstance, he was always fond of me – & used to regard me with a strange mixture of admiration & contempt...'³¹ Such ambivalent behaviour might well induce psychological damage, with the affection binding the younger brother, as it were, to the hammer blows of hatred. And he records an almost classically Oedipal memory of a double assault by Francis, together with the guilt it aroused:

> I had asked my mother one evening to cut my cheese *entire*, so that I might toast it: this was no easy matter, it being a *crumbly* cheese – My mother however did it – / I went into the garden for some thing or other, and in the mean time my Brother Frank *minced* my cheese.... I returned, saw the exploit, and in an agony of passion flew at Frank – he pretended to have been seriously hurt by my blow, flung himself on the ground, and there lay with outstretched limbs – I hung over him moaning & in great fright – he leaped up, & with a horse-laugh gave me a severe blow in the face – I seized a knife, and was running at him, when my Mother came in & took me by the arm – /I expected a flogging — & struggling from her I ran away, to a hill at the bottom of which the Otter flows – about one mile from Ottery.   (CL I 352–3)

In such a nightmare of mincing, knife play, seeming death, guilt and retribution, we are made directly aware of how psychologically harrowing Coleridge's childhood situation in fact was.*

* Cf. his statement to Sir George Beaumont in 1804: 'I was hardly used from infancy to Boyhood; and from Boyhood to Youth most, MOST cruelly' (CL II 1053). Douglas Angus points out that a fraternally Oedipal situation is also the burden of *Osorio*: 'If one doubts the highly autobiographical nature of Coleridge's writing during this period, he should read this play carefully. It is concerned with the rivalry of Osorio with an older brother, Albert, for the love of a woman named Maria.... It is, in short, his old rivalry with Francis that reappears in the play. Osorio plots to murder his brother so

As he here tried to solve the problem by removing himself, so, in a certain sense, did the double anxiety always remove him from himself, evacuate, as it were, his inner feeling of self. He felt 'self-deserted and bereft', that he was 'a crumbling wall, undermined at the foundation', that there was '*pith within* the trunk, not heart of Wood'.[32] The anxiety made him feel worthless and isolated. 'From my Youth upward', he wrote near the end of his life, 'the most unpleasant if not the most worthless Object of direct Thought has ever been my individual Self'. He speaks elsewhere of his 'sense of my own small Worth & of others' superiority'.[33] 'Mine is a sensibility gangrened with inward corruption', he writes self-loathingly in February 1794.[34] 'I feel, with an intensity unfathomable by words, my utter nothingness, impotence & worthlessness, in and for myself—'[35] Still again: 'My past life seems to me like a dream, a feverish dream! all one gloomy huddle of strange actions, and dim-discovered motives! Friendships lost by indolence, and happiness murdered by mismanaged sensibility.'[36] In a notebook entry of August 1805, the sense of isolation is poignantly connected with the fact that 'by poor Frank's dislike of me when a little Child I was even from Infancy forced to be by myself'.[37]

As a counter to his sense of being 'self-deserted and bereft', Coleridge developed a clinging reliance on his friends. 'I cannot be happy', he writes in a continuation of the note just quoted, 'but while awakening, enjoying, and giving *sympathy* to one or a few eminently loved Beings'; otherwise, he says, 'I *feel* my Hollowness'. 'To be beloved is all I need', he says at the conclusion of his recountal of night-horrors in 'The Pains of Sleep', 'And whom I love, I love indeed.'

In his reliance on his friends, Coleridge seems often to have sought not merely a single but a double dependency, that is, he

---

that he can have Maria, but instead he murders another character, Ferdinand. This murder is completely irrational from beginning to end. It is without motivation' ('The Theme of Love and Guilt in Coleridge's Three Major Poems', *Journal of English and German Philology*, LIX (1960), 658). Doubtless Francis's early death, by intensifying Coleridge's sense of guilt, made the fraternal relationship even more neurotically damaging. In this respect, of course, it is significant that the title of *Osorio* was eventually changed to *Remorse*.

seems to have attempted to replace the threatening brother and
cold mother with an accepting brother and warm mother. His
early enthusiasm for Southey is marked by such an emphasis:
'Remember me to your Mother – to our Mother – am I not
affiliated? I will write her when I arrive at Cambridge'.[38] He
was equally enthusiastic for his bachelor friend Thomas Poole
and Poole's mother. ('My filial love to your dear Mother | &
believe me, my best dear friend! | ever, ever most affectionately
your's'; 'In this hurly burly of unlucky Things, I cannot describe to you how pure & deep Joy I have experienced from
thinking of your dear Mother!')* And the friendship with
Wordsworth seems to have been enhanced by Dorothy's mother-
like concern that came with it. 'Wordsworth & his exquisite
Sister are with me,' he writes in July 1797: 'She is a woman
indeed!'[39] Even his strange willingness to be led by Southey
into a disastrous marriage perhaps derives from the unconscious
expectation that Sarah Fricker would form with Southey a
combination of mother and brother. Certainly Southey's agency
seems crucial in the venture.

After the estrangement from Wordsworth, Coleridge managed
to find still other combinations. The most lasting was the one
with the Gillmans. Here the longed for mother was transformed
into something like a daughter or younger sister, and the accepting older brother into a less potentially threatening son and
younger brother; and Coleridge often and fervently recorded his
gratitude to both James Gillman and his wife. They were people
'to whom under Heaven I owe my Life and more than words
can express!'[40] In short as De Quincey says,

> in one respect at least he was eminently favoured by Provi-
> dence: beyond all men who ever perhaps have lived, he found
> means to engage a constant succession of most faithful friends;
> and he levied the services of sisters, brothers, daughters, sons,
> from the hands of strangers. . . . Fast as one friend dropped
> off, another, and another, succeeded: perpetual relays were
> laid along his path in life, of judicious and zealous sup-
> porters . . .   (DQW II 210–11)

---

* CL I 381 (27 Jan 1798); I 480 (6 April 1799) and cf. CL I 529
(16 Sept) and, still more emphatically, CL II 758 (19 Sept 1801): 'She
was the only Being whom I ever *felt* in the relation of Mother . . .'.

Thus Coleridge sought to ameliorate both orders of anxiety by having himself adopted, as it were, by the various mother-brother combinations; for in the relation to his own family he always felt himself, as he angrily wrote his brother George, to be 'a deserted Orphan'.* In all of these relationships he assumed something of the situation of a child, for the neurotic nature of his needs froze him into certain infantile attitudes, as though (and Freud has emphasised the point†) in the psychic arena where the problem originated, there must it forever be ministered to. Ensconced benignly on the top floor of the hard-working Gillman's house in Highgate, Coleridge seems to us, by his obliviousness to many aspects of adult responsibility, to be something like a pink, friendly infant of enormous mental powers. Indeed, a constant feature of his rejection of adulthood was his lifelong refusal to work sensibly for money; and one of the necessary signs of love that he awaited seems to have been that, like a child, he be given money by someone. He was perpetually poor as a boy (he speaks of his 'want of money all the first two or three and 20 years of my Life'[41]), and his infrequent monetary gifts were presumably invested with great emotional significance against the penurious background of Ottery St Mary and Christ's

* CL III 103 (11 May 1808). Cf. CL III 31: '... releasing my conscience wholly from all connection with a family, to whom I am indebted only for misery'.

† For example, 'It seems quite normal that at four years of age a girl should weep painfully if her doll is broken; or at six, if her governess reproves her; or at sixteen, if she is slighted by her young man; or at twenty-five, perhaps, if a child of her own dies. Each of these determinants of pain has its own time and each passes away when that time is over.... We should think it strange if this same girl, after she had grown to be a wife and mother, were to cry over some worthless trinket that had been damaged. Yet that is how the neurotic behaves.... [He] behaves as though the old danger-situations still existed, and keeps hold of all the earlier determinants of anxiety' (XX 147). Again, after pointing out that 'a great many people remain infantile in their behaviour in regard to danger and do not overcome determinants of anxiety which have grown out of date', and that it is 'precisely such people whom we call neurotics', Freud speaks of 'the element of persistence in these reactions' and notes that 'the affect of anxiety alone' seems to enjoy the 'advantage over all other affects of evoking reactions which are distinguished from the rest ... and which, through their inexpediency, run counter to the movement of life' (p. 148). Cf. XVI 365.

Hospital. 'I am remarkably fond of Beans & Bacon – and this fondness I attribute to my father's having given me a penny for having eat a large quantity of beans, one Saturday'.[42] We hark back again to the unusual explanation that he could not visit his dying mother because the brother would not give him money; and he reacted almost hysterically to Poole's reasonable refusal to lend him fifty pounds that Wordsworth had begged in his behalf.[43] The gifts from the Wedgwoods, De Quincey, and Byron, or the Wordsworths' dividing of their money with him on the Scottish tour, in this respect all assume symbolic significance.

The attempt to find a forgiving brother was particularly important to his unconscious need to reinstate his sense of self. 'My anxieties eat me up', he laments to Poole, '... I want consolation, my friend! my Brother!' 'Dear Friend – and Brother of my Soul –', he writes to Gillman in October 1822, 'God only knows! how truly and in the depth you are loved & prized by your affectionate/Friend S. T. Coleridge.'[44] The ardour that marks these declarations recurs repeatedly throughout his career; although when directed to an older friend such statements frequently take on overtones of masochism. Poole, for instance, who himself had been hailed as 'the man in whom *first* and in whom alone, I had felt an *anchor*', somewhat jealously but also accurately accused Coleridge of 'prostration' with regard to Wordsworth.[45] How much anxiety was suspended in such relationships can be gauged from a dream Coleridge records about his friend, Thomas Middleton, who had been the object of his hero worship both at Christ's Hospital and at Cambridge:

> Wonderful Blending of Ideas in Dreams.... Middleton, who was my superior, my friend and Patron ... received me kindly ... he went away – & I lay down at the bottom of the Desk ... Then Middleton returned & reproved me severely for taking Liberties on the slightest encouragement, & sitting thus by *his Fire*/ Till that moment it had been the bottom of a Desk, & no Fire/ but now there was a little obscure Fire-place ... & I awoke—   (CN II 2539)

Middleton was only one of a number of older men who filled the role of accepting brother for Coleridge. His rather priggish brother, George, was also cast into that role:

My Brother George is a man of reflective mind & elegant Genius. He possesses Learning in a greater degree than any of the Family, excepting myself. His manners are grave, & hued over with a tender sadness. In his moral character he approaches every way nearer to Perfection than any man I ever yet knew – indeed, he is worth the whole family in a Lump. (CL I 311)

This was written in 1797. Earlier, in May 1794, he had written to George himself and closed with these ardent words: 'God bless you — my Brother – my Father!'[46] Inevitably, however, there came an estrangement, the nature of which is implicit in this statement of October 1794: 'I have heard from my Brothers – from him particularly, who has been Friend, Brother, Father – 'Twas all remonstrance, and Anguish, & suggestions, that I am deranged!!'*

The role occupied and relinquished successively by George Coleridge, by Middleton, by Southey and by Poole was filled longer and more deeply by Wordsworth. Indeed, in the relation to Wordsworth, we glimpse not only the depth of Coleridge's need to reclaim his evacuated sense of self by dependence on another, but see also the dim outlines of his compulsion to plagiarise. As he wrote in a note of 1806, 'absorption and trans-figuration of Consciousness' were what he groaned for. And in a note of 1805 he utters the clinging wish with reference to Wordsworth 'that my Spirit purged by Death of its Weaknesses, which are alas! my *identity* might flow into *thine*, & live and act in thee, & be Thou'.[47] In this poignant statement, Coleridge's masochistic submersion of his own self in his friend's strength becomes strikingly apparent.

The tendency to self-denigration is hardly less evident in a depressed statement of September 1807: 'W[ordsworth] is greater, better, manlier, more dear, by nature, to Woman, than I – I – miserable I!'[48] Masochism, however, is not an unalloyed misery to the masochist, and Coleridge accordingly can say that 'My instincts are so far dog-like/ I love beings superior to me better than my Equals.' Again: 'at times I derive a comfort even

* CL I 118. The immediate cause of the estrangement was George's informing Coleridge, in 1807, that because of the latter's impending separation from Sarah Coleridge, he would not 'receive' him (See CL III 102–5).

from my infirmities, my sins of omission & commission, in the
joy of the deep feeling of the opposite Virtues in the two or
three whom I love in my Heart of Hearts'.[49]

Of those two or three, Wordsworth was first. 'Wordsworth is
a very great man', writes Coleridge to Southey in July 1797,
' – the only man, to whom *at all times* & in *all modes of excellence* I feel myself inferior.' In March 1798, he speaks to Cottle
of 'The Giant Wordsworth – God love him! – even when I
speak in the terms of admiration due to his intellect, I fear lest
those terms should keep out of sight the amiableness of his
manners.'[50] And as late as 1822 he wrote to Allsop that 'in the
course of my past Life I count four griping and grasping Sorrows,
each of which seemed to have my very heart in it's hands, com-
pressing or wringing', and one of these was the estrangement
from Wordsworth, 'when all the Superstructure raised by my
idolatrous Fancy during an enthusiastic & self-sacrificing Friendship of 15 years . . . burst like a Bubble – but the Grief did not
vanish with it, nor the Love which was the Stuff & Vitality of
the Grief'.[51]

It was, I believe, this need to allay the castration anxiety in
his own ego by identification with the strength of an accepting
brother that provided the original basis for Coleridge's compulsion to plagiarise. Indeed, his need to merge himself with other
men's modes is witnessed by his very first published reference
to Wordsworth. In 'Lines written at Shurton Bars . . .', he
writes, in 1795, as follows:

> Nor now with curious sight
> I mark the glow-worm, as I pass,
> Move with 'green radiance' through the grass,

and in a footnote he then says:

> The expression 'green radiance' is borrowed from Mr.
> Wordsworth . . . whom I deem unrivalled among the writers
> of the present day. . . .   (PW I 97 and n)

The phrase 'green radiance' is unmistakably a kind of fetish, a
talisman that Coleridge clasps to himself. Of similar psychic
import was his later publication of some of Wordsworth's
juvenilia in *The Morning Post*, or the reworking of a youthful
Wordsworthian poem into his own poem 'Lewti'.[52] The function

of these Wordsworthian borrowings prefigures that of the un-acknowledged quotations, or 'plagiarisms', that exist as mosaic fragments throughout his work. All testify not to intellectual poverty but to the need to relieve his over-powering anxiety: to rejoin the brothers, as it were, and at the same time to reclaim the 'essential something' that he always felt to be wanting in himself.*

* Cf. De Quincey: 'Had, then, Coleridge any need to borrow from Schelling? Did he borrow *in forma pauperis?* Not at all: there lay the wonder. He spun daily, and at all hours, for mere amusement of his own activities, and from the loom of his own magical brain, theories more gorgeous by far, and supported by a pomp and luxury of images such as neither Schelling – no, nor any German that ever breathed, not John Paul – could have emulated in his dreams. With the riches of El Dorado lying about him, he would condescend to filch a handful of gold from any man whose purse he fancied ... applying ... to intellectual wealth, that maniacal propensity which is sometimes well known to attack enormous proprietors and million-aires for acts of petty larceny' (DQW II 146–7).

If we accept De Quincey's shrewd surmise that Coleridge's com-pulsive plagiarisms were in fact a variant form of kleptomania, then in this context psychoanalytical theory connects to both his mother and his brothers his haunted feeling that he was missing an 'essential something'. In view of the importance of the matter for our ultimate understanding of Coleridge's struggle, we must force ourselves to confront precise significances – no matter how strongly they are resisted by the psychoanalytically uninformed. Accordingly, we must entertain the possibility, with regard to Coleridge's damaged relation-ship with his mother, that the 'essential something' represents what he memorably terms the once imbibed but now lost 'milk of para-dise'. Cf. Fenichel: 'If it is true that the cleptomaniac is striving for a lost sexual satisfaction which has been protection, forgiveness and regulator of self-esteem simultaneously, the property stolen must of necessity symbolically represent milk.' (*The Psychoanalytic Theory of Neurosis*, p. 370.) And with regard to his damaged relationship with his brothers, we should be aware of the theoretical insistence, no matter what our reluctance to accept it may be, that 'In the clepto-manic strivings of patients who are not very deeply disturbed, the significance of "penis" will be in the foreground.' (Ibid.) In this same context of the formal theory of impulse neurosis, Coleridge's drug addiction would be related as an attempt 'to satisfy the archaic oral longing which is sexual longing, a need for security, and a need for the maintenance of self-esteem simultaneously. Thus the origin and nature of the addiction are not determined by the chemical effect of the drug but by the psychological structure of the patient.' (Ibid., p. 376.)

Coleridge's plagiarisms are not the only testimony to the compulsion to reclaim his identity by merging himself with the brothers. We see it also in his lifelong fondness for joining marginalia to the books he read, a form of composition that, in terms of the number and of the variety of books so adorned, and of the worth of the notations themselves, has no real counterpart in either English or continental literature. The compulsion appears in still another of its protean manifestations in his *Aids to Reflection*. There, late in life, he seems to attempt to give up his indulgence in explicit plagiarism, but substitutes instead a technique by which his own thoughts exfoliate around the work of another man, Archbishop Leighton. As he says in 1824,

> a little volume will soon appear under the title *Aids to Reflection*, which was at first intended only for a Selection of Passages from Leighton's Works but in the course of printing has become an original work almost.   (CL v 336)

Again, he found that he increasingly preferred to compose only when dictating to an amanuensis, especially a benign brother-figure such as Gillman or Joseph Henry Green.*

All such phenomena are symptomatic of Coleridge's attempt to restore the self that had been evacuated by his anxieties. As he said of himself, the 'first lesson, that innocent Childhood affords me, is – that it is an instinct of my Nature to pass out of myself, and to exist in the form of others'. 'My nature', he says again, 'requires another Nature for its support, & reposes only in another from the necessary Indigence of its Being.' Still again, he intended to write a biography of Lessing 'because it would give me an opportunity of conveying under a better name, than my own ever will be, opinions, which I deem of the highest importance'.[53]

If much of what Coleridge did in his literary career attests the pervasive demands of his anxiety, much that he did not do testifies as well. His procrastination and inability to work seem to be complications arising from his traumatically threatening anxiety situations.† 'I deeply regret', he writes in 1797, 'that

---

* Referring in 1825 to his 'friendly Amanuensis', he says that 'the slowness, with which I get on with the pen in my own hand, contrasts most strangely with the rapidity with which I dictate.' (CL v 423).

† Cf., e.g., Freud's statement, with regard to 'symptom-formation

my anxieties and my slothfulness, acting in a combined ratio, prevented me from finishing my "Progress of Liberty...".'[54] They prevented him from finishing, or even doing, many other things. 'I became a proverb to the University for Idleness', he writes of his later Cambridge days, ' – the time, which I should have bestowed on the academic studies, I employed in dreaming out wild Schemes.'[55] The inhibition of his ability to work continued throughout his career. 'He will tell me', writes Dorothy Wordsworth in 1810, 'that he has been writing, that he *has* written half a Friend; when I *know* that he has not written a single line.'[56]

The unfinished state of the legendary *magnum opus* is the most notorious monument to his procrastination, but it is not psychologically the most revealing; it is rather in Coleridge's minor procrastinations, his inability, for instance, not only to answer letters, but even to open them in the first place, that the roots of the inhibition in anxiety become most apparent. 'As to letters', recalls De Quincey, 'unless the address were in some female hand that commanded his affectionate esteem, he tossed them all into one general *dead-letter bureau*, and rarely, I believe, opened them at all.'* Coleridge muses on this deficiency in 1803:

> ... received a Letter which I knew would contain interesting matter – not quite certain whether it would be affectionate or reproachful, mournful or happy — this I have kept in my pocket sometimes half a day, sometimes a whole day – have opened it at length, just looked at the end ... – then let it lie on my Desk, or put it up once more in my pocket – & have

---

in obsessional neurosis', that symptoms 'which once stood for a restriction of the ego come later on to represent satisfaction as well', and that the 'result of this process ... is an extremely restricted ego which is reduced to seeking satisfaction in the symptoms. The displacement of the distribution of forces in favour of satisfaction may have the dreaded final outcome of paralysing the will of the ego ...' (XX 118). Thus Coleridge in 1808: 'I have been for years almost a paralytic in mind ...' (CL III 131). Cf. Southey's surmise (p. 134 above) that Coleridge was labouring under 'a disease of the volition', and Hazlitt: 'He was a man without a will' (HCR I 11). Cf. Freud X 241.

* DQW II 149. Cf. Coleridge's own anguished confession, in 1808, that on occasion he 'left every letter received lie unopened for weeks together, all the while thoroughly ashamed of the weakness and yet without power to get rid of it' (CL III 148).

walked about my garden or Study an hour or more, wasting the
activity & flutter of feeling excited by the letter in planning
compositions, or have sate & read a book of Kant/ & last of
all read my Letter, my spirits tamed—   (CN I 1517)

The trivial nature of his anxiety's object here testifies to the
authentic structure of the anxiety itself, for as Freud insists,
anxiety 'has a quality of *indefiniteness* and *lack of object*. In
precise speech we use the word 'fear' rather than 'anxiety' if
it has found an object.'[57]

Freud's distinction between anxiety (*Angst*) and fear (*Furcht*),
with the former being characterised by the lack of a definite
object, is parallel to, although independent of, Heidegger's
phenomenological distinction of the same two states. To Heidegger 'the object of anxiety is completely indefinite'.[58] *Furcht*,
to Heidegger, is fear of a definite danger;[59] *Angst*, fear of nothing
at all.[60] In Heidegger's conception, *Angst* comes about simply
from the fact of our being thrown into the world ('*das Wovor
der Angst is das geworfene In-der-Welt-sein*'); it arises from
the sense of 'naked existence cast into psychic homelessness'.[61]
And the conception corresponds closely to Freud's description
of anxiety's origin as the birth trauma of separation from the
mother.

It is useful to cross this bridge between the psychoanalytical
and the existential conceptions of anxiety, and to view Coleridge's drowning struggles from the existential shore. It is
possible to do so because both conceptions of anxiety, despite
their difference in focus, are attempts to analyse a psychic
phenomenon that arises in experience; neither conception is
merely the verbal construct of psychologist or philosopher. As
Sartre says in his own discussion of *angoisse*:

> Kierkegaard, in describing anxiety in the face of what one
> lacks, characterizes it as anxiety in the face of freedom. But
> Heidegger, whom we know to have been greatly influenced
> by Kierkegaard, considers anxiety instead as the apprehension
> of nothingness. These two descriptions of anxiety do not
> appear to us contradictory; on the contrary the one implies
> the other.[62]

The various descriptions of *Angst*, therefore, whether by Freud,
by Heidegger, or by Kierkegaard, are complementary rather than

mutually exclusive, and all provide perspectives on the sea of anxiety in which Coleridge was engulfed.

A second reason for crossing over to the standpoint of existential anxiety is that the Freudian analysis of the condition tends to make Coleridge seem, as it were, a special case, a patient. Existential analysis of anxiety, on the other hand, emphasises its human unavoidability. As Kierkegaard says, 'if a man were a beast or an angel, he would not be able to be in the state of anxiety. Since he is a synthesis he can be in such a state, and the greater the anxiety, the greater the man.'[63] To transfer such a contention to a Freudian matrix, one could point out that it was precisely Coleridge's unusual mental receptivity that made him so vulnerable to the unfavourable childhood influences that surrounded him. His neurosis is, as it were, the index of his intellectual power.

Kierkegaard further relates to Coleridge's situation by connecting anxiety with that original sin so often avowed by the English poet. 'I believe most stedfastly [writes Coleridge] in original Sin; that from our mothers' wombs our understandings are darkened; and even where our understandings are in the Light, that our organization is depraved, & our volitions imperfect; and we sometimes see the good without *wishing* to attain it, and oftener *wish* it without the energy that wills & performs.'[64]

Such a conviction is entirely consonant with the emphasis of Kierkegaard, whose primary definition of anxiety is 'the presupposition of original sin'.[65] 'The consequence of original sin', Kierkegaard says again, '. . . is anxiety.'[66] But original sin is the affliction of the race, not merely the problem of the individual, and for both Coleridge and Kierkegaard the conception socialises the woes of existence.

In these terms, Coleridge's anxiety, or dread, not only brings him into the communal fold, but actually becomes a special mark of spirit; for as Kierkegaard insists, 'the less spirit, the less anxiety'.[67] To accept this is to reverse the tendency of a long tradition, current no less in our own day than in an earlier one, that aproaches Coleridge with an attitude of moralistic finger-pointing and pious head-shaking. This tradition, I think, is mistaken. As Dr Johnson says of Savage:

For his Life, or for his Writings, none who candidly consider

his Fortune, will think an Apology either necessary or difficult. . . . nor will a wise Man easily presume to say, 'Had I
been in *Savage's* Condition, I should have lived, or written,
better than *Savage*.'[68]

So too for Coleridge. But I should go still further, and urge
the validity of Kierkegaard's formula: 'the greater the anxiety,
the greater the man'.[69] Despite Coleridge's own frequent laments
for his weakness, in a larger sense I do not find that term properly descriptive. Certainly the conception is a relative one. If
we see legs buckle under a burden, we might ascribe the effect to
weakness; but if the legs belong to Atlas, the ascription makes
little sense. Coleridge, I have always felt, is in a special way a
hero of existence: though life bore him down, he fought from
his knees.[70] He did not take refuge in suicide, which was the
way chosen by Kleist, by Chatterton, by Nerval; he did not
become mentally unbalanced, as did Hölderlin, Cowper, Ruskin;
he did not become misanthropic, as did Swift, or Schopenhauer,
of whom Nietzsche said that 'he raged for the sake of raging'.[71]

On the contrary, he preserved his life, his reason and his
humanity. Querulous and often feline he could be, but he was
not twisted or distortedly bitter. As Leslie Stephen noticed, 'at
his worst Coleridge was both loved and eminently lovable. . . .
He was always full of kindly feelings, never soured into
cynicism.'[72] Wordsworth, even after his estrangement from
Coleridge, spoke, as Henry Crabb Robinson records, of his
'goodness of heart'.[73] And after Coleridge's death, Lamb, who
knew the worst about his friend, said that 'his great and dear
spirit haunts me'.[74]

Coleridge's spirit manifested itself in other ways as well. He
warred constantly against the neurotic symptoms that in binding
his anxiety deprived his life of happiness. Thus De Quincey, no
ordinary observer of the drug habit, notes that 'Coleridge did
make prodigious efforts to deliver himself from this thraldom'.[75]
So, too, he struggled against the crippling inhibition of his
ability to work. During the very months of the deterioration that
Dorothy Wordsworth noted so vividly, he managed, despite his
diseased volition, a certain productivity. Thus the Wordsworths
record on 12 September 1809 that 'Coleridge has been very busy
lately'; on 18 November that 'Coleridge goes on with his work

briskly'; on 28 December that 'Coleridge has been very well of late, and very busy'.[76] But to Lady Beaumont, in February 1810, Dorothy revealed the internal struggle with diseased volition that this activity entailed:

> By the great quantity of labour that he has performed since the commencement of the Friend [she writes] you will judge that he has upon the whole been very industrious; and you will hardly believe me when I tell you that there have been weeks and weeks when he has not composed a line. The fact is that he either does a great deal or nothing at all; and that he composes with a rapidity truly astonishing, if one did not reflect upon the large stores of thought which he has laid up, and the quantity of knowledge he is continually gaining from books – add to this his habit of expressing his ideas in conversation in elegant language. He has written a whole Friend more than once in two days.
>
> (WLR (1806–11) 390–1)

It is in the way Coleridge met his death, however, that the element of heroism in his life becomes most apparent. For death, of all human possibilities, is the one most fraught with anxiety. As Shakespeare's Richard II says, 'The worst is death, and death will have his day.' For Heidegger, it is death that awakens man to his own authenticity, but this opening up of existence is achieved only through anxiety: '*Das Sein zum Tode*', he says, '*ist wesenhaft Angst*' – being toward death is in its nature anxiety.[77] As the nothingness that is the final object of all anxiety, as the anxiety in which existence confronts the possible impossibility of itself ('*In ihr befindet sich das Dasein vor dem Nichts der möglichen Unmöglichkeit seiner Existenz*')[78], death is the most genuine terror. It should, one thinks, have paralysed Coleridge, had he been truly weak. But he not only said throughout his life that he did not fear death, he actually proved as much when the moment of agony arrived. 'My father', recalls his daughter,

> since he first felt his end approaching had expressed a desire that he might be as little disturbed as possible . . . he then said that he wished to evince in the manner of his death the depth & sincerity of his faith in Christ . . . he then fell asleep – from

sleep into a state of coma, Torpor, as I understood it, and
ceased to breathe at half past six in the morning of Friday. . . .
In the middle of the day on Thursday he had repeated to Mr
Green his formula of the Trinity. His utterance was difficult –
but his mind in perfect vigour & clearness – he remarked that
his intellect was quite unclouded & he said 'I could even be
witty'.   (CL VI 991–2)

As his nephew, Henry Nelson Coleridge, remarked: 'He shrank
from mere uneasiness like a child, and bore the preparatory
agonies of his death-attack like a martyr'.[79] It was as though the
Nightmare Life-in-Death had indeed pre-empted the claims of
death itself.

If Coleridge's ruined existence thus contains elements of
heroism, so too does his fragmentary work function culturally
with no less power than work of more conventionally praised
structure. Both effects are possible because 'every life', as Ortega
y Gasset has insisted, 'is, more or less, a ruin among whose debris
we have to discover what the person ought to have been'.[80]
Accordingly, when Dr Leavis judges that 'Coleridge's prestige
is very understandable, but his currency as an academic classic
is something of a scandal', and that 'he was very much more
brilliantly gifted than Arnold, but nothing of his deserves the
classical status of Arnold's best work',[81] what seems to be called
in question is not so much Coleridge's achievement as the relevance of this conception of the academic classic.

There are actually only incomplete human lives and the
gestures that occur within them. Where, except in such an arena,
does the evidence arise that could make a 'prestige very understandable', or that could justify the conviction that Coleridge
was 'very much more brilliantly gifted than Arnold'? Coleridge's
ruin, in both life and work, is, I suggest, the true human fact;
the academic classic and the conventional achievement the
illusion. Such ruin is testimony to what the greatest philosopher
of our century – or at least the one nearest my heart – has
elucidated as '*die Zerrissenheit des Seins*': the tatteredness of
being. Coleridge's prestige could hardly *be* understandable to us
if he stood outside the mainstream of human experience; it *is*
understandable, on the contrary, because his tragic existence is
an icon for the larger nature of our situation.[82]

For tragedy and human existence are synonymous. Human life is not only nasty, brutish and short; it is also uncertain in its hopes, vulnerable in its affections, and unsatisfactory in its achievements. From the Biblical Preacher's 'vanity of vanities' to the universal 'foundering' described by Karl Jaspers,[83] our annals sound warnings of the shipwreck that awaits everyone.

Of those who foundered, and left a record of their foundering, Coleridge occupies an honoured role in our cultural memory. His life was tormented by anxiety and his work torn by imperfection. But neurotic anxiety, as Freud contends, is an intensification of the anxiety that all men feel; while to Kierkegaard, anxiety is the mark of the human spirit itself. And the imperfection so evident in Coleridge's work is, from the perspective of the larger truths of existence, nothing less than the final shape of every man's effort.

7

Coleridge on Powers in Mind and Nature

Dorothy Emmet

Coleridge's philosophy tends to be an embarrassment to the admirers of his poetry – or indeed a matter of resentment. Wordsworth hinted that it killed the poet in him and Quiller Couch said so explicitly:

> He had landed in Germany a poet . . . he embarked from Germany not yet perhaps the 'archangel a little damaged' (as Charles Lamb described him some sixteen or seventeen years later) but already – and worse for us – a poet lost. . . . The man came back to England intensely and furiously pre-occupied with metaphysics. *This*, I suggest and neither opium, nor Mrs. Coleridge's fretfulness, was the main reason why he could not recall his mind to poetry.[1]

Others have suggested that it was a way of propping up the faith he desperately felt in need of – Carlyle, for instance, had his taunt about 'transcendental life-preservers, logical swim-bladders'.[2]

My own belief is that for Coleridge philosophy was a matter of inner necessity. But the difficulty over trying to see just what he was saying is twofold: first, that most of it was put into the thought forms of the post-Kantian German idealists. These were unfamiliar to his contemporaries; indeed Coleridge was a pioneer in introducing them into this country. And they are also unfamiliar to our contemporaries – this kind of metaphysical philosophy of nature is out of fashion. Also Coleridge was always making fresh starts, prolegomena set out in notes, and until all this work is properly edited, we cannot really say how much was achieved and how much was left unfinished. But we can try to see what he was mainly wanting to say, particularly if it is something which need not be looked on as an unfortunate distraction from his poetry, but which helps to illuminate what he was doing in his poetry and in his other interests, for instance his political ones. This, moreover, is how metaphysics comes alive – as an attempt to see a more general significance in some particular kind of experience: we don't just say 'This is how this experience is', but 'This is how it is because this is how the world – life – what have you – is.' So the metaphysical notion has some empirical application, and the question is how far it can be extended without making it so vague that no distinctions are made and no further applications can be seen.

I believe the heart of Coleridge's philosophical interest lay in trying to understand the powers he found operative in his own mind, especially in creative work. Then he tried to see these powers as *connatural* (his word,[3] and also an older medieval word) with powers of life and growth in nature, and finally tried to see powers in the mind and in nature as alike depending on a spiritual ground.

What does he make, and indeed what can we make of this? In trying to face this question I am not going to concern myself with just what his sources were – how far, for instance, he plagiarised from Schelling and the German *Naturphilosophen*. I think Professor McFarland has dealt perfectly with this question – he doesn't deny liftings or borrowings, but turns attention to what Coleridge was making of them. He says[4] that Coleridge's borrowings, 'though skirting and sometimes crossing the boundary of propriety, were not the thefts of a poverty-stricken mind, but the mosaic materials of a neurotic technique of composition.' It is worth calling attention to this estimate in view of the sustained attack in Norman Fruman's recent book *Coleridge, The Damaged Archangel* – note, not an 'Archangel a little damaged' as Lamb had called him.[5] This is some 500 pages of indictment for plagiarism, disingenuousness and downright lies. Fruman represents him not only as a 'library cormorant' (Coleridge called himself that),[6] but as a magpie, lining his nest with shreds and patches – or even large pieces – of other people's clothes. But I don't think anyone who has read Professor Whalley's study, earlier in this series, or has browsed in what is now available of the notebooks, could subscribe to Fruman's saying that Coleridge got his images from books, and just took them and arranged them – that he didn't get them (as Wordsworth did) from his own first-hand perceptions. No one can deny that he jotted down images and phrases from his reading, but when they came out years after, they had passed through his own mind – they are not just 'fixities and definites'[7] rearranged by fancy, but used as new ways of seeing in a new context. (In the *Notebooks* he has a phrase about 'the Light purifying, and the purified receiving and reflecting the Light, sending it off to others, not like the polish'd mirror by rejection from itself, but by transmission thro' itself'[8].) When we come to the philosophical writings, borrowings are more frequent, and of longer passages. Coleridge makes use of thought forms from a succession of philosophies – Platonic, Spinozan, Kantian, post-Kantian idealist – to say what he wanted to say. (It is just as well he didn't come too close to Hegel – there would have been another, still more formidable vocabulary and still more obscure thought forms.) But rather than discuss his sources and plagiarisms, I shall invoke his own reference to truth as a divine ventriloquist – 'I care not from whose mouth the sounds are supposed to proceed, if only the words are audible and intelligible.'[9]

So can we make at least some of the words audible and intelligible?

They are audible enough, or if not, it is not for lack of repetition. 'Will', 'Reason', 'Ideas', 'Subject, Object', 'Nature' – great and familiar words, but are they intelligible, if we do not just use them as counters, but try and see what weight Coleridge is making them carry?

'Metaphysics and poetry and facts of mind'; including in the latter 'all the strange phantasms that ever possessed your philosophy-dreamers' was how Coleridge described his 'darling studies'. 'All metaphysical philosophy indeed is at last but an examination of our powers of knowledge,' he said later.[10] This sounds Kantian. Kant was uncovering the conceptual and perceptual schemata through which we organise a manifold of sensations into objects understood as causally interacting in space and time. But whereas Kant confines knowledge to the phenomenal world and has to rest agnostic about things in themselves beyond the phenomenal world (he has as it were an iron curtain between the phenomenal and the noumenal), Coleridge wants to take these 'facts of the mind' as clues to the character of a really existent nature, not just of nature as a phenomenal construct. And he tries to do this by seeing the same powers at work in the mind and in nature beyond the mind. He puts this central conviction in his last appendix to *The Statesman's Manual*: 'Whether Ideas are regulative only, according to Aristotle and Kant; or likewise CONSTITUTIVE, and one with the power and Life of Nature, according to Plato and Plotinus (ἐν λόγῳ ζωὴ ἦν, καὶ ἡ ζωὴ ἦν τὸ φῶς τῶν ἀνθρώπων) is the highest *problem* of philosophy, and not part of its nomenclature.'

Ideas are regulative according to Kant when they hold before the mind an ideal of unity and intelligibility, which guides it in trying to order and explain phenomena – for instance, the ideal of universal mechanistic explanation. As regulative, they could be logically tabled as prescriptions – instructions to look for this kind of cause – not as describing what is presumed to be the case. As constitutive, ideas are thought of in Locke's phrase[12] as 'the real internal constitution' of something, an inner principle according to which its parts form an operative unity – a kind of unity of which a living organism is the paradigm case.

Can one make the word 'Idea', or even 'principle', do this work, thinking of Ideas as dynamic powers, not as *entia rationis*, abstractions with which we think? Coleridge was well aware of the difficulty of using the term 'Idea' for something which was not just an abstract concept but a living power, but he decided none the less to use it. He was well aware that 'Idea' had other meanings in the history of philosophy – he lists some of them in *Biographia Literaria*.[13] To some extent he links his use with Plato (he was as much Platonist as Kantian, and not quite either.) So in the *Friend*:

A distinguishable power, self-affirmed and seen in its unity with the Eternal Essence, is, according to Plato, an Idea, and the discipline by which the human mind is purified from its idols (εἴδωλα) and raised to the contemplation of Ideas and thence to the secure and ever-progressive, though never ending investigation of truth and reality by scientific method, comprehends what the same philosopher so highly extols under the title of Dialectic. (*Friend* I 492)

Remember that for Kant Dialectic was the seed bed of endless controversies. And note how many questions are raised in this one complex sentence.

To begin with, let us look closer at this notion of Ideas as dynamic powers. It sounds like primitive animism, but this does not just mean it should be dismissed. Primitive animism may not be all nonsense, but that is another story.

I think a way into making some sense of it is through Coleridge's concern with psychology, particularly the psychology of poetic creation. Metaphysics, he said in the Philosophical Lectures of 1818, must not be estranged from experimental philosophy (physics) and psychology.[14] The psychology was something he did *not* buy from Kant. 'In Psychology', he remarks, 'Kant is but suspicious Authority.'[15] Nor did he buy it from the associationist psychology of Hartley, which had attracted him in his early days, no doubt because it was an attempt to give an account of how the mind worked. Perhaps I. A. Richards is right in saying that he abandoned it not as altogether untrue, but as 'the intellectual equivalent of his uncreative moods'.[16] His concern was for a psychology which would be true to his creative moods, and he did not see this in Hartley, or for that matter in Kant.

What was true of his creative moods was a kind of psychology which brought the body as a feeling, sentient instrument into the process of knowing. 'Metaphysics make all one's thoughts equally corrosive on the Body by the habit of making momently & common thought the subjects of uncommon interest & intellectual energy.'[17] Certainly any theory of knowledge has to allow for sense perceptions, and these depend on sense organs. Hume has to say 'If it be perceived by the eyes, it must be a colour'. But many philosophers, having said this, leave the body behind and construct knowledge out of sense data, concepts and logical relations. Coleridge uses the expression 'Psycho-somatic Ology'[18] for the kind of study needed. This psychosomatic interest comes out in what he says about what nowadays would be called the unconscious. Without benefit of Freud or Jung, he was deeply concerned with states of fringe awareness, where feelings are emerging into consciousness and then finding expression in a symbol. Indeed this is the creative state, and it depends on feelings, which are the bridge between mind and body. A notebook entry for February 1805 runs: 'Deep Sky is of all visual impressions the nearest akin to a Feeling/ it is more a Feeling than a Sight/ or rather it is the melting away and entire union of Feeling & Sight.'[19] In fact the dualistic way of speaking of mind and body is misleading. We have these states of consciousness emerging from an organic life in which we are part of nature. But the body-mind which is part of nature is not just a passive reactor – or at least it need not be. Also our perceptions of nature depend on our own constitutions. He writes in the *Friend* that a man's knowledge of objects 'derives its whole and sole evidence from an obscure sensation, which he is unable to resist or comprehend, which compels him to contemplate as without and independent of himself what yet he could not contemplate at all, were it not a modification of his own being'.[20] In perceiving as well as thinking we are active, forming unities out of confusions, whether through a perceptual schema, or in a symbol expressing in image form what is seen and felt, or in an intellectual form in an interpretative theory. These are activities in which not just the 'faculties of the mind', but in which the whole sentient organism is involved. Coleridge does, it is true, sometimes speak of 'faculties of the mind' as though these were a set of separate instruments, but he also struggles against this way of talking – the different faculties are different ways in which the whole person behaves in knowing and perceiving. (Remember, 'faculty' means 'power'). In 'Understanding' one is proceeding according to fixed rules, in 'Reason' the person as a whole is unified with his feeling, and is forming an integrative idea or symbol, which is not just an application of, or deduction from what he already has before him. Note that Reason and Will are here spoken of as coextensive with the person. They are not organs; they are the whole person as involved in thinking and acting. 'My will & I seem perfect Synonimes – whatever does not apply to the first, I refuse to the latter.'[21] This may be why Coleridge also insisted on the importance of 'keeping alive the heart in the head'. This is taken unsympathetically to mean he was letting his desires dictate his metaphysics, especially in matters of religious faith, but I think that it should be taken in this context to mean that the creation of an idea involves the whole person.

So on the subjective side Coleridge is wanting to show ideas being produced in an ambience of feeling and will. On the objective side, he wants to exhibit an idea not just as an abstract definition, but as the principle which gives a thing its distinctive unity, or as an operative ideal which can move people (perhaps the French expression *idée force* comes near this).

The antithesis of such ideas would be what Whitehead calls 'inert ideas' – notions entertained without any feeling of live interest.[22] (Whitehead thought the transmission of inert ideas was the curse of a good deal of our education.) Coleridge remarks that this can happen even to truths that were once 'the most awful and interesting'. 'They lose all the power of truth, and lie bed-ridden in the dormitory of the soul, side by side with the most despised and exploded errors.'[23] Again, he speaks of

> Education of the intellect, by awakening the *method* of self-development ... not any specific information that can be *conveyed into* it from without: not to assist in storing the passive mind with the various sorts of knowledge most in request, as if the human soul were a mere repository or banqueting-room, but to place it in such relations of circumstance as should gradually excite the germinal power that craves no knowledge but what it can take up into itself, what it can appropriate, and reproduce in fruits of its own.[24]

He also spoke of the capacity to form living ideas as being killed not so much by carrying along a lot of luggage of inert ideas (there was plenty of luggage in his own notes), as by finding what he called 'Preventive substitutes of occupation' – the ways the 'busy indolent' find of using their energies without rousing themselves to think:

> Reconciling two contrary yet co-existent propensities of men, the Indulgence of Sloth with the Hatred of Vacancy; and which Class, besides Novels, contains in it, *Gambling*, Swinging or Swaying on a chair, Spitting over a Bridge, Smoking, Quarrels after dinner between Husband and Wife when tête à tête, the reading word by word of all the advertisements of a Daily Advertiser in a Public House on a rainy Day.[25]

So much for living, as distinct from inert ideas. But are the ideas themselves living powers, or is the liveliness in the mind that entertains them, and that can kindle other minds in communicating them? Or is this a wrong antithesis, coming from ways of thinking of an idea as like a ghostly inhabitant of a mind, instead of the mind itself actively thinking and using symbols – images, words – which can be put down in sounds and marks on paper to express what it is thinking? There is the active thinking, and then the thought as embodied in a symbol, not 'some spectral woof of impalpable abstractions, or unearthly ballet of bloodless categories'.[26] So by an idea as a living power can be meant a mind in an active state, creating symbolic expressions which can kindle feeling and interest, perhaps excitement, in other minds.

In *On the Constitution of the Church and State according to the Idea of Each* he says that the Constitution is an idea arising out of the idea of the State, and that 'we speak and have a right to speak, of the idea itself, as actually existing, i.e., as a *principle*, existing in the only way in which a principle can exist – in the minds and consciences of the persons, whose duties it prescribes and whose rights it determines'.[27] Coleridge is here speaking of a *prescriptive* principle. When we turn to *theoretical* principles, his interest is in Reason as the productive process, rather than the idea as the product. In judging truth and adequacy, it is the product not the process we have to consider. Coleridge, of course, recognises that ideas have to find expression, and that symbols, and especially language, give them an external form as products, but his main concern is with the productive process.

Is there a counterpart of this in the workings of nature, or are the symbol-creating powers of the mind, issuing in communications between mind and mind, quite different from any 'goings-on'[28] in nature?

One bridge would be the use of the term 'Idea' which I have already noted, as in 'The Idea of a Political Society' where it is used to describe the operative ideal (if indeed there is such) which makes a complex institution tick. In this instance it is being used of something which, if not the expression of an individual mind, is the embodiment of the purposes of a number of individual people. Coleridge was, I believe, the first to use 'Idea' in this way, speaking of 'The Idea of the State' (as Newman was to speak of 'The Idea of a University').

> By an *Idea* [he says] I mean (in this instance) that conception
> of a thing which is not abstracted from any particular state,
> form, or mode, in which the thing may happen to exist at this
> or at that time; nor yet generalized from any number or suc-
> cession of such forms or modes: but which is given by the
> knowledge of *its ultimate aim.*   (C & S 5)

Can we go from this to ideas of the cat or the oak tree, or of
a crystal structure, taking examples of ordered wholes in nature,
where it becomes less and less plausible to think of them as being
shaped by active purpose?

I do not think Coleridge ever intended to be as teleological,
as anthropomorphic about nature, as this sounds. The most
telling passage of how he did try and think of these powers in
nature is also in *The Statesman's Manual*, in an appendix. Contemplating Nature, he says,

> I seem to myself to behold in the quiet objects, on which I
> am gazing, more than an arbitrary illustration, more than a
> mere *simile*, the work of my own Fancy! I feel an awe, as if
> there were before my eyes the same Power, as that of the
> REASON – the same Power in a lower dignity, and therefore a
> symbol established in the truth of things. I feel it alike,
> whether I contemplate a single tree or flower, or meditate on
> vegetation throughout the world, as one of the great organs
> of the life of nature.

And he speaks of how a living thing 'with the same pulse effectuates its own secret growth . . . upholding the ceaseless plastic
motion of the parts'.[29]

'The same power as that of the Reason.' We have seen that
the power of Reason (as distinct from Understanding) for Coleridge is not primarily one of drawing deductive inferences, but
of bringing a unity into multiple material, above all holding
together and reconciling contrasts (his beloved polarity principle)
and finding a symbol in which this unifying vision can be
expressed. I think what he is saying in this passage is that in a
lower degree the characteristic of a natural organism is to hold
itself together in a unity which grows by assimilating material
into its own constitution. But the unity is not something the
organism expresses in a symbolic form which is then a creation

apart from itself – a poem or picture. It is its own self-creation.

If this is what is meant, the analogy cannot be pressed too far. I made a start on it in my Rylands' Lecture 'Coleridge on the Growth of the Mind'[30] and Stephen Prickett in *Coleridge and Wordsworth: the Poetry of Growth*[31] takes it a long way further. But there are difficulties in making the notion of physiological growth an analogue for the mind's symbol-creating power. The growth of an organism is indeed, as D'Arcy Thompson said in *On Growth and Form*, a process and a force. Coleridge himself said, 'Life itself is not a *thing* – a self-subsistent *hypostasis* – but an *act* and *process*.'[32] But a living thing reaches a peak of maturity and then falls away. Moreover, an organism is an open system, assimilating and rejecting nutriment from its environment, whereas the nutriment of the symbol-making process may be combinations of unlikely, even apparently incongruous elements. (Remember Coleridge's love of 'polarities'.) The creation of the symbol depends on the capacity to find unexpected congruities, new ways of seeing one thing in terms of another. 'Only connect', but in an original way, not in the way in which an organism can go on selecting and eating the same kind of food day after day. Indeed the growth of an organism depends on a steady diet without too many surprises, while the growth of the mind depends on being able to master variety.

So there are limitations in seeing the creative powers of the mind as an extension of the powers of growth in organic nature. But there may also be a positive analogy, indeed more than just an analogy. The notion of growth as a psycho-biological force, having a spear-head in the kind of development that can happen in contemplative mystical experience, was used by Margaret Masterman in a pioneer paper 'The Psychology of Levels of Will.'[33] Some of the group associated with the journal *Theoria to Theory* (a journal concerned with the borders of science and religion, where these are not just being distinguished and kept separate, but can be mutually fructifying) are wanting to look further into this notion of growth. Whether there can be continuities in biological, psycho-physiological and spiritual growth is a question of enormous complexity, needing contributions from people with skills in cytology, endocrinology, depth psychology (to name only some of the relevant sciences) as well as in the psychology of religion. These were in fact the kinds of things that Coleridge was interested in, in terms of the sciences of his day. They concern what it is to be a *living* creature. To emphasise the aspect of life and growth can all too easily be dismissed by talk about 'Vitalism'. I do not think that Coleridge should properly be called a Vitalist in the sense of one who believes that the life in an organism is not the whole organism in an active state, but depends on the existence of some distinct vital factor. Certainly Coleridge does sometimes talk about living principles in ways that suggest they are distinct existences. But we can recall the parallel with Ideas as living powers, when I suggested that in such talk an Idea is not a ghostly inhabitant of the mind, but the mind itself – indeed the whole thinking and feeling person – finding a form to express a theme which is holding its attention. Is this a possible meaning of the phrase 'the unity of subject and object' which Coleridge was always invoking? The theme, like the Idea, is a form in which thinking is given external embodiment in symbols which can be used to connect one part of experience with another.

If we take the analogy thus far, the link with organic life is in the powers of Reason as the active energy of thinking and feeling, bringing into operation the whole embodied person, who, as embodied, is part of nature. That something in nature has these powers is itself a significant fact about nature. Indeed, the more purely mechanistic one makes one's view of nature, the more dualistic one may have to be about the mind-body relation. The more one sees thinking as including the states of the body, and yet also as creative, the less possible it is to be purely mechanistic about the living organism, which in our case is an idea-forming organism. Coleridge sees the commerce of mind and nature as a two-way process. We are active in our experience, so that even our perceptions are shaped by powers of the mind; at the same time the powers of growth in nature are energising in us and shaping the mind. The difficulty, with Coleridge (as with Whitehead, who does not seem to have considered Coleridge, though he was constantly quoting Wordsworth) is in stretching these organic concepts of living systems down into the inorganic on the one hand, and up into mental and aesthetic activities on the other. But the alternative is to have irreducible breaks between the different levels. Coleridge did not want to have such breaks. He was nothing if not a would-be unifier, a synthesiser. In so far as his conception of continuities between powers of the mind and the living powers of natural organisms was more than a piece of speculative metaphysics, its empirical grounding was in the way in which states of the body were integral parts of the kind of thinking that he called Reason and Imagination (it is noteworthy how the two are often coterminous). Feelings emerging into consciousness on the fringes of awareness are physiological as well as psychological happenings, and each of these ways of thinking of them, the physiological and the psychological, may be misleading if taken alone. Hence his 'Psycho-somatic Ology'.

Also this symbol-creating state of mind, especially in poetic creation, is for Coleridge a state in which the person is not closed up into himself, but is in some kind of communication with other persons or things in nature, whether actually present or recollected, and so it is a process of making 'the external internal and the internal external'.[34] F. J. A. Hort wrote that to Coleridge, Man was 'a being who belongs to both worlds [nature and spirit] at once, and is capable of beholding glimpses of the one reflected from the unconscious face of the other'.[35] Here neither what is called a projectionist nor a realist view of the relation between the symbol and the external reality holds. The former says that the poet projects his feelings on a neutral or alien nature by interpreting nature in terms of his own feelings. The latter takes the symbols as describing actual goings-on in nature.

Coleridge, I think, came nearer to a 'rapport' view than to either of these – though rapport with nature, as a way of feeling oneself in communion with nature, and then turning this feeling into poetry, is, I think, a more adequate way of describing Wordsworth's attitude than Coleridge's. Coleridge had very exact perceptions of nature, but in looking at nature I think he was often seeking an analogue for something in the mind. In a notebook entry for 'Saturday night, April 14, 1805' he writes:

In looking at objects of Nature while I am thinking, as at yonder moon dim-glimmering thro' the dewy window-pane, I seem rather to be seeking, as it were *asking*, a symbolical language for something within me that already and forever exists, than observing any thing new. Even when that latter is the case, yet still I have always an obscure feeling as if that new phænomenon were the dim Awaking of a forgotten or hidden Truth of my inner Nature/ It is still interesting as a Word, a Symbol! It is Λόγος, the Creator! (and the Evolver!).[36]

With Coleridge 'nature' was, I think, first and foremost his experience of his own embodied self – an embodied self usually in pain and ridden with addictions, with feelings breaking out in nightmares, giving uncreative as well as the occasional creative symbolic vision:

> A sense of weakness – a haunting sense, that I was an herbaceous Plant, as large as a large Tree, with a Trunk of the same Girth, and Branches as Large and shadowing – but with *pith within* the Trunk, not heart of Wood – that I had *power* not *strength* – an involuntary Imposter – that I had no real Genius, no real Depth – This on my honour is as fair a statement of my habitual Haunting, as I could give before the Tribunal of Heaven. (CL II 959)

Sometimes, as for instance in *Christabel*, he was able to turn nightmare anxieties into poetry, and he had a strong metaphysical interest in producing a synthesis, an overall world-view.

I have been representing this synthesis as a form of what the German romantics and post-Kantian idealists called *Naturphilosophie*, a speculative attempt to describe continuities and analogues between powers of the mind and powers in nature, though with Coleridge this was not just speculative, since there was always the empirical grounding in his introspective concern with the workings of his own embodied mind and his interest in experimental science. Besides looking at nature for symbols of his subconscious states, he also had a wide scientific interest (more, I think, than Wordsworth had) in natural phenomena as studied in current experimental work. I think it is right to characterise his philosophy as a form of *Naturphilosophie*. But to say no more than this is to leave out its theological and religious side. Here I can only make a few very inadequate remarks in conclusion. Ever since his early Unitarian days, Coleridge was unhappy with 'anthropomorphitism' – the personal notion of the Deity as a magnified non-natural man. His philo-

sophical approach drove him in the pantheist direction, and
Professor McFarland in *Coleridge and the Pantheist Tradition*
has written definitively about both his sympathy and his
struggle with pantheism. Indeed, given his approach to the
powers of mind and nature, pantheism was surely very nearly
the right conclusion for him to have come to. It was only not
quite right because he thought it failed to do justice to the
creative process and above all to the individual 'I am' – the
individual person as a centre of thought and will and striving,
as well as a part of a great overall system of nature (however
spiritualised the notion of nature). He therefore tried to see the
powers of the mind in the embodied person and the powers of
life and growth in nature as dependent ultimately on a single
ground, which was the creative source and sustainer of nature,
and not only a description of nature in spiritual instead of in
material terms. The notion of a 'Ground of Being' has come
back into contemporary philosophy of religion. Bishop Robinson
popularised it from Tillich, but Tillich himself drew it from
Schelling and Boehme, in whom Coleridge saw a 'genial coincidence' with his views.[37] When Coleridge speaks of a Ground
of Being, he uses the words Will and Reason in an extension
of the sense we have seen he gives to these as ways of describing the power which holds the psyche in unity and enables it to
express itself creatively. So in using these words he was searching for a notion of the Ground of Being as the root of the
dynamic power which does just this, not only in our own
embodied psyche, but in everything that is. And he thought he
saw the outline of such a way of thinking in the notion of the
creative Logos in the Greek Christian Platonist theologians. As
with the Reason, and indeed with its Ideas, it was crucial that
this Logos should not be the hypostatisation of an abstraction but
a dynamic power. He wrote in a notebook that as we recede from
anthropomorphitism we must go either to the Trinity or to
Pantheism.[38] Of the Trinitarian doctrine of the unity in multiplicity of this power he also wrote (commenting on John Scotus
Erigena) that the doctrine of the Trinity has to draw on language
accommodated to our minds, for the human intellect 'must
define and consequently *personify* in order to understand/ and
must have some phantom of Understanding in order to keep
alive in the heart the substantial Faith. They (*sic*) are Fuel to

the sacred Fire – in the Empyraean it may burn without Fuel/ and they who do so are Seraphs'.[39] 'For a poet,' he says, in a notebook entry for 1833, 'is a transfigured philosopher with seraph wings on his shoulder'.[40]

Perhaps he was closer to being a Seraph than to being an Archangel, even 'an Archangel a little damaged'.

In an appendix to *The Statesman's Manual* Coleridge makes a 'half apology for the supposition of a divining power of the human mind'.[41] I have been mainly concerned with his meta-physical views, drawing them mostly from prose writings, notes and letters. But of course he was first and foremost a poet, and in his great poems he had a divining power for which no half-apology is needed. We meet this when it becomes a feeling which goes beyond a sense for quiet, steady processes of organic life and growth, and which takes us into a world where these powers become more numinous, more disturbing, more daemonic – a word Coleridge himself uses in its proper Greek sense. To me, this is where his principle of 'bipolarity' at the base of everything comes alive. I find it very hard to do justice to his use of this principle in what he says about organic processes in nature. (A treatment which does take this as central is given in Owen Barfield's *What Coleridge Thought*.) But I can see the significance of 'bipolarity' in the daemonic as a creative power which can be corrupted into the demonic or raised into the divine. We meet this in *Kubla Khan*, where Xanadu does not only contain a garden and stately pleasure dome, but

> A savage place! as holy and enchanted
> As e'er beneath a waning moon was haunted
> By woman wailing for her demon-lover.

We meet daemonic power again in the community of guilt and love, deeper than moral right and wrong, where the Ancient Mariner's senseless act in shooting the albatross awakens the guilt, and his capacity (even in his own unhappiness) to bless the water snakes – 'happy living things' – awakens the love. It meets us in *Christabel* in the fascination and fear of some unknown evil associated with Geraldine. And it meets us in *Dejection*, where he can salute joy when he himself is in a state of dereliction.

Norman Fruman has given a simple Freudian-like interpretation of the anxieties symbolised in these poems: *Kubla Khan* may be an incest fantasy, the *Ancient Mariner* expresses Coleridge's suppressed wish for his father's death, *Christabel* his ambivalent feelings about his mother, *Dejection* impotence anxiety.[42] He introduces these interpretations tentatively, but the tentativeness disappears as he elaborates them. Some suppressed sexual fears may well be there, though I am sceptical about these particular interpretations. But surely the strange world of daemonic powers into which the poems take us includes more than such fears.

These powers, however strange, are not visitors from an alien world. As Hort says in the essay to which I have referred, Coleridge never cuts his 'spirits' off from the rest of creation: 'they are not ghosts haunting an alien earth, but have their appropriate homes in some region of land, or air, or water... When they have passed quite away, the mystery of their power is thenceforth transferred to nature herself.'[43]

Professor Irving Babbitt had some scathing remarks about 'the Ancient Mariner, who, it will be remembered, is relieved of the burden of his transgression by admiring the colour of water snakes'.[44] This is to be blind to the way in which these powers for good and ill can be released in unexpected ways. Just as the senseless killing of the albatross brought the curse of death in life, so the Mariner's responding to the joyful play of the water snakes when he himself was in profound misery, brought the beginning of healing.

> O happy living things! no tongue
> Their beauty might declare:
> A spring of love gushed from my heart,
> And I blessed them unaware:
> Sure my kind saint took pity on me,
> And I blessed them unaware.
>
> The self-same moment I could pray;
> And from my neck so free
> The Albatross fell off, and sank
> Like lead into the sea.

The symbols of daemonic powers may indeed be charged with the fears, anxieties, guilt, which arise in our relations with nature, and that part of nature which is our fellow human beings. But they can also be symbols of joy and healing. For when these relations are right they are channels of healing and creative power, stemming from our common roots in the Ground of Being. Then the daemonic powers which were the Eumenides, the Furies, become the Eumenides, the kindly ones, powers of grace.

8

Coleridge and Kant

D. M. MacKinnon

Coleridge is commemorated chiefly, if not entirely, as a poet. If one who is professionally concerned with philosophy and theology ventures comment on his treatment of Kant, he must therefore do so in full awareness that in Coleridge's appraisal of the philosopher he has to do with a poet's understanding of one of the most commanding figures in the whole history of Western philosophy. It therefore becomes him to eschew any form of pedantry and to be ready to receive insights as unexpected as they are unsystematic; he must not be deterred by the presence of sharp contradiction in the poet's expressed attitude towards the philosopher. After all, no one who has studied Kant to any depth has any excuse for forgetting the extent to which that philosopher's thought developed and underwent significant changes before his *Inaugural Dissertation* of 1771, then again between the delivery of that formidable lecture and the publication of the first edition of the *Critique of Pure Reason* in 1781, then again between the publication of that edition and of the second edition of 1787, and indeed in the whole period during which the massive structure of the critical philosophy was itself being elaborated. The philosopher in whose works the poet quarried was a man whose many-sided thought pursued a course that was at once relentless, rigorously concentrated, yet continually aware of the complexity and diversity of human experience.

In view of Norman Fruman's recent book, there is one issue to which attention must be briefly directed at the outset of this essay, and that is the charge of plagiarism which has been directed against the poet with renewed force and unprecedented wealth of reference in Fruman's long study. Inevitably he includes widespread borrowing from Kant. In the calendar of charges of alleged conversion of others' ideas to his own use which he draws up against the poet, indeed, he implies that in the unpublished *Opus Maximum* Coleridge in fact sought to present the central ideas of the *Critique of Pure Reason* as if they were his own.* It is not for me to defend Coleridge in detail against Fruman's charges; but as a student of Kant, I may observe that for any man to suppose that he could present as his own a work as idiosyncratic in language and style as Kant's masterpiece is to suppose him guilty of quite extraordinary stupidity. Plagiarism is, after all, a kind of confidence trick, and it is not the practice of confidence men to attempt tricks which they have good reason to suppose totally unlikely to succeed. Further (and this is much more important), the accusation of so crudely conceived a project totally neglects the diversity of Coleridge's references to Kant. Again, we shall see that he is surprisingly inconsistent in his evaluation of Kant's work, setting store now by one strand in his thought, now by another. Again, he will sometimes praise aspects of Kant's work that in other places he will sharply criticise. It is, indeed, this dauntingly unsystematic aspect of his treatment that irritates the professional philosopher and scholar, and inclines them to reject the poet's references to Kant as the random jottings of a dilettante. Plagiarism should surely be made of sterner, subtler, less vulnerable stuff. Thus, if Coleridge seriously sought to offer the *idées maîtrises* of Kant's system as his own, he would never have allowed himself continually to suggest that the *Inaugural Dissertation* presented in concentrated summary the central theses of the *Critique of Pure Reason*. Whereas, the philosopher who seeks to come to terms with Coleridge's understanding of Kant may find that what puzzles him and interests him most is just this obstinate insistence on the part of the poet that the *Inaugural Dissertation* does contain the very marrow or substance of Kant's mature thought. There was something in this most formidable of all

---

* Fruman 136–7. (Mr Fruman is, however, wrong to suggest that the remarks which he quotes from Miss Snyder refer to the *Opus Maximum* MSS as a whole. The central MSS are not, as he mistakenly states, in the British Museum, but in Victoria College Toronto and in the Huntington Library; Miss Snyder is writing only of the preliminary 2-volume *Logic*. (Ed.))

philosophical inaugural lectures which spoke to the poet's condition, and it could be that an attempt to answer this question
would take us some way along the road we require to travel in
order to make our own what the poet found in the philosopher.
But the charge of plagiarism neglects also altogether the extent
to which Coleridge found in the study of Kant's work what he
required in order to free himself from bondage to the ideas of
the speculative, romantic Schelling, to whom he was enormously
attracted. More seriously still, the charge of plagiarism, where
Coleridge's relations to Kant are concerned, ignores altogether
passages in the former's writings in which most certainly we can
trace Kant's influence, of which we can say with conviction that
he never would have written thus if he had not profoundly
studied Kant, but of which we must also acknowledge that here
he shows himself the continuator of his master's work, rather
than the sly borrower of his ideas. It is with these considerations
in mind that I dismiss as irrelevant to consideration of Coleridge's
relations to Kant, detailed assessment of the charge of plagiarism.

It is certainly true that Coleridge did borrow from Goethe the
suggestion that in philosophy, men and women were either by
nature Platonists or Aristotelians.[1] He might have qualified out
of his own intellectual experience that dictum by the suggestion
that the very greatest philosophers had, as a condition of their
claim to greatness, something in their intellectual make-up both
of the Platonist and of the Aristotelian. This was most certainly
true of Kant, and although Coleridge himself is not a philosopher
in the sense in which Kant was, one might say that his own
incursions into the world of philosophy show a comparable
readiness to respond to the claims of the two traditions he had
learnt from Goethe to contrast. The Platonist is, traditionally, a
man whose devotion to the one over against the many encourages
him to neglect the rich diversity and complexity of that many
in zealous pursuit of the one which he seeks. He is the man who
seeks a single, all-embracing final vision through which he hopes
to secure a true perspective on the multiplicity of the world
around him, both natural and human. Whereas, the Aristotelian is always in the last resort ready to study things as they are,
insisting that we do not lose sight of their concrete particularity
in pursuit of any single comprehensive vision. If we suppose
that there is a wisdom which we can treat as a pearl of great

price, for which we must be ready to sacrifice all we have and hope for, we must be quite sure that the conception of such an all-embracing insight is not itself a supreme folly leading us away from that which is, rather than towards it. The Aristotelian temper is that of the man who prefers to advance step by step, to acknowledge that he may find answers to some questions but not to others, that there are irreducible diversities in the world that must be accepted and not treated as if they were unreal under the consuming influence of a single all-embracing intellectual aspiration.*

There is a passage in a letter which Coleridge wrote to Sotheby on 10 September 1802 in which he follows a discussion of some of Bowles's later poems with these words:

> ... Never to see or describe any interesting appearances in nature, without connecting it by dim analogies with the moral world, proves faintness of Impression. Nature has her proper interest; & he will know what it is, who believes & feels, that every Thing has a Life of it's own, & that we are all *one Life*. A Poet's *Heart* & *Intellect* should be *combined, intimately* combined & *unified*, with the great appearances in Nature – & not merely held in solution & loose mixture with them, in the shape of formal Similies. (CL II 864)

In his excellent Clark Lectures of 1951–2 on Coleridge, the late Mr H. House[2] states that in his view 'a full commentary on those sentences would go far into Coleridge's heart'. He remarks that the poet takes the strength of impression made by external nature on the mind as the essential starting-point, going on from there to insist that nature has her own proper interest, irrespective of a secondary act of application to human morality.

But he concludes that this proper interest derives from the dual fact that everything, 'including a human being', has its own life, and yet shares in what is properly described as the common life of all. This letter belongs to a time when Coleridge had already known something of Kant's philosophy for several years. And we must remember that it is the comment of a man

---

* On the relations of Aristotle to Plato, as here presented, see especially Aristotle's criticism of Plato's conception of the 'Idea of the Good' in *Nicomachean Ethics* I 6.

who, in *The Rime of the Ancient Mariner* had shown as a poet a quite remarkable capacity for invoking changing natural phenomena as virtual, perceptible projections of spiritual experience, which assumes without loss of overwhelming, personal intensity, communicable structure, through its suggested resonances in the mariner's natural environment. The comment is also the work of a man who, in other places of his voluminous writings, showed sharp impatience with the Newtonian model of the world, finding indeed in Schelling's natural philosophy the suggestion of an alternative way of conceiving its processes. Yet, in what he says in this letter, he shows a readiness to insist that men must be interested in the natural world for its own sake, clearly implying by this insistence that they must submit to the sharp discipline of learning the most effective ways of wresting its secrets, and not in self-indulgent moralism, suggest that it comprises patterns quickly traceable for our edification. Inevitably, one recalls Kant's remark that he was moved to reverence (*Achtung*) by contemplation of the starry heavens above as well as by contemplation of the moral law within. For the philosopher it was by the methods which Newton had perfected, the fusion of constructive mathematical effort with patient observation that the ordering principles of those heavens were disclosed. If there is a quite unmistakable element of Platonism in Kant's insistence on the unconditional worth of characteristically moral excellence, and indeed in his sense of the power and significance of mathematics in scientific explanation (in his case, of course, applied mathematics), there is also a clear indebtedness to Aristotle. This most obviously in his doctrine of categories, but also more pervasively in his repeated insistence that there are diversities of method appropriate in different fields. In the passage which House rightly praised, we see the extent to which Coleridge has learnt such lessons from his master.* The indebtedness extends, indeed, to the third and last point which Coleridge there makes, where he reminds his reader that he is familiar with Kant's third and last *Kritik*, the so-called *Critique of Judgement*, in which the philosopher is concerned not simply with principles of aesthetic evaluation, not simply with the analysis of such concepts as that of *das Erhabeme* (the

* This in spite of the immanentist metaphysical remark that 'we are all one Life', which Kant would have intensely disliked.

Sublime), but also with the methodological schemata involved in the specifically biological sciences, arguing in the end that in natural explanation, mechanical and teleological principles must both of them be regarded as indispensable, even though we could not see how their use, both together, could be reconciled.

But the reader will remember here that at the outset of this essay I insisted that in Coleridge's Kant we had to reckon with a poet's Kant and it may fairly be commented on the immediately foregoing that it is unusually prosy even for a philosopher and theologian! Yet the very heaviness is a witness to Coleridge's intellectual seriousness. It may well be that he received the work of the German philosophers whom he would seem first to have encountered in the last years of the eighteenth century as men whose work seemed to him to contain answers to questions in the philosophy of mind posed to him by his experience as a poet. He had been deeply influenced by the associationist psychology, which he had learnt from Hartley, and in his own poetic experience had in some measure confirmed. The so-called 'laws of association of ideas', of contiguity, of succession, of resemblance, did in fact summarise recurrent patterns of individual mental history. In such ways the mind worked, the complex being fashioned out of the simple, the unfamiliar wrought out of the stuff of the familiar. Yet, that was not the whole story and, notoriously, Coleridge sought to supply its deficiencies and, by their supply, to correct the story he had already told, by his treatment of imagination. The outline account he offers in *Biographia Literaria*[3] of the imagination of which he would write, the distinction he draws between primary and secondary Imagination, and the distinction of both alike from Fancy, is too well known to require recapitulation. But it is worth while our recalling that he insists that Fancy is 'no other than a mode of Memory emancipated from the order of time and space' which – 'equally with the ordinary memory' – 'must receive all its materials ready made from the law of association'.[4] To distinguish Fancy from Imagination would seem to depreciate the former; yet to link it with memory would equally seem to afford the power its own dignity in as much as the world of memory is a world that most certainly Coleridge knew and feared. There is an ambivalence in his attitude towards association that springs from his half-comprehended endurance of the depths of memory-experience, when recollections spring unbidden from sudden encounter with items of awareness which force upon the subject the task of coming to terms with elements in his past that have made him what he is, which he would rather remained obliterated from conscious recall.

For our purposes in this study, it must simply be emphasised that the Imagination of which Coleridge wrote bore little more than verbal identity with the *Einbildungskraft*, on which Kant had much to say in the *Analytic of Principles*, of which the philosopher says in one place that it is 'the understanding working blind' whose role in perception of the world around us (and in particular in application of 'objectivity-concepts'*) he continually stresses; but which he will always in the end seek to show as standing under the sovereignty of *Verstand*. In perception of the world about us it is to imagination that Kant assigns the work of the second synthesis which, significantly, he calls the synthesis of reproduction in imagination, thereby making plain that for him imagination is something closely akin to memory and therefore to Coleridge's fancy, protected against the arbitrariness that may beset the latter by subordination to conceptual understanding. We cannot, on Kant's view, identify what is in front of our eyes as a tree forming part of our immediate environment unless fragmentary, intermittent, interrupted sense awareness is filled out by the resources of recollection, imagination, even (in Coleridge's sense) Fancy. Yet the haphazard flow of such imaginings or indeed imagings must be disciplined by conceptual definition whereby the random is dismissed as mere association and the awareness endowed with objective import. Again, it is by imagination that according to Kant we are enabled to lay hold of the sense for us of those notions (e.g. substance and cause) which, in rendering possible awareness of a single common time to which our world and ourselves both alike belong, constitute the fundamental forms of our thinking. This activity which Kant calls by the name of Schematism, he clearly regards as deeply significant, but allows himself in writing on the subject to speak of its essential mystery and its obscurity. Yet here again Imagination is cast by him for a mediating role between sense and understanding.

* I owe the useful characterisation of Kant's categories as 'objectivity concepts' to Professor Jonathan Bennett.

Coleridge's Imagination is vastly different, whether one thinks of the primary or the secondary imagination. Of the former he writes notoriously in frankly metaphysical or even theological vein, speaking of it as 'a repetition in the finite mind of the eternal act of creation in the infinite I AM'. In this sentence there are, I repeat, frankly metaphysical implications of a deeply pantheistic kind. The mood is a long way removed from the disciplined idiom of the letter to Sotheby quoted above. But where the secondary Imagination is concerned, while he speaks of it as 'an echo of the former', he also says that 'it dissolves, diffuses, dissipates, in order to recreate; or where this process is rendered impossible, yet still at all events it struggles to idealise and to unify'; he adds that 'it is essentially *vital* even as all objects (*as* objects) are essentially fixed and dead'. Again, that final sentence is pantheistic in its suggestion; but where in the sentence immediately before, Coleridge speaks of the dissolving, diffusive, dissipating powers of secondary Imagination, he is certainly writing boldly, but not necessarily committing himself to pantheistic doctrine.

Earlier in *Biographia Literaria* (in Chaper X), Coleridge had touched on the distinction between reason and understanding, quoting from the fifth book of Milton's *Paradise Lost*;

> Both life and sense,
> Fancy, and *understanding*; Whence the soul
> *Reason* receives, and REASON is her *being*,
> DISCURSIVE or INTUITIVE: discourse
> Is oftest your's, the latter most is our's,
> Differing but in *degree*, in *kind* the same.
>
> (BL I 109)

The distinction between Reason and Understanding, which Coleridge of course found in Kant, was for him of the very greatest significance. Indeed, one of the aspects of Kant's thought, to which he responded with a peculiar immediacy, was precisely this distinction which was of course for the philosopher one of the pivots on which his argument in the first *Kritik* turned. If many questions of Kantian exegesis are hard, none is more difficult than grasping the precise sense of the relation in which Kant supposed Reason to stand to Understanding. There are, moreover, long stretches of his exposition of this distinction which are not only extremely obscure but also unbearably tedious. When Coleridge met the distinction in the way in which Kant drew it in his first *Kritik*, he was already familiar with the analogous distinctions drawn (as it seemed to him) elsewhere. Thus, it is no accident that in the passage quoted above he invokes the authority of Milton. In other places he writes as if Kant had done little more than revive with the massive force of the major philosopher, distinctions familiar to those who, like Coleridge, regretted the eclipse, under the pervasive intellectual authority of John Locke, of the different traditions of the Cambridge Platonists. Yet Coleridge was too obstinately persistent a student of Kant to allow himself the easy interpretation of that philosopher's work which would take the form of treating him as an exceptionally powerful late eighteenth-century counterpart of Herbert and More. It is certainly true that Locke was one of Coleridge's blind spots. He could never have devoted his energies, as Newman was later to do in his *Grammar of Assent*, to the minute analysis of a particular stretch of the argument of Locke's *Essay concerning Human Understanding*. The treatment of the empiricists in the *University Sermons* of Newman's Anglican days, which often in their style anticipate parts of the later *Grammar of Assent*, is the sort of treatment which one would expect from one whose intellectual formation was Aristotelian and whose bent (to invoke again the classification of philosophers Coleridge borrowed from Goethe) was always towards Aristotle rather than Plato. We cannot escape the sense that Coleridge approached the sorts of issue that the empiricists seemed to him to have raised often as a seer or prophet rather than as a philosopher. He mourned the eclipse of the tradition in which in differing ways such men as the Cambridge Platonists and indeed William Law had stood, and part of Kant's appeal to him was the appeal of a man who, with the most strenuous intellectual energy, seemed to recreate the intellectual world that Locke's influence (in Coleridge's view more than his explicit argument) had overshadowed.

There are times in which Coleridge seems to belittle the level of understanding in ways that go a long way towards contradicting the implications of the passage from the letter to Sotheby quoted above; but it is not only that passage that compels

revision of this facile judgement. Discussing deduction and induction in his *Table Talk*, he criticises the inductivists for
claiming that 'facts gave birth to, and were the absolute ground
of, principles' by insisting that unless a man 'had a principle
of selection, he would not have taken notice of those facts upon
which he grounded his principle'. He goes on to say: 'You must
have a lantern in your hand to give light, otherwise all the
materials in the world are useless, for you cannot find them; and
if you could, you could not arrange them.'⁵ The passage immediately recalls Kant's insistence that we can only achieve insight in answer to questions which we have ourselves framed
according to plans that we have conceived, awaiting the outcome
of experiments we have ourselves devised, always dependent
where questions and answers are alike concerned on the skills we
command, the sorts of mathematics at our disposal, the technical
possibilities open to us, etc.* Coleridge shows here the influence
of that part of Kant's doctrine of the understanding whose
authority Professor Karl Popper has invoked in criticism of the
claims made for induction. Yet, it is the Reason that reaches
beyond Understanding that Coleridge is concerned with. The
strangely lyrical language which on occasion the philosopher
will allow himself in respect of reason's pretensions awakens an
immediate response in the poet. It is here that he traces the outline of the imagination that he would distinguish from fancy,
that is indeed no arbitrary power, but which yet finds its
discipline in itself and not, as in some measure for Kant understanding does, in the total circumstances of human involvement
in the world. It is because the *Inaugural Dissertation* seems to
Coleridge to deploy this reason in its essential working (in Kant's
account of the *real* as distinct from the *logical* use of the intellect)
that Coleridge esteemed that work as highly as he did. He wrote
of it on a blank leaf at the front of Volume II of his copy of
Kant's *Vermischte Schriften* as a 'Masterwork of profundity and
precision', a 'model of steady investigation, clear Conception
and . . . *elegant* Demonstration'.⁶ The language is fascinating,
suggesting that in the *Dissertation* Coleridge, the Platonist,
found the sort of fusion of mathematical precision and transcendent vision the Platonist has so often sought as the term of
the philosophical quest. If, however, it was as a poet that

* It also recalls Plato's *Meno*.

Coleridge came to Kant, with problems raised by his poetic experience to which he sought an answer, it was as a poet that he read his German master; as a poet he responded to him and a considerable, if not the main, part of what he has to teach professional philosophers concerning Kant is the presence in the work of that formidable thinker of elements to which a poet immediately responds. So, our understanding of Kant is deepened. It is with this in mind that we must now turn to the detail of the *Dissertation*.

The work is divided into two parts, the first concerned with the forms and principles of the sensible world, the second with the forms and principles of the intelligible world. In the first part Kant sets out in bold outline a much simplified version of the doctrine of space and time which he developed with far greater subtlety and sophistication in the *Critique of Pure Reason*. But in the *Dissertation* Kant exploits the status of space and time as subjective forms of outer and inner sense to depreciate the ontological dignity of the world revealed to us by the senses, of which space and time are the pervasive forms. Although the middle section of this daunting inaugural lecture is very obscure, it is clear that the author is contrasting with the world of space and time a realm with which we are enabled to enjoy intellectual commerce through the use of pure concepts which he claims to be derived '*e legibus menti insitis*'. Here he makes play with the distinction he draws between the 'real' and the 'logical' uses of intellect. Through the latter we are enabled to order what we know without reference to the material differences in the subject-matter of our concern, in bland indifference to the mode of our contact with the subject-matter in question. Whether we be chemists, botanists, social scientists, historians, archaeologists, we are still compelled to order and classify our material, going on to establish interrelations between the concepts we employ in the initial ordering and classification. In Kant's relatively simple doctrine here in the *Dissertation* it is only principles of formal consistency that we need to observe in this organisation of the matter of our knowledge. It is true that there is another phase in his argument which shows him concerned with the peculiar status to be assigned to the sorts of law regarded as uniquely fundamental in the physical science of his age. But the central direction of his thinking is controlled by his conviction that for all its diversity, the material which human beings seek to organise by exercise of the 'logical' powers of their intellect is always temporal in its form and for the most part spatial and temporal at once. While Newton was right against Leibniz in insisting that neither space nor time were reducible to systems of relations, but must be regarded as ontologically independent of and prior to that which was said to fall within them, according to Kant he had been very wrong to treat them as if they were unique, self-existent entities. Rather they were to be understood as ways in which human beings were affected at the level of sense experience by that with which through such experience they had contact.* Therefore Kant believed himself free in the *Dissertation* to argue that, however comprehensive, conceptually sophisticated, even aesthetically elegant the structures of our knowledge concerning what belonged to space and time, these structures still related only to that which owed its most fundamental forms to the conditions of characteristically human awareness.

Over against the 'logical' use of the intellect, Kant set its 'real' use wherein by use of such concepts as substance, causality, existence, possibility, necessity, freed from any imagined association with aspects of the world of space and time, we are enabled to establish irrefutable truths concerning the unconditioned. The kind of liberation from misleading association of which Kant speaks seems to the reader sometimes more akin to an ascetic discipline than to an exercise in conceptual analysis. A modern reader might be tempted to suppose that where existence is concerned, Kant is pleading in old-fashioned language for the kind of formal treatment which the notion has received at Professor Quine's hands as against the more informal approach characteristic of those who attend to the varied circumstances in everyday life in which we invoke the distinction between the real and unreal, the actual and the non-actual, that which we regard as existent as an element in our world and that which we dismiss. But Kant goes a very long way beyond this.

It may be that we will go some way towards understanding him if we look at the argument of an earlier work, namely his Essay on *The Only Possible Proof of the Existence of God* of 1763. In this work Kant insists that the only admissible proof is to

---

* The word 'contact' is of course used metaphorically.

be found in the idea of a necessary being, that is one whose concept necessarily entails his existence. It is Kant's conviction that if our idea of God is adequately framed it must be the idea of a being about whose reality there can be no dispute. If we offer a definition of God and then find ourselves disputing whether or not there is anything answering to that definition (as we do argue concerning, e.g., the existence of living beings on Mars, where recent space-probes have shown traces of water), we know that that concerning whose reality we are disputing is not God. If God exists, he exists necessarily. If therefore our concept of God is adequate, it must be the concept of a being whose existence is seen to be necessarily involved with what he is. We are here, of course, meeting the 'ontological argument' in one of its forms; but it is a form in which such notions as possibility, actuality, necessity and indeed substance in the sense of self-existent being are in play. Further, it is clear that we have to do with an argument which claims as a condition of its validity that we must be able to conceive God as he is in himself, and not content ourselves with representing the relation in which the world stands to him. It will be remembered that Aquinas rejected the so called 'ontological' argument on the ground that while God's essence entailed his existence *quoad simpliciter*, and therefore, if we could conceive God as he conceives himself we would grasp his existence as entailed by his essence, we do not grasp God as he is in himself, but only in terms of the relation in which the world of which we are part, and whose existence is contingent, stands to him. Therefore our concept of God is not of God as he is in himself.

The historical pedigree of the sort of argument Kant is discussing in this work is as old as Plato's rejection of the literary representation of divine metamorphosis as contradictory of that which we knew of the perfection of the divine nature. Where the version of 'the ontological' argument here in play is concerned, we have to reckon with an argument whose inspiration is partly derived from a deeply religious sense of God as directly disclosing himself as the self-authenticated concretion of absolute perfection. The kind of intellectual activity Kant sought to vindicate in the *Dissertation* and less than eleven years later sharply criticised in his massive onslaught on all forms of transcendent metaphysics in the *Critique of Pure Reason* is a kind of theoretical anatomisation of the ultimate that is made to the measure of a deeper aspiration towards the unconditioned. It is characteristic of Kant that in the Antinomies in the *Kritik*, while he insists that neither thesis nor antithesis can be proved to the exclusion of the alternative, he insists that his readers are all the time aware which side they wish to prevail.

No one reading the *Dissertation*, after submitting to the discipline of the first *Kritik*, finds it easy to enter in to the earlier work's peculiar fusion of rarefied quasi-logical argument with eloquent aspiration. Yet a close study of the text of the *Kritik* shows the extent to which Kant remained haunted by the dream of the sort of transformation of human knowledge in which, set free from the conditions through which alone he then supposed it possible, men might enjoy not simply comprehensive synoptic vision but the sort of insight which would render perspicuous to their understanding their very experience itself. One might say that he saw human beings beset by a craving to 'jump out of their cognitive skins'. It was indeed his view that, properly disciplined, such dreams could be the source of creative dissatisfaction with a science that contented itself with description and eschewed the more precarious tasks of comprehensive, conceptually economical, mathematically elegant explanation. But in his criticism of transcendent metaphysics it was with the illusory quality of this dream that Kant engaged, and it is surely clear enough by now that in terms of Goethe's distinction the dream was Platonic rather than Aristotelian in shape.

Coleridge was very wrong to regard the *Dissertation* as a summary of the first *Kritik*. Indeed anyone seeking to defend him against Fruman's charges of plagiarism, where his philosophical work was concerned, might well ask whether anyone seeking deliberately to present Kant's work as his own would be guilty of such an extraordinary gaffe. Yet although it is a gaffe, Coleridge's response to the earlier work is impressive evidence of the extent to which the later work for all its rejection of the earlier's mystique of the pure intellect, is continuous with it in as much as the author is struggling all the time to come to terms with questions raised for him by the way in which he had hoped in his *Dissertation* to assign to Newtonian dynamics its proper field and to reveal the pure intellect as equipped by nature to allow men commerce with the ultimate. One can read the first *Kritik* as an elaborate essay in self-knowledge, enabling the reader to take stock of the limits of his intellectual powers. This is of course by no means the only way in which it can be or indeed should be read. But if one so approaches it with Coleridge's peculiar sensitivity for the quality of the *Dissertation*, one can see how out of the longer, greater work, a poet might learn lessons he can only communicate in his practice concerning the significance, for the deepest sort of self-scrutiny, of the logically inadmissible aspirations which Kant indulged in the *Dissertation*. We do well to remember the extent of the poet's preoccupation with the problem of self-knowledge and if at the conclusion of this essay I quote in full a poem belonging to the last stages of his life on this theme, I do so partly because it seems to me possible that the key to his strange gaffe concerning Kant's work may lie in the extent to which he found in the *Dissertation* an attempt to formulate the kind of pure unfettered intellectual ascent to the ultimate which he desired, and then in the *Kritik* a massive argument, which, while it protected him against whole-hearted commitment to Schelling's speculations, at the same time counselled a deep, yet not unsympathetic caution concerning the styles of thinking through which he supposed his dreams might find fulfilment. One has to remember that in the opuscula of his last years, Kant, for all his disdain of examples and strenuous search for the maximum degree of abstraction in exposition, came increasingly to rely on illustrative examples, always carefully qualified but sometimes extremely illuminating in respect of his deepest sense.

Yet the matter does not end here. Coleridge was deeply affected by Kant's doctrine of the primacy of the practical reason. Thus in one place he insisted that 'Religion . . . must have a *moral* origin; so far at least, that the evidence of its doctrines could not . . . be wholly independent of the will'.* Indeed historians of religious thought often write as if Coleridge's emphasis upon the moral dimensions of faith represented for the first generation of his readers the occasion of their deliverance from bondage to the artificial apologetic associated with Paley's name. It is indeed in the highly individual use which

---

* BL I 135. For a long analysis of the relationship involved, see LS 59–70.

Coleridge made of Kant's doctrine of human beings as always, in all times and in all places morally committed, and therefore involved unceasingly with the unconditioned, whatever the changing mood of contemporary speculation, that Coleridge's great contribution to Christian apologetic has allegedly been made. A commentator might remark that here he effectively revived the traditions of Joseph Butler (who was, of course, among John Henry Newman's masters) with the peculiar effectiveness born of his poetic genius, and given strange force by reason of his wide-ranging philosophical culture. It was the poet in Coleridge which led him impatiently to reject John Locke's work, as if it were no more than an elaborate variation on the theme of the mind as a *tabula rasa*, and as if that philosopher had never offered for his readers' reflection such profoundly suggestive and illuminating sections as that in which he defends the distinction between nominal and real essences.

Coleridge's attitude to Kant was by no means constant. There is an unresolved contradiction between his readiness to welcome the philosopher's doctrine of the primacy of the practical reason and his long brooding over the significance for his experience of the issues raised for him by study of the *Dissertation* and of the first and third *Kritiks*. Thus in a marginal jotting in his copy of Taylor's *Proclus* (1792) he writes, 'It seems clear that the Critical Philosophy, as contained in the works of Immanuel Kantius is a Junction of the Stoic *Moral* with the Platonic *Dialectic*, which Kant has unfairly confounded with the *Sophistic* (Logik der *Schein*).'[7] One can guess the mood of disappointment with the conclusions of the dialectic expressed in that sentence; yet the poet is right to emphasise the Stoic influence on Kant's ethics. This though he shows elsewhere how much he has learnt from Kant's moral philosophy, and not least the late work on the philosophy of religion in which Kant towards the end of his life, sought with considerable subtlety, and with the deep vein of moral pessimism discernible in his earlier ethical writings fully displayed, to establish both the role of religion in human life and the conditions of its subordination to morality.

In *Aids to Reflection*, Coleridge wrote as follows:

He who begins by loving Christianity better than Truth, will

proceed by loving his own sect or Church better than
Christianity, and end in loving himself better than all.

(AR 101, MR xxv)

One must remember that the author of this profound and
illuminating statement was also the author of a work on the
constitution of Church and State in which he pleaded for
Church establishment in the characteristically Anglican form.
No student of that work can acquit Coleridge of complicity in
what has been since the seventeenth century arguably the worst
flaw in Anglican Christianity, namely the bland assumption
that the Church of England effectively embodies the authentic
norm, not simply of English, but of British Christianity. Few if
any mistakes of fact in the history of the Christian Church have
been more sheerly disastrous both in the perpetuation of un-
necessary antagonisms and (more gravely) in encouragement of
the uglier forms of spiritual pride, both individual and collective.
But in the sentence which I have quoted from *Aids to Reflection*
where Coleridge's debt to Kant is quite unmistakable, he offers a
devastating critical judgement on the heresy of which he was
in the years of his religious commitment not infrequently guilty.
Moreover, as a comment on Kant's philosophy of religion, it
goes to the very heart of the matter in that the poet shows that
he has learnt from his intellectual master not to repeat his ideas
but to assimilate their sense and to advance beyond their first
formulation by a novel application. Coleridge recognises that in
his subordination of religion to morality Kant was not pursuing
a simple essay in reductionism; rather he was insisting that
religious ideas should be used not as a means of confirming men's
belief in their individual significance and the validity of their
purposes, whether personal or collective, but rather imagina-
tively to enlarge their perceptions by giving them a vivid sense
of that absolute by which their conduct was continually judged,
of which indeed as autonomous members of the realm of ends
they were in some sense the bearers. Yet that of which they were
thus the bearers stood over against them, even as Kant saw it
standing over against Jesus, whose authority (and this is certainly
the teaching of the Fourth Gospel) rested not on himself but on
a vindication which he was powerless to command, only seeking
by his total innocence to receive it. In writing in these terms I

go beyond Coleridge and Kant alike; but I do so following a
route which the former has suggested.

In the poem written towards the end of his life entitled 'Self-
Knowledge', Coleridge returned to a theme which had occupied
him across the years:

Self-Knowledge

—E cœlo descendit γνῶθι σεαυτόν   Juvenal, xi. 27.

Γνῶθι σεαυτόν!—and is this the prime
And heaven-sprung adage of the olden time!—
Say, canst thou make thyself?—Learn first that trade;—
Haply thou mayst know what thyself had made.
What hast thou, Man, that thou dar'st call thine own?—
What is there in thee, Man, that can be known?—
Dark fluxion, all unfixable by thought,
A phantom dim of past and future wrought,
Vain sister of the worm,—life, death, soul, clod—
Ignore thyself, and strive to know thy God!
[1832.]   (PW I 487)

The language of this poem recalls the poet's early fears of what
might be suggested concerning the stuff of which his self was
fashioned by empirical study pursued in accordance with the
associationist psychology of David Hartley. If Coleridge rejected
the adequacy of Hartley's development of Hume's treatment of
the mind as a 'bundle of perceptions' to give account of intellectual and imaginative activity, he had yet learnt from Hartley
to reckon with the element of the uncontrollable unknown in
what went to make us what we individually are. If James Mill
found in associationism ground to justify his hope that, given
time, he could 'make the workings of the human mind as plain
as the road from Charing Cross to St Paul's Cathedral',[8] Coleridge, as he brooded on what he had learnt from his early master,
found only occasion for disturbing uncertainty and insecurity.
Of course the self with which he is concerned in his poem is in
Kant's terms the 'empirical Ego'; and if we say that the study of
Kant's philosophy taught Coleridge important lessons in self-
knowledge, those lessons related more to the disciplining and
proper assessment of his intellectual powers and activity than to
the elusive detail of his autobiography. For Kant the self-knowledge expressed with varying accuracy in varying forms of

autobiography was as much empirically based as knowledge of the world around us. It is true that Kant insisted that self-knowledge of this sort was not something we could achieve in abstraction from our response to the world around us; thus he rejected any suggestion that the 'empirical Ego' was transparent to our scrutiny in the sort of way which would allow us to treat it as the primary datum of our awareness. He was as adamantly hostile to the suggestion that empirical self-awareness could be enjoyed apart from our total response to the world with which he had to deal as he was to the attempt to establish the immortality of a substantival soul from reflection on the unique role of an identical consciousness in experience. What we knew about ourselves we had to learn the hard way. But what Kant would claim that self-knowledge – in the special sense proper to defining the task of the critical philosophy – made possible was a proper mastery of the standing human conditions of all individual self-awareness and the significance of that self-awareness itself, once gained. We should not be deluded by recognition of its possibility into supposing that through it we gain a total grasp of what we are. If, in the mood of the *Dissertation*, the metaphysician is tempted to suppose the ways of the unconditioned open to his scrutiny, there are still human constants with which the dogmatic empiricist fails to reckon.

And among these we have to include Kant's doctrine of the primacy of the practical reason in the individual and frequently inconsistent form in which Coleridge made it his own. As I read this late poem by the author of the *Rime of the Ancient Mariner* I am aware of the confluence of lessons the poet had learnt from Kant. At first this may seem strange in view of the last line. But self-forgetfulness was a very important element in Kant's conception of the way in which human beings should live. Admittedly it was a self-forgetfulness obtained by cultivation of an austere objectivity. No student of Kant's ethics at any depth can fail to remark the paradox in his marriage of spontaneity and rationality. Yet this paradox at least emphasises the difficulty involved in an authentic self-forgetting. We may be betrayed by the burden of empirical self-knowledge into rejecting the continuing fact of our moral responsibility. Yet the very acceptance of what we painfully learn concerning our motives and intentions involves the exercise of practical reason.

But in this poem it will be said that Coleridge, in a manner vaguely suggestive of Augustine, bids the reader turn from self-scrutiny to knowledge of God. It is indeed hard to find Kantian inspiration in such language. Yet if we recall the complexities of Kant's work on *Religion* and also its certain influence upon the poet, it is just possible to construe knowledge of God in the sense of which Coleridge writes of it here, as the sort of knowledge born of continuing fidelity to that 'realm of ends', of which Kant insisted that all human beings were members, constrained by that membership to a deep respect for their common human dignity. It is from a self-knowledge that is at once a duty from which individual human beings cannot escape, but which may in the manner in which they achieve it destroy them, that Coleridge bids his readers turn to knowledge of God. He almost uses that phrase to indicate a sustaining illumination they will receive for their fidelity. In a recent study of Kant's philosophy of religion,[9] M. Jean-Louis Bruch has remarked that where the relations of grace to human freedom and responsibility are concerned, Kant's attitude could be summed up in the Jesuit tag, *Facienti quod in se est, non denegat Deus gratiam*. One might extend the principle to what Coleridge writes in this poem and find in it a plea for the sort of knowledge of God that springs from faithfulness in reckoning with the reality of oneself, both as reward and as authentic consolation.

Kant's influence on Coleridge can be traced only by a tortuous study concerned to follow the windings of the confused, many-sided, yet continuous engagement of the poet with the work of the philosopher. What Coleridge saw in Kant was one who like himself (apart e.g., from the doctrine of the Categories and of the Paralogisms of Pure Reason) was Platonist rather than Aristotelian, and who when the fever of the *Dissertation* was past, made himself less the exponent of an English-style empiricism than of a new sort of 'negative theology', even one Socratic rather than Neoplatonist in inspiration. There was of course another factor at work here, in Schelling's influence upon the poet; and here it might be said that Kant's own critical rejection of the early German Romantics served his disciple well. Because Kant's own achievement was many-sided, one must expect that many-sidedness to be reflected in the response to his work of a man as complex as Coleridge. No student of Kant's philosophy can fail to learn something from attending even briefly to the poet's evaluation of one he acknowledged his intellectual master. It is always illuminating; indeed there are implications concerning the relations of the critical philosophy to poetry on which it has not been possible to touch except indirectly. There is also the deep impact of Coleridge's study of Kant on his religious thought, of which rather more has been said, enough perhaps to suggest that if it was an influence Kant could hardly have foreseen, it might have been one that the philosopher would have welcomed, especially if he could have complemented his own very interesting remarks on matters of Christology along lines indicated in the reference above to John's Passion-narrative. We have to reckon with many-levelled response on the part of the poet to the philosopher whom he had studied. We need not acquit him of an element of vanity in the sense that he was on his way towards making his own an intellectual achievement of which for the most part his countrymen were unaware; on occasion he may certainly have sought to pass this or that characteristically Kantian insight off as his own. But philosophical plagiarists are made of simpler and less confused stuff; as the late Professor J. L. Austin once remarked, they are often clever young men who know a good idea when they hear one or meet with one in some little-known article. No one can dispute the seriousness of the charges Fruman rightly brings against the writer whom he criticises as a 'damaged archangel', but where his intellectual apprenticeship to Kant and his argument with him are concerned, we move at a deeper level: and the poet's work receives sufficient vindication if those who approach Kant primarily as philosophers, at the end of their efforts to make sense of Coleridge's treatment of Kant's formidable work, admit that they can never see it in quite the same way again.

9

Coleridge's Enjoyment of Words

Owen Barfield

There is a little volume in the series known as the Home University Library entitled *The English Language*. It is rather more than sixty years old now, but it is a book I always recommend very strongly to anyone who either enjoys words already or is anxious to begin enjoying them. But what does one mean when one speaks of 'enjoying' words?

When I was a very young man, I was for a brief period in rather close touch with the author of that book, Logan Pearsall Smith. In fact he took me to a certain extent under his wing as the result of an article I had published. Pearsall Smith was a literary friend of the poet Walter de la Mare, and I remember him telling me that, in one of his conversations with the poet, they had agreed there ought to be a word to denote a person with a certain easily recognisable but hardly definable kind of feeling for, or delight in, or enjoyment of words. They decided to invent one and they further decided that, in doing so, they would apply a new principle of coinage. This was, to look around for some especially lovely word, with which there happened to be no available rhyme, and to invent a rhyme for it. The existing word they hit on was 'silver' and the word they invented was 'milver'. A 'milver' was to be a man who enjoyed words in the way they both meant.

I believe I am right in saying that that was as far as it went and that neither of them ever did actually use the word in public. So, at all events, de la Mare himself told me many years later. If so, this is the occasion on which it makes its début. And the anecdote will have been worth recording if it draws attention at the outset to the rather elusive quality I had in my mind when I fixed on the title for this lecture. It is not quite the same as a 'feeling for language'. Every decent writer must have that. Nor does it equate with a scientific or historical interest in language, though it may well overlap all these things. What is exuded by the milver is more like a kind of flavour. It comes through on startlingly different levels, from a taste for puns upward. Lewis Carroll was a milver; but so was Sir Thomas Browne; and so, above all, was Milton. Then there is the long array of what I will call affectionate etymologists, stretching from Horne Tooke, through Archbishop Trench, to Ivor Brown and Eric Partridge. And there are others at other levels. Perhaps I may attempt a comparison. There is a certain flavour we must acknowledge in one of the consecrated elements of the Eucharist; but that does not alter the fact that we must acknowledge the same flavour in that particular species of custard-pie that is called a Trifle. In this case it has a name, and the name is *wine*. I am suggesting that there is a similar 'unity in difference' in the relation to language of different minds, and again of the same mind on different planes of its activity. And, after a good deal of searching about, the best name I could find for that pervasive unity was 'enjoyment of words'.

I emphasised a moment ago that Milton had it, and I shall be returning briefly to that a little later on. Meanwhile it may help to pinpoint the indefinable if I now add that Wordsworth, who in other respects has sometimes been associated with Milton, in my opinion rightly, did *not* have it. M. Paul Deschamps, in his truly admirable book on the formation of Coleridge's thought, contrasts him in this respect with Coleridge. For Wordsworth, he says,

> poesy is a photographic reproduction of reality, every metrical or metaphorical ornament being an artifice it is desirable to eliminate; for Coleridge on the contrary the poet feels himself seized by a lyric and creative emotion in the actual manipulation of the words. There is a magic of words; the word has a living reality in itself ... (Deschamps 532)

It is, as he puts it '*substance vivante*'. It is because of Coleridge's insatiable, shall I say, appetite for words – almost any word – as *substance vivante* that, when I think of that myriad-minded man,

I must think of him, among all his other eminences, as a Prince
of Milvers. And it is so that I hope to present him.

For he had the appetite on *all* its different levels. Let me begin
with the lowest – the punning and funning one. I have recently
been reading the two final volumes of Professor Griggs's monu-
mental edition of the *Collected Letters*. They are sometimes
heavy going, especially the long-winded apologies for not having
written before, including an apology for the length of the
apology. There is a great deal about family and domestic problems, both his own and the Gillmans', and they frequently
stress his physical sufferings and the lowness of his spirits. It is
however extraordinary how pervasively they are leavened by the
recurring ebullience of just that zestful appetite. However low
those spirits, and perhaps at their very lowest point, Coleridge
always felt up to having a lark with a word. Not so much any
particular instance as the frequency of its occurrence is refreshing to the reader, as no doubt it was refreshing to him. However
black things were, and however blue he felt, somewhere underneath it all the old Nether Stowey Coleridge, one is made to feel,
is still very much alive, the Coleridge who jumped over the fence
to save time in reaching Alfoxden, the Coleridge who explained
that the reason why a man swings his walking-stick, when he is
out for a walk, is that he is using it as a kind of lightning-
conductor in reverse, to distribute his own high spirits to as
many points of the compass as possible,[1] the Coleridge who, when
he needed a milkmaid, asked Thomas Poole in a letter to recommend a girl 'simple of heart, *physiognomically* handsome, and
scientific in vaccimulgence';[2] and who added: 'That last word is
a new one; but soft in sound, and full of expression. *Vaccimulgence!* – I am pleased with the word.' Incidentally I sometimes
wonder whether his enthusiasm for the Pantisocracy scheme
would have burned quite so fiercely if he had not also been rather
pleased with the word 'Susquehanna'.

Actual puns, which mark the lowest level, are not very frequent, though they are always liable to appear, as when he describes his intestinal symptoms to Allsop as 'increased pain in a
wrong place altho' *in recto*', or when he describes those Thursday evenings at Highgate, at which he himself did most of the
talking, as '*one*-versazioni'.[3] Usually they involve Latin or Greek
allusions, perhaps at a schoolboy level, like the Latinising of his

own name, when he once chose to refer to himself as 'Samsar-
torius Carbonijugius' – 'Coal-ridge!'[4] He certainly understood, as
every good punster does, that the best puns are the worst, and
the more excruciating the better: or, as he put it himself: 'And
puns then best when exquisitely bad.'[5]

Very much more common is a semi-humorous use of his close
familiarity with the classical languages, to invent or compound
a new word, with which to rub in his meaning. *Nimis* is the
Latin adverb for 'too much', and we find him remarking in his
Table Talk: 'There is a nimiety – a too-muchness in all Germans.
It is the national fault.'[6] And what of his own faults? It is not
enough that he was over-fond of parentheses in writing, not
enough that he was aware of it; he must invent a new word and
call himself a *philoparenthesist*.[7] And since he was also fond of
mottoes, he must also remark, in a letter to Estlin; 'You know,
I am a *mottophilist*, and almost a *mottomanist* – I love an apt
motto to my Heart';[8] hybrid formations these last, between
Latin and Greek, which was most uncharacteristic of him. On
another occasion he labels himself, justifiably I think, as an
idoloclast.[9] And so on.

What are we to call this habit? Humorous pedantry perhaps,
but the line between humorous pedantry and actual pedantry is
a wavering one, and some of his inventions, like *psilanthropy*,
psilosophy, *misosophy*, *aspheterize*,[10] and the better-known
Pantisocracy that went with it, or Schelling's *theanthroposophy*,[11]
or even the world-famous *esemplastic*,[12] may be thought neither
particularly humorous, nor particularly useful. Actually it is
not always easy to be sure whether he was in fact inventing or
only resuscitating. I had always assumed that he invented that
word *nimiety* on the spur of the moment, and I am still inclined
to think he did, though I find it had already been used in the
sixteenth century. So had *coadunation*, the Latin name for the
'esemplastic' activity. We have no means of knowing whether
Coleridge had come across it in his reading, or if he reconstructed
it for himself.

But if the boundary between humorous pedantry and mere
pedantry is unfixed, so also, and much more so, is the boundary
between mere pedantry and something much more important.
Let us hear Coleridge himself on the subject. In a letter of 1821
to William Blackwood, he adds a footnote on the word *aesthetic*,

which was then a recent and 'insolens verbum', but which he hopes, he says,

> will be brought into common use as soon as distinct thoughts and definite expressions shall once more become the requisite accomplishment of a gentleman. So it was in the energetic days, and in the starry court of our *English*-hearted Eliza; when trade, the nurse of freedom, was the enlivening counterpoise of agriculture, not its alien and usurping spirit; when commerce had all the enterprize and more than the romance of war; when the precise yet pregnant terminology of the schools gave bone and muscle to the diction of poetry and eloquence, and received from them in return passion and harmony; but, above all, when from the self-evident truth that what *in kind* constitutes the superiority of man to animal, the same *in degree* must constitute the superiority of men to each other, the practical inference was drawn, that every proof of these distinctive faculties being in a *tense* and *active* state, that even the sparks and crackling of mental electricity, in the sportive approaches and collisions of ordinary intercourse, (such as we have in the wit-combats of Benedict and Beatrice, of Mercutio, and in the dialogues assigned to courtiers and gentlemen, by all the dramatic writers of that reign,) are stronger indications of natural superiority, and, therefore, more becoming signs and accompaniments of *artificial* rank, than apathy, studied mediocrity, and the ostentation of wealth.　　　　　　　　　　　　　　　(CL v 169)

We perceive here the smooth transition, in Coleridge's judgement, from what sounds like pedantry, whether humorous or otherwise, to what is very much the concern of literature and, through that, of mental activity in general. A nice choice of words is not merely a matter of ornament; it is one of the marks which distinguish a literature of depth from the literature of mere surface reactions. And, as we follow him in this transition, the phrase 'enjoyment of words' itself begins to change its colour a little. There is more than one kind of enjoyment. There is the onlooker's enjoyment, of a firework display for instance; but there is also the hungry man's enjoyment of a meal; and there is the craftsman's enjoyment of his tools, the enjoyment a good cabinet-maker feels in handling his favourite screwdriver; which soon becomes also an enjoyment of, or a feeling for, the screw-driver itself.

This kind of feeling for words is not easily separable from some awareness, explicit or implicit, of their past history. For Coleridge at all events I think the two were inseparable. Moreover, the history of the English language is such, its vocabulary is derived so predominantly from Latin (whether directly or indirectly through French) and from Greek words that the awareness I am speaking of easily, perhaps even necessarily, takes the form of an awareness of the Greek or Latin original still peering, as it were, through some particular English word it has turned into. Among the poets I suppose Milton is the one in whom this awareness is most evident and most effective. If I now proceed to illustrate from him, and if you hear me going on for a surprisingly long time about one or two particular words used on one particular occasion by one particular poet, please be assured that my aim in doing so is, not to be wonderfully precious about them *à la* Walter Pater, but to evoke for my present purpose, or (as Coleridge himself might have said) to 'objectize', a possible *way* of experiencing most, or at all events, many words with varying degrees of intensity. It is the submarine way; but in the instances I shall dwell on it happens to be easier than usual to detect, because it has been brought nearer than usual to the surface.

Suppose we take the epithet *affable*. In its ordinary use, it tends to suggest an avuncular figure with its thumb in its waistcoat arm-hole and perhaps a cigar between its lips, leaning back after a good dinner. And I gather from the quotations in the Oxford English Dictionary that its normal overtones were not so very different in Milton's time. But when Milton characterises Raphael as 'the affable archangel',[13] we are drawn back, so to speak, through this rather shrivelled meaning to the naked Latin source of it; not, mark you, merely to the Latin epithet *affabilis*, which had already begun to acquire the avuncular meaning in addition, but to its origin in *ad*-and-*fari*: to 'speak to'. An archangel, but an archangel who could be spoken to by a mere man. And of course the epithet loses none of its appeal from the fact that it is not mere substitution. We do not lose sight altogether of the shrivelled meaning. The earlier appears, transpires, through the later. In being called *affable* Raphael is *also* rendered very slightly avuncular.

So also, the *secure* delight with which the upland hamlets in *L'Allegro* invite us to dance in the chequered shade[14] is not simply 'secure' in the sense of being free from danger; it is not even simply Latin *securus*; it is also *se-cura* – free from care. And so again, when the sun in *Paradise Lost* appears enlarged by its looking through 'the horizontal misty air',[15] the insipidly geometrical term is invigorated by this reappearance of its old connection with the 'horizon', the great circle that is the *horos*, or boundary of our earthly vision. More often than not, the earlier, the unshrivelled, meaning has just this kind of concreteness about it. It was figurative – imaginal – metaphorical in the looser sense of the term – and this is even true of most of the words we use. A writer, who has the feeling for them, will tend accordingly to awaken in his reader, by the way he uses them, what M. Bréal, the author of the book *Semantics*, once called 'the satisfaction ... of feeling a metaphor, whose value has not hitherto been understood, suddenly open and reveal itself'.[16]

That Coleridge habitually enjoyed words in just this way is certain. That he attached to the habit, and not for himself alone, an importance going far beyond the little aesthetic thrill that may well accompany it we learn from observations he let drop here and there, such as his advice in a letter to Gillman's schoolboy son, who was studying Greek:

> In your Greek never be satisfied with the Latin-pretended Equivalent, or Equivalents, of Lexicon or Translation. With the few exceptions of words imitating sound, every word has its primary visual image, as its proper, at least its original sense – and a man cannot be said to understand the WORD, tho' he may the whole sentence in which it occurs, unless he sees how that image was capable of such and such applications ...   (CL VI 700–1)

It must be added that, in Coleridge (with the grand exception of his potent uses of archaism) the sort of enjoyment I am at the moment speaking of is more evident in his prose than in his verse. Notice that, although he is contrasting Coleridge and Wordsworth *as poets*, the actual examples with which M. Deschamps (whom I quoted earlier) illustrates Coleridge's sense of the '*magie*' and the '*substance vivante*' of words are all taken from his *Letters* and *Notebooks*.

If I may be allowed my previous distinction between a literature of depth and a literature of surface-reactions, I would
suggest that Coleridge aimed at a *poetry* of depth by two routes,
one of which was successful and the other not. Overtly philosophical poetry is not, as is sometimes affirmed, a contradiction
in terms. It is not a thing impossible to be written, as both
Lucretius and Dante have sufficiently demonstrated, but it is no
service to Coleridge to maintain that his attempts at the genre,
in 'Religious Musings' and 'The Destiny of Nations', were other
than failures. By the other route to the depths on the other hand,
the way of symbolism, the way of the *Ancient Mariner*, of *Kubla
Khan* and *Christabel* and in a lesser degree, as we now realise, of
the 'Conversation Poems', he was rather more than successful.
He gave us great poetry. For that very reason I find it rather
strange that this enjoyment of words I am speaking of should be
so much more evident in his prose writings than in his verse.

In what way is it evident? As a preliminary to answering that
question, let me refer once more to Milton, or rather to a certain
accusation which has been levelled against him. It has been said
that Milton 'exhibits a feeling *for* words rather than a capacity
for feeling *through* words; that we are often, in reading him,
moved to comment that he is "external" or that he "works from
outside"'. I believe the accusation may have originated in Cambridge, but you will not wish the laws of hospitality to restrain
me from voicing the serious doubt I feel whether so large a
quantity of error has ever been compressed into so small a
quantity of words. You have not invited me to lecture to you
on Milton; but my point is, not that these observations are
wrong about Milton, but that they are wrong about Milton
because they must be wrong about anybody. It is the supposed antithesis itself that is misconceived. It is not simply
untrue; it is the painstakingly precise opposite of the truth.
Words and things are just not related in that way, so that the
more you feel of one, the less you feel of the other. It was a nearly
contemporary poet who casually remarked that names meant
so much to him that he regarded them as an important part of
a plant. 'What excites me', he added, 'about a west-country
orchard in spring, is to see not just yellow flowers but, as it were,
the visible words, Wild Daffodils.'[17] And he was there speaking,
not as a poet or a critic, but as a botanist.

Coleridge's feeling for words was an integral part of his whole deeply-felt philosophy of the true relation between words and thoughts, between thoughts and things, and thus, and thus only, between words and things. Language does not reproduce things; it gives '*outness* to thoughts'.[18] Why is some acquaintance with etymology important? Because it gives us a pretty-pretty feeling for words as distinct from the reality behind them? He could hardly agree less. Let us hear him on the subject:

> In disciplining the mind one of the first rules should be, to lose no opportunity of tracing words to their origin; one good consequence of which will be, that he will be able to use the *language* of sight without being enslaved by its affections. He will at least save himself from the delusive notion, that what is not *imageable* is not *conceivable*.[19]

He will be emancipated, in fact, from that 'despotism of the eye' which is at the root of all shallowness. Imagination is not the slave of images; it is their master. Etymology does not imprison you in words; it frees you from them. It is not the man who knows something of the history of the words he is using, who perhaps instinctively breaks them up into their old component and more concrete parts; it is not he who will use language 'externally'. On the contrary it is only *he* who really *uses* words at all; the others are more often used *by* them. And that, in the last resort, is the difference between literature and journalism.

There are two ways in which the mind can relate itself to reality; and both of them have their importance. If you care to imagine reality as a vast solid sphere and the individual mind as an ant on its surface, one of the things the ant can do is to crawl about over as much of the surface as it has time for. The other thing is to begin from any point where it happens to be, and bore its way in towards the centre. This is rather what can happen when anyone enjoys, studies and meditates on a particular word. That word, the point where he happens to be, becomes the point of penetration. This was very much Coleridge's way. And one of the first things this kind of ant discovers is that language is not, as he at first supposed, a kind of thin film spread over the surface of a wordless sphere (a film which he can penetrate by taking care to feel *through* a word and not *for* it), but that the entire sphere is composed of a substance for which 'word' and 'thing' are *both* correct names in different contexts. 'I would endeavour', Coleridge wrote to Godwin in 1800, 'to destroy the old antithesis of *Words* and *Things*, elevating, as it were, words into Things, and living Things too. All the nonsense of vibrations etc. you would of course dismiss.'[20]

In other words, if your goal is reality, or truth, or Life with a capital 'L', or whatever your favourite nickname may be for the sphere *as* a sphere, and if you are anxious to get at it *through* words, one of the sharpest instruments you can use is a deep feeling *for* words, and for their history. You will be all the better equipped for finding out how *things* came to be what they are, if you know something of how *words* came to be what they are. Of this Coleridge was profoundly aware and in this respect also he is a true representative of the Romantic school. For a new, and above all a historical, approach to language, as evinced by such men as von Humboldt and Friedrich Schlegel, can almost be said to have presided over the birth of the movement.

We have begun the transition to yet a third level of meaning in my carefully chosen title. For the word 'enjoyment' is used not only of impact experiences, as when we speak of enjoying a meal or a play, but also of states or conditions of the whole organism, as when we speak of enjoying good health. Indeed in the strictest sense – that in which the philosopher S. W. Alexander disjoined it from its opposite, 'contemplation'[21] – it would be equally appropriate to speak of 'enjoying' ill health! The relation it now expresses is nearly one of identity. Identity, I mean, between the enjoyer and what is enjoyed. And I believe Coleridge enjoyed words in this sense also. He was somehow aware of them as a motion in the depths of his being, and very little that he thought about anything was altogether disengaged from that motion. He saw, he felt, the face of nature and the whole process of creation as the self-division of one active Power into two forces, the one relatively active and the other relatively passive; he saw, he felt, the whole development of language as the self-division of the I AM that is neither verb nor noun (or that is both at the same time) into verb and noun respectively; and as consisting at all stages of its development of parts of speech, some of which have more of the verb and others more of the noun quality in them. And these were not two processes, the one of which is analogous to the other, but one single process. One of his names for it was 'Separative Projection'.[22]

In that direction so far, and no further. It is not my intention to expound the 'dynamic philosophy'. What I do want to suggest is that it is perhaps because of such an intimate union of his own genius with the genius or spirit of language that his positive contributions to the thought of his age, and I would say of posterity, are so often to be found focused or concentrated in some particular word. And the same is true of those prophetic anticipations, to which attention has often been drawn, of whole modes of thought which were later on to become part of the intellectual climate of every day. For example, it is almost a commonplace now that Coleridge was exploring, writing and philosophising about the unconscious mind a hundred years or so before it became the fashion to do so. And in Chapter iv of the *Biographia Literaria* we find him running together the words 'collective unconscious';[23] it is true with a comma between them, as parallel adjectives; not as adjective and noun; but all the same there they are lying on the page together, and with the authentic synthesised meaning.

But let me try to arrange things in better order; because I want to conclude with a few examples that will illustrate not only this element of semantic prophecy, but also the various ways of enjoying words of which I spoke earlier; and, which (as I pointed out) you find in Coleridge at many different points in the gamut between seriousness and levity. One of these was the evocation of etymologically latent meaning. Here I found it convenient to wander off into Milton; but I ought not to let it go without a few overt examples from Coleridge himself. In one of his letters he takes to pieces the word *acquaintance*,[24] contrasting it with two imaginary parallels, *in-quaintance* (which baby Hartley had invented at the age of five) and *con-quaintance*. In another, accusing himself of *indolence*,[25] he goes on to break down the word into its components *in-* and *dolere*, as he points out that one of the three meanings he assigns to it is simply 'freedom from pain'. The etymology of *enthusiasm*[26] naturally attracts his attention, as it had done that of others before his time. In the *Theory of Life* the concrete, the planar significance of the – *plan* – in *explanation* is important for the distinction he draws between an *explanation* and a *hypothesis*.[26] In his *Essays on*

Method he imparts a certain movement to the word *method* itself by at once dissecting and reinvigorating it into a *meta-hodos*, a road or way that is a 'progressive transition' towards a goal.[27] The fact that *uttering* means 'outer-ing' did not escape his notice.[28] The very root of both his psychology and his philosophy is not indeed dependent on, but neither is it wholly extricable from, the intimate connection between *conscious* and *conscience*, or from the fact that both words break down into *con-scire*.[29]

It would be wrong, I think, to omit all reference to the numerous disused or abandoned words which he reintroduced, even though many of them have since been abandoned again; and perhaps it is well if, in doing so, we bear in mind those remarks on the 'pregnant terminology', the 'bone and muscle' he detected in the diction of the schools.[30] If a single word was available for conveying a whole complex of meaning, he was glad to snap it up, never mind how old-fashioned it might sound; *coadunation* (to which I have already referred), *alterity, ipseity,*[31] *objectize,*[32] *circumvolving,*[33] *solifidian,*[34] *illapse,*[35] *radicative,*[36] *involvent.*[37] What he disliked much more than being unfashionable was vagueness and confusion of thought. To avoid that, if he could not find an old word, he was prepared to coin a new one, though he held that, if possible, both the unusual and the newly-made should be avoided. Or so he claimed. 'Unusual and new-coined words', he remarks in Chapter xii of the *Biographia*, 'are doubtless an evil; but vagueness, confusion and imperfect conveyance of our thoughts, are a far greater.'[38]

In view of this principle it is perhaps surprising to see how often he found the evil unavoidable. For he did in fact employ a great many unusual words and coin a great many new ones, some of which, like *potenziate,*[39] *neuropathology,*[40] *psychosomatic,*[41] are still with us today (in the last case very much with us), while others, like *generific,*[42] *instinctivity,*[43] *centro-peripheric*[44] and *clerisy,*[45] have not been picked up, though some of them at least might well have proved equally useful. *Esemplastic*, focusing his whole concept of creative imagination, lies somewhere between the two. It *has* been picked up, but only by the English School.* Before I add any more examples, however, let

* For a valuable account of this and other critical terms coined or reintroduced by Coleridge, see J. Isaacs, 'Coleridge's Critical Termin-

me concede that to affirm positively that Coleridge or anyone
else 'coined', i.e. was the first to use, a word should nearly always
be qualified by 'as far as we know'. Except in the occasional
instances (*esemplastic* is one of them), where he actually *tells* us
he is coining, and why, all I really mean by it is that his own
use is either the earliest one quoted in the Oxford Dictionary or
else is earlier than the earliest. Exhaustive research in such a
field is of course impossible and I am not criticising that monument of learning, which I so much admire and love, when I add
that each of the following words was used by Coleridge before
the date of its earliest citation in the Dictionary: *idoloclast*,[46]
energic,[47] *organific*,[48] *narcissism*,[49] and *heuristic*;[50] while his
synartesis and *impetite*[51] (by analogy and contrast to 'appetite')
are not included in the dictionary at all.

All these, and no doubt many others I have failed to notice,
could be added to the examples (*psilosophy, pantisocracy*, and
so forth) which I included under the heading of humorous
pedantry. One that I have not yet mentioned under any heading
is *desynonymise*,[52] which is of particular interest, because it is
not only one of Coleridge's inventions but is also his name for
one of the most fruitful contributions that, in his view, can be
deliberately offered by a writer to the development of his native
language. Its meaning is, I think, fairly obvious. He was operating with it, when he carefully distinguished his *multeity*[53] from
the current *multiplicity* (which implies not simply 'many', but
a 'great many'), and when he sought to distinguish the pre-
valent notion of *synthesis*, as a fairly crude kind of joining
together, from his own notion of it as total interpenetration –
and to do so by reserving *synthesis* for his own notion, and
allocating *synartesis* to the cruder one.[54] But desynonymisation
need not necessarily entail coinage. It may demand only a vigil-
ance to detect and seize and use what is already there. A potential distinction between two existing synonyms may be already
stirring dimly within the genius of a language, 'an instinct of
growth', as he calls it in that fourth chapter of the *Biographia*
to which I have already referred, and where once again we do
actually see the word being coined – 'an instinct of growth, a

certain collective, unconscious good sense working progressively to desynonymize . . . words originally of the same meaning'.

This occurs of course in the passage where he is introducing *the* desynonymisation, for which he is most widely known, his distinction between *fancy* and *imagination*. Actually I think Coleridge's influence on *meanings* is a profounder and, in the long term, a more interesting study than his additions to our stock of words. I would say there is room for more than one dissertation on it; but of course it soon takes you away from language as such and into deeper waters. Concerning his influence on the meaning of the word *imagination* itself much, and perhaps too much, has already been written. But there are others which have received no attention at all. If you look up the word *interpenetration* in the Oxford Dictionary, the earliest quotation you will find for it is from Coleridge. Can we therefore say that he 'coined' the word? It would be a fairly rash assumption, and I am not sure that it matters much. What does matter is the way in which, the meaning *with* which, he used it. Shelley, we should find, was also quite fond of it, but for him it usually, perhaps always, signified merely an intenser degree of ordinary 'penetration', uni-directional penetration, if I may use the term. In Coleridge it normally signifies mutual, *reciprocal*, either-other penetration – penetration of A by B as well as of B by A – and that is a process which is not only beyond precise conception, but even beyond imagination, though not, I think, beyond that intimate marriage between precise conception and imagination which Coleridge himself desiderated. Or again, look up the word *polarity*, about which his commentators have been so lukewarm, although he himself insists so firmly and frequently that it is the basis of his whole system. You will find, not indeed that he was the first to use it, but that he *was* (as far as the O.E.D. is aware) the first to use it in the all-important sense '2b', that is, the *general* sense of 'exhibiting opposite or contrasted properties or powers in opposite or contrasted directions'.[55] Look up *energy* and you will find him heading the citations illustrating 'Sense 3'. But this line of inquiry, though it may begin with the enjoyment of words, soon takes us beyond, beneath and above it. It could launch us on the whole question of Coleridge's thought and of the significance it may or may not have for the thought of the future. Not a bad threshold perhaps to have reached at the latter end of the last of a series of lectures celebrating his bicentenary.

But not one to cross. Indeed there is much more I could have said without crossing it. For instance, although I have said much of his *use* of words, I have said almost nothing of his frequently shrewd and penetrating *comments* on them and on their history; I had hoped in that connection to retail his fascinating gloss on the name *haemony*,[56] which Milton gave to the magic herb in *Comus*. However, there is just not time for it, and anyway I have said more than enough about Milton already. What I may perhaps hope I have done is to illustrate fairly fully the way in which that faculty for enjoying words informed all the different levels of Coleridge's mentality, all of them, from the level of jesting, and even rather silly jesting, to the highest and deepest concerns of the human spirit.

Leigh Hunt's son tells how his father and Charles Lamb were once subjected to a long monologue by Coleridge concerning the blessings of faith. As they came away, Hunt said to Lamb: 'What makes Coleridge talk in that way about heavenly grace, and the holy church, and that sort of thing?' To which Lamb, who had a slight stammer, replied: 'Ah, there is a g-great deal of fun in Coleridge!'[57] I have wondered, and perhaps I may leave you wondering, whether this gentle snub was simply a piece of Elian mischief (it was certainly that as well), or whether it may not have sprung from a subtle perception – and Lamb could be very perceptive – of the subtle interpenetration that went on between those contrasted levels of his old friend's mind, of the intricately organic unity that informed that whole vast, sprawling, complicated structure which in 1772 was christened Samuel Taylor.

A Stream by Glimpses:
Coleridge's later Imagination*

John Beer

It is not unfitting, considering the unobtrusive but important contributions of his later writings to the development of nineteenth-century theology, that a lecture to commemorate Coleridge should be given in a church; it is more particularly fitting that it should take place in this church, where, some ten years ago, his body was finally reburied after many years of neglect – and where a large congregation (including the late T. S. Eliot) gathered to honour him in a ceremony which was more like a serious marriage-feast than a second funeral. Yet one is also driven to reflect that when his most brilliant work was achieved he was a unitarian preacher veering towards pantheism; while this in turn recalls an immortal exchange with Lamb. 'Lamb', said Coleridge once, 'You have heard me preach, I think?' 'Coleridge', he replied, 'I have never heard you do anything else.'[1]

Dealing with Coleridge often brings one up against such disparities. It is the eccentric and comic aspects of his career that are likely to strike the newcomer most sharply: the scheme of Pantisocracy by the Susquehanna; the enlistment as a dragoon under an assumed name; the later tendency to buttonhole people (or whole groups of people) for hours on end. Yet through the humorous and sometimes exasperated recollections of his friends there breathes a different sense. For some reason, it seems, he mattered immensely to them – as if there were something rare and special about him – almost as if (as someone said of Johnson

* Coleridge Memorial Lecture for the bicentenary year given in St Michael's Church, Highgate.

after his death) 'no-one else could be said to put you in mind of him'. Carlyle once declared that he never heard him discourse without feeling ready to worship him and toss him in a blanket.[2] Two hundred years later, we are still left asking just what it was that made him so maddening yet also so attractive.

Perhaps we ought to begin a stage further back. Towards the end of Benjamin Britten's opera, *Noye's Fludde*, there comes a moment which is at once splendid and curiously poignant. The flood is over. The surviving animals and human beings stand on dry land and, as sun, moon and stars move slowly into sight, they sing a hymn to the creation. The music of the hymn is a grand and stately version of Thomas Tallis's Canon and the opera is based on a medieval morality play, but the words that are being sung belong to a different age again. For the hymn is Addison's 'The Spacious Firmament on High' – a poem which is, in its way, about the death of the Middle Ages. There is, after all, no physical heaven above the dark universe; there is no music of the spheres. Yet Addison is undismayed:

> What though in solemn silence all
> Move round the dark terrestrial ball;
> What though nor real voice nor sound
> Amid their radiant orbs be found;
> In reason's ear they all rejoice,
> And utter forth a glorious voice;
> For ever singing as they shine,
> 'The hand that made us is Divine.'

In the music of the opera, the last line goes on reverberating through the parts of the canon, giving a sense of distance and splendour; but if one pays attention to the actual words one may feel a certain disquiet. Addison is calm, rational and neo-classical: 'What though in solemn silence all . . . In reason's ear they all rejoice . . .' But one has only to shift one's view a little to find oneself saying, 'What though in reason's ear they all rejoice . . . there is no *real* voice or sound'. The vision correspondingly darkens; and by Coleridge's time, at the end of the century, there were many who were beginning to pose the question in that second, more sombre form.

From Coleridge himself, in his early poetry, we hear a different question. Where Addison had been content to ask, in dignified self-assurance, 'What though?' Coleridge is willing to expose himself with a more daring 'And what if?' How can we be so sure that Newton has had the last word? Can we be certain that we live in a universe which is, in the ultimate infinity of its time and space, darkened and silent? Could it be that after all – and in a physical sense – the forces of light and life are more dominant than we think? Can we be sure that the creative force stands outside the universe, making it no more than a vast machine? May it even be that it energises in every living thing?

> And what if all of animated nature
> Be but organic Harps, diversely fram'd
> That tremble into thought, as o'er them sweeps
> Plastic and vast, one intellectual breeze,
> At once the Soul of each, and God of all?   (PW I 102)

So he writes in 'The Eolian Harp'; and in 'Religious Musings', having described the spirits 'of plastic power' that 'Roll thro' the grosser and material mass/ In organizing surge', he goes on to ask, parenthetically, 'And what if Monads of the infinite mind?'

There is something other than speculative inquiry in such questions; something more like delight in a magical view of the universe – a Blakean sense that we may understand the universe better in a moment of wonder than we do in the process of anatomisation and dissection. It was a side of him that his friends commented on. From Lamb we hear of the adolescent discoursing in the cloister of Christ's Hospital, holding the casual passer-by spellbound while 'he weighed the disproportion between the speech and the garb of the young Mirandula' (Lamb is probably thinking not merely of Pico della Mirandola himself, but of another young prodigy, John Donne).* He describes how Coleridge, translating Schiller in 1799, would sit in a dressing-gown and look like a conjuror.[3] Sixteen years later he wrote of him, now returned to London and at Highgate, '"Tis enough to be within the whiff and wind of his genius, for us not to possess our souls in quiet.'[4]

Again, one thinks of Hazlitt, finding new worlds open to him as he heard Coleridge preach at Shrewsbury and was then invited

---

* The spelling 'Mirandula' is that used by Isaak Walton, describing Donne at the age of eleven. Cf. my *Coleridge the Visionary* (1959) p. 308.

to visit him at Nether Stowey: '*I was to visit Coleridge in the spring.* This circumstance was never absent from my thoughts and mingled with my feelings.'[5] Or of De Quincey, some years later, when misfortunes had begun to overtake Coleridge, going to meet him for the first time in Bridgwater, seeing the man who must be him in a gateway yet finding it hard to bring him out of his reverie into a sense of daylight realities.[6] Or, for that matter, of Wordsworth, declaring in old age that Coleridge was the only *wonderful* man that he had ever known.[7]

If Coleridge's sense of magic, and his power to impress that sense on others, was his most memorable characteristic, it also created problems for him. It was not just that he sometimes succumbed to the temptation to dazzle with borrowed learning when his own resources refused to flow; he was also forced to distinguish continually in his own mind between the compellingly delusive fantasy and the genuine imaginative insight. Yet he never lost the conviction that, however far the attractions of human fancy might sometimes lead one astray, it was possible to trace, within the deeper workings of human imagination, a key to the nature of ultimate reality. Of Boehme, for example, he wrote in 1818:

> Behmen was a Visionary in two very different senses of that word. Frequently does he mistake the dreams of his own over excited nerves, the phantoms and witcheries from the cauldron of his own seething Fancy, for parts or symbols of a universal Process; but frequently likewise does he give incontestible proof that he possessed in very truth 'The Vision and the Faculty Divine!'[8]

and a few years later he wrote to Allsop:

> It is a source of strength and comfort to know, that the labors and aspirations and sympathies of the genuine and invisible Humanity exist in a social world of their own, that it's attractions and assimilations are no platonic fable, no dancing flames or luminous bubbles on the magic cauldron of my Wishes; but that there are even in this unkind life spiritual parentages, and filiations of the soul . . .   (CL v 176)

By this time, Coleridge had passed through many disillusion-ments and could write (in paradoxically imaginative prose) that Nature was bound to win the unequal struggle in the end:

> But alas! alas! that Nature is a wary wily long-breathed old Witch, tough-lived as a Turtle and divisible as the polyp, repullulative in a thousand Snips and Cuttings, *integra et in toto!* She is sure to get the better of Lady MIND in the long run, and to take her revenge too – transforms our To Day into a Canvass dead-colored to receive the dull featureless Portrait of Yesterday ... (CL v 497)

Yet to the end of his life what he had been in the past left its mark. John Sterling wrote:

> It is painful to observe in Coleridge, that with all the kindness and glorious far-seeing intelligence of his eye there is a glare in it, a light half unearthly, half morbid. It is the glittering eye of the Ancient Mariner.[9]

Our difficulty, of course, is to locate more precisely the quality to which his friends alluded. One thing that most of them agreed on was that his published works – with the exception of his greatest poems – gave no adequate picture of him. The best of Coleridge, they said, came out in his conversation. But even the records of his conversation are not as helpful as one might hope. There are partial exceptions – Hazlitt's Essay 'My first Acquaintance with Poets', or some of De Quincey's writings, for instance – but even here there is a note of underlying disenchantment.

The most fascinating and tantalising account of all is a swift record in one of Keats's letters. Walking towards Highgate, he met Mr Green, who had been his demonstrator at Guy's Hospital, in conversation with Coleridge in the lane by Ken Wood. 'After enquiring by a look whether it would be agreeable – I walked with him at his alderman-after-dinner pace for two miles I suppose. In those two miles he broached a thousand things – let me see if I can give you a list – Nightingales, Poetry – on Poetical Sensation. ...'[10]

At this point the reader sits up, remembering that the year is 1819 and that shortly afterwards Keats is to write a poem entitled 'Ode to a Nightingale'; but since the rest of the account consists of no more than a line of headings, he falls back disappointed. The biographers of Keats have generally agreed that

its main service is to indicate how Coleridge could never keep
to any subject for more than two minutes at a time.

Another dramatic and less sympathetic account was given still
later by Thomas Carlyle. I am thinking of the chapter in his
Life of John Sterling which begins, 'Coleridge sat on the brow
of Highgate Hill, in those years, looking down on London and
its smoke-tumult, like a sage escaped from the inanity of life's
battle...'. Carlyle has previously given a picture of Coleridge
some five years after Keats had met him: 'a fat, flabby, incur-
vated personage, at once short, rotund, and relaxed, with a
watery mouth, a snuffy nose, a pair of strange brown, timid, yet
earnest-looking eyes, a high tapering brow, and a great bush of
grey hair ... a kind good soul, full of religion and affection and
poetry and animal magnetism'.[11]

Carlyle, too, describes Coleridge's conversation. This account
is tellingly destructive, for one remembers the dart of the author's
incisive wit rather than his accompanying touches of admiration:

> He began anywhere: you put some question to him, made
> some suggestive observation: instead of answering this, or
> decidedly setting out towards answer of it, he would accumu-
> late formidable apparatus, logical swim-bladders, transcen-
> dental life-preservers and other precautionary and vehiculatory
> gear for setting out; perhaps did at last get under way,—but was
> swiftly solicited, turned aside by the glance of some radiant new
> game on this hand or that, into new courses; and ever into
> new; and before long into all the Universe, where it was
> uncertain what game you would catch, or whether any.
>
> (Carlyle 73)

By now the damage is too great for the reader to pay much
attention to indications of a different kind; sometimes, says
Carlyle, those who had started conversations of their own in
despair would stop and turn back:

> Glorious islets, too, I have seen rise out of the haze; but they
> were few, and soon swallowed in the general element again.
> Balmy sunny islets, islets of the blest and the intelligible: —
> on which occasions those secondary humming groups would
> all cease humming, and hang breathless upon the eloquent
> words; till once your islet got wrapt in the mist again, and
> they could recommence humming.   (Ibid. 74)

Any ameliorating effect is in any case shattered a moment later
when Carlyle drops us, a thousand fathoms, to his picture of
Coleridge being offered a cup of tea by Mrs Gillman at one of
those gatherings:

> 'Ah, your tea is too cold, Mr Coleridge!' mourned the good
> Mrs. Gilman once, in her kind, reverential and yet protective
> manner, handing him a very tolerable though belated cup. –
> 'It's better than I deserve!' snuffed he, in a low hoarse mur-
> mur, partly courteous, chiefly pious, the tone of which still
> abides with me: 'It's better than I deserve!'   (Ibid. 75)

A truly bathetic moment; yet, when we reach it – if, that is, we
are reading with some degree of sympathy for Carlyle's victim
– we may begin to glimpse something that has become increasingly evident with the publication over the past twenty years of
his letters and notebooks – that there survives in the records of
Coleridge one of the most extensive documentations for the
picture of the totality of a sensitive human being that has ever
existed – one which registers not only the full range of an
extraordinary and wide-ranging intelligence but the heights and
depths of a brilliant yet mercurial temperament.

For some modern critics, indeed, such an approach might
seem the most profitable one. Suspicious of anything that savours
of the 'bardic', they find Coleridge's career an *exemplum*, a
brilliant disaster, furnishing one either with a series of occasions
to point the finger of moral disapprobation or (if one is of a more
generous turn) with a vivid exposé of conditions that subsist in
each one of us. But is this really enough? Is Coleridge's career,
then, no more than a fascinating and instructive case-history?
We look back to that enigmatic figure at Highgate and wonder.

I remember that when I first came across Carlyle's account I
was struck by a curiously familiar – almost nursery-rhyme –
note in that first phrase: 'Coleridge sat on the brow of Highgate
Hill . . .'. It was a long time before I attended closely enough to
identify it, though when I did the echo was obvious: it was
Dick Whittington, of course, who also sat on Highgate Hill –
and heard the London bells sounding 'Turn again'. In the context of Carlyle's account, however, any such echoes are sombre.
Coleridge did not arrive in Highgate until 1816, when he was
43; if a voice was sounding in his head by then one would expect

it to have been more like the refrain in a poem which T. S. Eliot published in his forties: 'Because I do not hope to turn again . . .'. Yet it may be that Highgate did have some retrospective significance of the kind, allowing him as it did to contemplate from a distance the city to which he could never quite return, yet could never quite leave. London, after all, was the place where he had spent his schooldays and (both then and at later times) had dreamed some of his brightest dreams.

The everyday life of the city had not attracted him particularly, to judge from the few descriptions of it that survive among his voluminous writings. Occasionally he will refer to the Exchange, or to a popular preacher, or to current literary fashions; just occasionally one comes across something like this, in a notebook:

> Bright Reflections in the Canals of the blue & green Vitriol Bottles in the Druggists' shops in London.   (CN I 1081)

Even here, however, one feels that his basic preoccupation is elsewhere. It is to Lamb that one goes for a more vivid sense – Lamb, who wrote to the Wordsworths that he could not consider living in the Lakes as an alternative to London:

> O! her lamps of a night! her rich goldsmiths, print-shops, toyshops, mercers, hardwaremen, pastry-cooks! St Paul's Churchyard! The Strand! Exeter Change! Charing Cross, with the man *upon* a black horse! These are thy gods, O London!   (LL I 251)

For Coleridge, I suggest, London had always meant something more elusive. And here we might do worse than look again at that sentence of Carlyle's: 'a kind good soul, full of religion and affection and poetry and animal magnetism'. It is the last two words that are unexpected; and I believe they may provide an important key to the character of Coleridge's lost self.

London in his youth had been full of unusual speculations. Various echoes from the intellectual ferment that accompanied the French Revolution had crossed the English Channel, so that ideas that a few years before would have been dismissed as quackery could be taken for a time more seriously. *And what if* the universe were a more mysterious place than had been supposed in the heyday of eighteenth-century rationalism? New discoveries in electricity and chemistry were already bringing new ideas and images into play; the cult of Gothic romance had drawn attention to strange depths in human nature. Now there arrived the 'animal magnetisers', or hypnotists, who enjoyed an enormous fashionable success. At the height of the craze, it was said, 20,000 people besieged the house of one of them, trying to gain admission.[12]

It was not surprising then, if Coleridge too was fascinated by the phenomenon, for here, it seemed, physical proofs of powers which had nothing to do with the rational were actually being exhibited before men's eyes. And his interest in the subject has been discussed from time to time. Many years ago Professor Lane Cooper collected a surprisingly large number of references to 'the power of the eye' from his poetry,[13] including lines from the first version of *The Ancient Mariner*:

> Listen, O listen, thou Wedding-guest!
>   'Mariner! thou hast thy will:
> For that, which comes out of thine eye, doth make
>   My body and soul to be still.'   (PW II 1040)

Generally, however, Coleridge's interest in animal magnetism has been treated as an isolated phenomenon – just another subject among the many that crowded his inquiring mind. What I want to suggest here is that it had a more basic importance for him than has generally been recognised, and that during those early years in London and Bristol and Nether Stowey he was exploring an ingenious and complicated version of the idea, by which, he hoped, the phenomena of magnetism between living creatures would throw light on the nature of human consciousness itself.

In his notebooks and manuscripts there are occasional references to a theory which he never properly explains, but which he refers to by the terms 'single touch' and 'double touch'. One of the most striking comes in an annotation made, some time after 1815, at the end of a book on animal magnetism. Here he argues that faith, understood as a sort of unifying energy, is most likely to exist in weak and credulous, but sincere, sensitive and warm-hearted men; this is often, he thinks, the case with those who believe in animal magnetism. And he goes on:

> I think it probable, that Animal Magnetism will be found
> connected with a Warmth-Sense: & will confirm my long long
> ago theory of Volition as a mode of _double Touch_.
>
> (PL 423–4)

Fascinating words, certainly; but what do they mean? No one
has been able to suggest a convincing explanation to these and
other references, yet Coleridge's nostalgic language suggests that
the theory was of continuing importance to him.

I believe it is possible to throw more light on the matter once
one discovers that the term 'double touch' was used in the
field of ordinary magnetism in Coleridge's time. It had been
remarked that it was very difficult to obtain a sustained magnetic
effect simply by rubbing one pole of the lodestone (a process
which was called 'simple touch'). If, on the other hand, one
employed what was known as 'double touch', involving both
poles, a much more strong and permanent magnetic effect could
be obtained – apparently because a 'vortex' had been created.

What happened, I would further suggest, is that Coleridge
carried over this observation from the ordinary magnetism of
physics to phenomena associated with animal magnetism. And
one need only consider such a collocation to see the kind of
theory, concerned with the development of human consciousness
in relation to the sense of touch, which might then begin to
emerge. _And what if_ the phenomenon observed in the magnet
were really true of human beings as well? Let us suppose that
all human touch, all human perception contains a magnetised
and magnetising element. It will then follow that, magnetically
speaking, the human being is born into a world of 'simple
touch' or, as Coleridge called it, 'single touch', and gradually
learns a world of 'double touch'. At first all he knows is the
immediacy of the mother's breast and the mother's touch, by
which he remains totally magnetised to and identified with her;
but slowly, and often rather painfully, he learns to explore the
outer world, always through modes of 'double touch'. He learns
to relate the sight of things outside himself to his touching of
them – and as he does so becomes magnetised to them, losing
his pure dependence on the original single human being who
bore him. Slowly, too, he learns to measure the world and control
it, until he does not have to rely on any magnetic relationship

beyond that supplied by his masterful understanding: he is now totally at home in the world of space and time. Nevertheless, beneath the secondary consciousness that has been developed there will remain always a primary level of consciousness, surviving rather like a spring under ice, hidden but in touch with other life-springs in the universe and directly available to the hypnotist's art. If a human being ever becomes so preoccupied with analysis and measurement, however, that he loses touch with that initial magnetism, by which he is enabled to respond directly to other living beings, he will find himself delivered into a world of fixities and definites – a very satisfying world in one sense, perhaps, but one which also has the disadvantage of being basically dead.

This, I believe, is the speculation which seized Coleridge at an early stage in his career and which continued to haunt him for years afterwards. It is not possible here to pursue the various ramifications and the bypaths which it seems to have opened up in his intellectual life,* though to do so helps to illuminate a number of puzzling passages. Nor, of course, am I arguing for the truth of the theory itself. What I am concerned to suggest is that by giving Coleridge a framework by which he could think of human consciousness as operating at distinguishable levels, it brought into focus for him a great many phenomena associated with such things as dreams, trance states, poetic imagination and effective modes of education – and even, at the height of his speculations, helped to open up the new poetic modes which we find at work in his poems of the supernatural.

As an example of a poem in which some elements of the speculation seem significantly operative, we may turn to 'The Nightingale', written in April 1798. The central theme of the poem, as in some of Wordsworth's at the same period, is exposure to nature. The poet rebukes that false, substituted artifice which causes 'youths and maidens' who spend their time in 'ballrooms and hot theatres' to 'heave their sighs/O'er Philomela's pity-pleading strains' when, if they listened to actual nightingales, they might discover their song to be not melancholy but joyful.

In the middle of the poem, Coleridge introduces a passage

* I hope to explore some of them in a forthcoming study.

concerning a maiden who sometimes goes into a nearby wood to listen to the nightingales. It is here that we become aware of a more esoteric note – as if the nightingales are transmitting an inward joy that is always present in nature; as if, indeed, they are physically stimulated to do so by a radiation from the moon.

> A most gentle Maid,
> Who dwelleth in her hospitable home
> Hard by the castle, and at latest eve
> (Even like a Lady vowed and dedicate
> To something more than Nature in the grove)
> Glides through the pathways; she knows all their notes,
> That gentle Maid! and oft, a moment's space,
> What time the moon was lost behind a cloud,
> Hath heard a pause of silence; till the moon
> Emerging, hath awakened earth and sky
> With one sensation, and those wakeful birds
> Have all burst forth in choral minstrelsy,
> As if some sudden gale had swept at once
> A hundred airy harps! And she hath watched
> Many a nightingale perch giddily
> On blossomy twig still swinging from the breeze,
> And to that motion tune his wanton song
> Like tipsy Joy that reels with tossing head.

Coleridge concludes by telling of an occasion when he had comforted his baby son, who had woken crying, by hurrying him into their little orchard:

> And he beheld the moon, and, hushed at once,
> Suspends his sobs, and laughs most silently,
> While his fair eyes, that swam with undropped tears,
> Did glitter in the yellow moon-beam! (PW I 266–7)

'Well!' he continues, 'It is a father's tale . . .' But even as he says so we may sense the underground working of his speculative mind. *And what if* the known power of the moon to affect not only the tides but the mental balance of the disturbed mind indicates the presence of some more powerful magnetism, which operates on all living things and induces the sense of magic that is sometimes experienced in looking at a moonlit scene? Could it be that Hartley's sudden change of mood was not just a simple movement of delight but a physiological reaction to an actual impulse?

Such a speculation, carefully guarded in 'The Nightingale', could be indulged more freely in an avowedly supernatural poem such as *The Ancient Mariner*. That poem, also, appears in a new light when examined in the context of the speculation I have suggested: it seems, indeed, to have been written (among other things) on the supposition that if one were to deprive a man of all the props which are normally set up by his customary, reinforced perceptions in time and space he might be enabled to see more clearly his place in the nature of things through the terrors involved in that loss. After his crime the Mariner finds himself delivered into a world without sense of motion; where time has ceased; where there is nothing to relieve the blazing scene before his eyes – not even water to assuage his thirst. In that state, a nightmare state of enforced 'single touch', where even the eyes of his shipmates are 'fixed' upon him, the Mariner finds no solace until he is able to respond to the movement of the moon and feel delight in the play of the watersnakes. When that happens, however, he perceives the link of all life, the fountain of his heart is suddenly opened ('a spring of love gushed from my heart, and I blessed them unaware') and he is restored to the most rapturous form of 'single touch' – rain after thirst, the breeze on the cheek after throbbing heat. There is even a visionary moment at dawn in which he sees and hears sounds flying back and forth from the spirits who have entered his dead shipmates to the sun, as if to a fountain of light and music. He returns to his own country with a new depth of knowledge.

Yet that knowledge is also a curse; if it has transformed the world of sense experience for him, making him see blessing where he might previously have seen no more than dull routine, it has also isolated him from men who have lost such vision, forcing him to seek out those who will be responsive to the power of his magnetic eye and willing to listen to his story. He can renew himself by the catharses of repeated tellings, it seems, but he cannot restore himself to the central harmony which he was momentarily allowed to glimpse.

After he had written *The Ancient Mariner* and begun work on *Christabel* Coleridge went to Germany and there, it seems, fell into disenchantment concerning animal magnetism. We hear

no more from him on that subject for many years, apart from a
disparaging reference in the *Friend* of 1809.[14] But the secondary
speculations that had been set in motion seem to have continued
unabated for a time; particularly when he was in conversation
with Wordsworth. Did the two poets talk together about the
noise of streams and their relationship to the inner consciousness? Certainly we find among Wordsworth's early drafts for
the poem which became *The Prelude* the melancholy reflection:

> Was it for this
> That one, the fairest of all rivers loved
> To blend his murmur with my nurse's song
> And from the alder shades and rocky falls
> And from his fords and shallows sent a voice
> To intertwine my dreams . . .
>
> (MS JJ; W Prel 633)

Did Coleridge talk about the work of spring breezes in giving
us a sense of freedom and wholeness as human beings in the
world of sense (counterfeiting the original, paradisal 'single
touch', so to speak)? Again, we find Wordsworth addressing
himself to his poem in a more cheerful vein and starting his
final draft for *The Prelude* with the lines,

> O there is blessing in this gentle breeze
> That blows from the green fields and from the clouds
> And from the sky: it beats against my cheek,
> And seems half-conscious of the joy it gives . . .
>
> (W Prel (1805) I 1–4)

Coleridge, meanwhile, continued to introspect and investigate
anything that might bear on his idea. Magnetism, as such, may
have dropped away, but he was still convinced of an important
relationship between the 'double touch' by which human beings
dealt with the external world and that 'single touch' which
occasionally delivered them into a different state. We find this,
for example, in the notebooks:

Night-mair is . . . a state not of Sleep but of Stupor of the
outward organs of Sense . . . and when ever this derangement
occasions an interruption in the circulation, aided perhaps by
pressure . . . the part deadened – as the hand, or his arm, or

the foot & leg, on this side, transmits double Touch as single Touch: to which the Imagination therefore, the true inward Creatrix, instantly out of the chaos of the elements ⟨or shattered fragments⟩ of Memory puts together some form to fit it.   (CN III 4046)

Or we find him investigating the way that his own children learn to speak, and trying to discover whether the whole process does not involve some subtle and immediate process through a primary sense of touch. 'Hartley,' he writes, 'seemed to learn to talk by touching his mother.'[15]

Such trains of speculations were given a new force many years later when he learned that certain German philosophers were giving new attention to the phenomena of hypnotism itself, and that the Blumenbach who had been sceptical on the subject at the time when he heard him lecture at Göttingen had since been convinced concerning hypnotic powers. For several years Coleridge returned to the subject with renewed interest, though forced in the end to confess a state of 'philosophical doubt' on the subject. The evidence was 'too strong and consentaneous for a candid mind to be satisfied of its falsehood' yet 'too fugacious and infixable to support any theory that supposes the always potential, and under certain conditions and circumstances, occasionally active, existence of a correspondent faculty in the human soul'.[16] The dream, in other words, of discovering a firm key to human nature through study of magnetic effects had after all eluded him.

At the same time, the sense that some sort of truth was involved – that there was a mystery involved in the depths of the human consciousness which might correspond to the mystery at the heart of the universe, seems never to have finally deserted Coleridge. It was perhaps one of the secrets of his success with younger men that the marks of the suffering through which he had passed, coupled with a surviving, magnetic earnestness in his discourse, forced them to listen. To such younger people he preached a form of Christianity which had its own relation to his theories of the mind, arguing for an acceptance of Christianity on the grounds that in the act of commitment a human being comes to know the truth of a movement or a relationship in a way that could never be discovered by standing outside it.[17]

For him, evidently, an awareness that action magnetises the mind into 'knowledge' had breathed new life into religious sayings such as the ancient 'Believe and thou shalt know'.

By then, however, Coleridge had long passed into a more sombre phase. Ill-health, drugs and the burden of a hopeless love had sapped the powers on which he had previously drawn. To the Wordsworth household he had ceased to be a fountain of life and new ideas, becoming instead a listless and brooding presence. When the rift widened further he had left the Lakes, never to return. He had passed through periods of gross ill-health and despair; sometimes, in his attempts to keep going, he had resorted to prevarications which are unpleasant to contemplate.

Yet it would have been easy for him to have given up altogether, or to have chosen some easier literary path. If he did not, the motive would seem to have been something other, or more, than pride. There was a persisting sense of urgency, a sense that he had important things to say to his generation. And if this now came to crystallise itself in religious statements, appeals to the old forms of belief on the grounds that these were the truths that 'find' a man, such appeals may still be seen to draw on his old sense of a subconscious force in human beings, causing them to thirst for restoration to a primal condition in which all are linked, all drink at the same infinite sun-fountain.

Nor could Coleridge wholly dissociate his religious sense from his feeling for nature, even in old age. On Midsummer Day, 1827, for example, his nephew records his response to an unusually fine sunset:

The sun was setting behind Caen Wood, and the calm of the evening was so exceedingly deep that it arrested Mr Coleridge's attention. We were alone together in Mr Gillman's drawing-room, and Mr C. left off talking, and fell into an almost trance-like state for ten minutes whilst contemplating the beautiful prospect before us. His eyes swam in tears, his head inclined a little forward, and there was a slight uplifting of the fingers which seemed to tell me that he was in prayer. I was awe-stricken, and remained absorbed in looking at the man, in forgetfulness of external nature, when he recovered himself, and after a word or two fell by some secret link of association upon Spenser's poetry ...   (TT 24 June 1827)

One poem which he chose for particular comment was 'Protha-lamion', with its refrain that keeps the sense of a stream running through the whole: 'Sweet Thames! run softly till I end my song'. Henry Nelson Coleridge recalls the 'sensible diversity of tone and rhythm' with which he repeated the lines, and then records how Coleridge 'talked a volume of criticism that day, which, printed verbatim as he spoke it, would have made the reputation of any other person but himself'. He concludes wryly, 'I left him at night so thoroughly *magnetized*, that I could not for two or three days afterwards reflect enough to put anything on paper.'

A similar obsessive strain may also be traced in Coleridge's philosophical writings, his sense that the human psyche operates at more than one level giving rise to a number of original insights. A central theme of his philosophy, as Thomas McFarland has shown in his book,[18] was the assertion of a qualitative distinction between the sort of statement involved in saying 'I am' and the sort of statement involved in saying 'it is'; we might add that the Coleridge who never ceased to see the wonder that is in-herent in things most often taken for granted, saw at the centre of all his wonder the miracle involved in communicative lan-guage. The fact that human beings are able to recognise one another's signals (however inadequately at times) is, as soon as one begins to consider it, one of the great wonders of the world. On this he never ceased to ponder; and it was this that drew him back again and again to that mysterious statement which opens one of the Christian gospels: 'In the beginning was the Word, and the Word was with God, and the Word was God'.

He hoped, indeed, to build a part of his great projected philo-sophical work around the theme. A volume was planned, 'on the LOGOS, or the communicative intelligence in nature and in man, together with, and as a preliminary to, a Commentary on the Gospel of St John . . .'[19] in which, we may surmise, he would have tried to convey his sense of a mystery inherent in the very idea of a 'creating word' – all words as being acts of communica-tive intelligence, presupposing the existence of initiating and imitative powers below the level of consciousness, and so, at one and the same moment, both thoughts *and* things – the balance varying between the degree of reflective awareness involved in the words 'I am' and the acknowledgement of objective presence involved in saying 'it is'.

The great work was not to be completed; and in the course of time Coleridge accepted the fact with sad serenity. Many hints and seminal thoughts survive; the system eluded completion. Yet the obsession at the heart of the project never, it seems, wholly left him. Even on the day before his death, having endured months of illness, he was still driven on: that evening he said that there were some final words he wanted to dictate to Joseph Green. He spoke 'with the utmost difficulty':

And be thou sure, in whatever may be published of my posthumous works, to remember that First of all is the Absolute Good, whose Self-affirmation is the 'I AM,' as the Eternal Reality in itself, and the ground and source of all other Reality. And next, that in this Idea, nevertheless, a Distinctivity is to be carefully preserved, as manifested in the person of the LOGOS, by whom that Reality is communicated to all other Beings.[20]

In that distinction is there not still detectable an attempt to isolate the two elements in consciousness – the one that says 'I am' and the one that says 'it is' – and relate them to the central mystery at the heart of the universe?

Coleridge went on to write a long note, giving directions for provision to be made for his servant – it was typical of him not to have done it before, typical of him to have done it just in time – and fell into a coma. His friends were left with an acute sense of loss. 'His great and dear spirit haunts me', wrote Lamb.[21] Wordsworth declared that, although he had seen little of him for twenty years, 'his mind has been habitually present with me';[22] he also paid tribute to his intellectual brilliance, and to his conversation, which he likened to

a majestic river, the sound or sight of whose course you caught at intervals, which was sometimes concealed by forests, sometimes lost in sand, then came flashing out broad and distinct, then again took a turn which your eye could not follow, yet you knew and felt that it was the same river: so there was always a train, a stream, in Coleridge's discourse, always a connection between its parts in his own mind, though one not always perceptible to the minds of others.

(W Pr W III 441)

This observation of Wordsworth's not only serves as a corrective to accounts of his conversation such as Carlyle's but may, on this occasion, be allowed to prompt a final Coleridgian speculation of our own, concerning that tantalising record left by Keats. Keats, too, was preoccupied by the mystery inherent in unusual sensuous and trance-like experiences. And *what if*, we may ask, he recognised in that Highgate conversation with Coleridge a stream, a connection between its parts, a set of speculations linking with ideas of his own? By 1819, as we saw earlier, Coleridge had recovered his respect for animal magnetism. Could it be that his mention of the nightingale was the beginning of a long resuscitation of long-standing ideas, re-emerging, during his hour's discourse, in connected, intelligible order?

It is easy, following the leads of Keats's account, to see how such a train of discourse might have proceeded. He spoke of nightingales – it is even possible that he spoke, as he was to speak a year later (looking towards Ken Wood), of his wish that he could die 'amidst flowers, and the sight of meadowy fields, and the chaunt of birds'.[23] Is it not also conceivable that as he spoke of the nightingale old thoughts revived, reminding him of the sense of joy that he had always associated with their song; and that he spoke of the sensation that responded to their song as running deeper than normal sensation – closer indeed to that central core of warm, vital sensibility where the central act of poetry-making took place?

Once started on the track, he might have gone on to relate this to philosophical issues, declaring that what was central to poetry was central also to metaphysics – that there was a level, below that of straightforward understanding, at which we were conscious of being in touch with reality in a quite different, sometimes frightening, way. This he might have illustrated from dreams: there were different sorts of dreams, some straightforwardly linked to waking consciousness, but others, such as certain nightmares, in which, through some unusual pressure, normal modes of sense experience were disrupted, and the imagination, always present in the primary consciousness, was left to deal with what was given to it as best it could, reacting through terror, or through images associated with previous terrors. And what if Coleridge then went on to recall his 'long long ago theory' of 'double touch' – the double touch by which we link ourselves to the outside world and the single touch which, in its pure form, links us, whether horrifically or beatifically, to infinity? This, he might have argued, could be illustrated not only by the investigation of dreams, but by the presence, in everyday life, of a primary level of consciousness beneath our secondary, perceiving awareness – constantly giving unity and wholeness to what was perceived by the secondary consciousness as a succession of fragments – and linked in turn to the difference between will and volition. Normal volitions were consequent upon accidents of our relationship to the world about us, but the movement of the will was dependent on some working in the primary consciousness – and therefore on more fugitive causes. 'If only philosophers would learn to differentiate between primary and secondary consciousness', we can imagine him saying, 'there would be far less dispute about questions of metaphysics.' He might then have urged the need to infer the operation of the primary consciousness from the workings of superstition. Would people believe in fictitious beings if there were not something deep in their consciousness that *needed* to believe in them? After all, when it came to phenomena like monsters or mermaids one found very rational, sober-minded men ready to credit their existence, even if their belief was so thin that it could not link on to any true cultivation of creative power. For that matter, did not human readiness to interpret some unusual happening, apprehended in fear, as the work of a ghost show the same universal propensity, the same shaping imagination always waiting behind our response to events, ready to step in at the onset of terrors or disorientations and clothe them in an appropriate form?

It is all a fascinating possibility; but of course, we cannot know in detail what Coleridge talked about that afternoon – and we probably would not find it worth while to pursue the attempt were it not for the fact that after that meeting with Coleridge there does seem to be a subtle change in the way that Keats confronted sense-experience. It is as if he became much more aware of the contrast between that state of warm, lulling, life-consciousness in ourselves during which we find it impossible to imagine that we shall die and that bleak contemplation of the bare forms of the world which reminds us that we shall. The clear emergence, for the first time in the 'Ode to a Nightingale' of that twofold conception makes it fair to ask whether something, at least, of the sort did not pass from Coleridge to him that afternoon.

And we do still have the rough heads of Coleridge's discourse in Keats's letter, so that it is at least possible to look at them in their original, bare presentation and see how closely or otherwise they correspond to the sort of speculation that has just been projected around them. Keats's account reads in full as follows:

I walked with him at his alderman-after dinner pace for near two miles I suppose. In those two miles he broached a thousand things – let me see if I can give you a list – Nightingales, Poetry, on Poetical sensation – Metaphysics – Different genera and species of dreams – Nightmare – a dream accompanied by a sense of touch – single and double touch – a dream related – first and second consciousness – the difference explained between will and volition – so many metaphysicians from a want of smoking the second consciousness – monsters – the Kraken – mermaids – Southey believes in them – Southey's belief too much diluted – a ghost story – good morning – I heard his voice as he came towards me – I heard it as he moved away – I had heard it all the interval – if it may be called so.[24]

Or, as he wrote a little later,

> ... thy plaintive anthem fades
> Past the near meadows, over the still stream,
> Up the hill-side; and now 'tis buried deep
> In the next valley-glades:
> Was it a vision, or a waking dream?
> Fled is that music: – do I wake or sleep?

Keats, I believe, saw more deeply into the paradox that was Coleridge than did Carlyle: he glimpsed inside that corpulent body, walking at its alderman-after-dinner pace, a mind that was quite other; haunted still by a sense that in its own depths and workings, if he could only tease it all out, there was a key to everything – a key which would solve all the arguments between science and religion simply by assigning them to different levels of human consciousness; a key to the mysterious fact that in a universe of isolated individualities we do all, in some way, succeed in signalling to one another; a key to our ability to perceive the wholenesses of things and the continuities of things. The originality of Coleridge lies in those obsessive concerns, and in his ability to make us look at the work of imagination in dreams, or the phenomena of friendship and love – or even simply at the power of the mind to see things as unities – and notice them, as if for the first time, as magical.

It is impossible to sum up a man like this in a phrase; the most one can do is to find ways of contemplating the paradoxical relationship between outer man and inner mind; on the one hand the man, searching incessantly for an adequate place in the world for himself, sometimes acting nobly, sometimes prevaricating, sometimes giving in munificent generosity, sometimes cowering in despair, looking always for love from others while demanding in that love an impossible perfection – and on the other the absorbed, inquiring Coleridge that is revealed in his writings:

> A late Physiologist represents the nervous system as a Plant, of which the spinal Cord is the Stem and the Brain the compound Flower – and if you have ever watched a Humble-bee at a Fox-glove or a Monkshood, visiting one Bell after another, and bustling and humming in each, you will have no bad likeness of the dips and dives I have been making into the several cells and campanulae of my Brain.   (CL V 464)

That is Coleridge at his best – a man exploring the riches of his reading and thought and bringing them back with the sense that the cell in which he works is at one with other cells, that at the deepest level he is working in warm sympathy with all other beings who enjoy the cultivation of sweetness and light. Yet it is essential to the man that there should also be a driving impulse (whether to be assigned to personal ambition, or to the age's demand for sublimity, or simply to the 'Eagerness' that his first love found characteristic of him – 'hurrying him into the sad Extreme')[25] that causes him at times to expand to a sense of himself as a centre of radiation, a sun-god figure about whom others, responding in recognition from their depths of consciousness, may weave an enchanted circle – and then, in the sequel, to plunge just as deeply into a vortex of despair, where he is hounded by a sense of guilt and worthlessness. It was not for nothing that when he came to publish *Kubla Khan* he immediately appended to it a poem about his terrible nightmares entitled 'The Pains of Sleep'.

The career of Coleridge confronts us with a series of such paradoxes and self-contradictions – most agonisingly in the relationship with the Wordsworths and Sara Hutchinson, that relationship which seemed to offer him everything he was looking for and yet which turned ineluctably sour, plunging him into the deepest despair of his career. It is perhaps fitting, then, that Sara, the woman whom he loved hopelessly for ten years, should be allowed the last word on Coleridge the man. What she herself felt about him, we hardly know: she left no personal record. But she visited him in his last days; and when she heard of his death and the subsequent post-mortem, this was what she wrote to a friend:

> . . . poor dear Coleridge is gone! He died a most calm & happy death – tho' he had suffered great pain for some time previous – He was opened – the disease was at his Heart.[26]

That last phrase is admirable in the discreet terseness of its charity; yet in summing up the man it instantly returns us to the paradox of his career – for it was precisely in the heart that he had looked for the spring, the fountain that he believed to be opened by the magic key of 'single touch', and to be magnetically linked with all other such life-springs in the universe. And however mistaken that quest may have been, it gave him so much in the way of magical verse and materials for perceptive psychological speculation that we ourselves are left asking whether those obsessive ideas may not, after all, conceal some important truths about the human imagination and its workings.

Coleridge's career, in its intricate processes and riddling self-contradictions, continually beckons one in this way to further thought and investigation rather than to attempts at sweeping evaluation. But this, at least, can be said – that the more one's eye succeeds in penetrating the crust of its admonitory shape to

glimpse the processes of his imagination, for ever gyring between
a warming, evolvent sense of the 'one Life' and chill engulfing
vortices of nightmare, the more one is driven to complement
Sara Hutchinson's factual, resonant statement with some words
from another young prodigy who became a notable preacher in
old age:

> But this infinite Hive of honey, this insatiable whirlpoole of
> the covetous mind, no Anatomy, no dissection hath discovered
> to us . . .[27]

Notes

Introduction

1. Dorothy Emmet, 'Coleridge on the Growth of the Mind', *Bulletin of the John Rylands Library* (Manchester), XXXIV (March 1952); reprinted *Coleridge*, ed. Kathleen Coburn (Twentieth-Century Views) (Englewood Cliffs, N.J., 1967).
2. William Walsh, *Coleridge: The Work and the Relevance* (1967) pp. 85, 89.
3. BL I 15.
4. Sh C I 68–9; II 270; I 20, 54–6, 67.
5. Ibid., I 74.
6. *Friend* I 108.
7. I borrow the phrase from J. A. Appleyard, *Coleridge's Philosophy of Literature* (Cambridge, Mass., 1965). Preface, ix, where, in the singular, it is used as a synonym for 'idea'.
8. Misc C 136.
9. This, and the following examples, ch. xv.
10. BL I 19, II 117. Cf. *Essays in his own Times*, ed. Sara Coleridge (1850) II 543.
11. BL II 117.
12. *The Romantic Age*, René Wellek, *A History of Modern Criticism, 1750–1950* (1955) II 186.
13. BL II 117.
14. *Political Tracts of Wordsworth, Coleridge and Shelley*, R. J. White (ed.), (Cambridge 1953) Introduction, xvi.
15. I 46.
16. *Cambridge Essays, by members of the University* (1856) pp. 324–5.
17. Sh C II 94.
18. CL II 680.

1. Coleridge's Poetic Sensibility

1. House 37.
2. CL I 330–1.
3. CL IV 574.
4. Ibid.
5. BL I 202.
6. Cf. BL I 65–93.

7. BL I 56.
8. CN I 213, 214, 216, 217, 219, 220, 226, 227, 229, 231. At 231 the forward-writing of the notebook ends, and the entries begin from the other end of the book.
9. PW I 226. Ernest Hartley Coleridge however (*Christabel*, 1907, p. 18) referred these lines to observations on Derwent in Oct–Nov 1800, citing CN I 835.
10. See for example CN II 2546, quoted below, pp. 177–8.
11. BL II 121.
12. CL V 496.
13. CN II 1589.
14. *Friend* I 499, where the phrase has to do with the development of 'our cognitions as with our children'.
15. *The Correspondence of G. M. Hopkins and R. W. Dixon*, ed. C. C. Abbott (1935) p. 14.
16. CN III 3708; quoted in part in, House 146, and in my *Coleridge Sara Hutchinson* (1955) p. 111. With the image of the fire attracting the fuel that feeds it, cf CN II 3136: 'Tho' Genius, like the fire on the Altar, can only be kindled from Heaven, yet it will perish unless supplied with appropriate fuel to feed it – or if it meet not with the virtues, whose society alone can reconcile it to earth, it will return whence it came, or at least lie hid as beneath embers, till some sudden & awakening Gust of regenerating Grace αναζωπυρει, rekindles and reveals it anew.'
17. IS 30.
18. CN I 1554.
19. CN I 886.
20. CN I 1649.
21. BL I 178.
22. CN III 4225.
23. CN III 4040.
24. CN III 3295.
25. CN III 3372.
26. David Jones, *An Introduction to 'The Rime of the Ancient Mariner'*, (1972) p. 25.
27. CL I 416. Cf. CN I 335 and *Friend* II 193.
28. CN I 886.
29. PL 67.
30. TL 84–6 (Ashe ed. 418).
31. *Friend* II 187.
32. CL III 5.
33. See for example CN III 4351.

2.   *Coleridge as Revealed in his Letters*

1. Henry James, *Notebooks* (New York, 1947) p. 152.
2. CL I 310.

3. CL I 354.
4. CL V 462; VI 837.
5. E. H. Coleridge (ed.) *Letters of Samuel Taylor Coleridge* (1895) I vii–viii.
6. CL I 294.
7. CL I 454–5.
8. E. K. Chambers, *Samuel Taylor Coleridge* (Oxford, 1938), p. 230.
9. CL II 990–1; I 330–1; II 1015; II 668.
10. CL V 115; VI 903; V 368; VI 790.
11. Virginia Woolf, *Collected Essays* (1967) III 219.
12. Ibid.
13. CL I 534.
14. CL I 279; 295; 294; II 866–7; 1080–3.
15. CL VI 736.
16. CL II 812.
17. CL II 830.
18. CL II 865; 1034.
19. CL III 125–6.
20. CL IV 675.
21. CL I 18.
22. CL I 249–50.
23. CL I 394. See also above, pp. 5, 7.
24. CL I 558.
25. CL III 476; IV 626–7; V 79–80.
26. CL II 740.
27. CL II 767.
28. CL II 884.
29. CL II 888–9.
30. CL II 726.
31. CL III 127.
32. CL III 415.
33. Ibid.
34. CL III 490–2.
35. CL III 477.
36. CL III 490–2.
37. CL III Introd., xxxix–xl.
38. *Huntington Library Quarterly* (1954) XVII 374.
39. CL VI 894.
40. WLR (1787–1805) 212.
41. CL IV 574.
42. Helen Darbishire, *The Poet Wordsworth* (1950) p. 90.
43. Walter Raleigh, *Wordsworth* (1925) pp. 23, 82, 85.
44. Jonathan Wordsworth, *The Music of Humanity* (1969) pp. 200–1.
45. WLR (1787–1805) 264.
46. CL I 631.
47. PW I 447.
48. CL IV 636 and n.
49. CL IV 559–63.

50. Peter Quennell, *Byron, a Self-Portrait* (1950) I 317.
51. Byron, *Letters and Journals*, ed. R. E. Prothero (1901) VI 113.
52. CL IV 888.
53. CL V 453.
54. CL VI 776.
55. CL V 131.
56. CL V 92.
57. Ibid.
58. CL V 28.
59. CL V 12.
60. CL III 533.
61. CL IV 561; 584.
62. CL IV 588.
63. CL V 431.
64. CL III 480.
65. CL V 28; V 340; VI 714.

3. *Ice and Spring: Coleridge's Imaginative Education*

1. Basil Willey, *Samuel Taylor Coleridge*; Owen Barfield, *What Coleridge Thought*; William Empson, Introduction to *Coleridge's Verse: A Selection*, ed. Empson and Pirie; David Jones, *An Introduction to 'The Rime of the Ancient Mariner'*.
2. F. D. Maurice, *The Kingdom of Christ* (1842) Dedication, p. viii.
3. Norman Fruman, *Coleridge, the Damaged Archangel*.
4. DQW V 197.
5. Leigh Hunt, *Autobiography*, ed. R. Ingpen (1903) 185.
6. Hunt, *loc. cit.*, I 85–91; LW I 142.
7. LW II 12, 14.
8. LW II 14.
9. Fruman 117.
10. LL I 172.
11. Gillman 23.
12. CL IV 750–1.
13. Fruman 117.
14. *Aurora*, ch. xiv.
15. Ibid., ch. ii 13 and i 6–14.
16. Ibid., ix 82.
17. L. Smith, 'Reminiscences of an Octogenarian', *Leisure Hour* (1860) IX 633–4. Reprinted in my note 'Coleridge at School', *Notes and Queries* (1958) 114–15.
18. *Aurora*, ch. viii, 14–17.
19. WPW II 127–8.
20. PW I 179, 181.
21. A. L. Barbauld, *Works*, ed. L. Aikin (1825) I 188–9. (The poem addressed to Coleridge himself appears on page 209.)
22. CL I 295.

23. House 82–3.
24. See Griggs's account, CL V 57–78.
25. CL IV 937 and n.
26. CN II 2224 n (cf. Fruman 11).
27. *Aurora*, ch. xi, 255–6.
28. BL II 19; cf Sh C II 128.
29. C & S 233.

4. Coleridge: A Bridge between Science and Poetry

1. See CN I, Index I, under Beddoes, for further references.
2. See above, p. 59.
3. See her letter of 8 Oct 1802, quoted Sir Harold Hartley, *Humphry Davy* (1968) p. 44.
4. J. Davy, *Memoir* (DW I 13).
5. CL I 209.
6. E. Darwin, *Phytologia* (1800) pp. 560–3.
7. J. A. Paris, *Life of Sir Humphry Davy* (1831) I 74–5.
8. IS §52, p. 67.
9. Hartley, op. cit., p. 42; R. Sharrock, 'The Chemist and the Poet: Sir Humphry Davy and the Preface to the *Lyrical Ballads*'. *Notes and Records of the Royal Society* (1962) XVII 63.
10. Sharrock, loc. cit., 62, 66; Hartley, op. cit., 25.
11. J. Cottle, *Reminiscences of S. T. Coleridge and R. Southey* (1847) p. 329.
12. DW V 42.
13. F. W. J. von Schelling, *Darlegung des wahren Verhältnisses der Naturphilosophie zu verbesserten Fichte'schen Lehre*, etc. (Tübingen 1806) pp. 125–6. (BM copy C. 126.f.7[2]).
14. J. A. Paris, op. cit., 138.
15. CN I 1098 f. 11.
16. Ibid., ff. 15v–16.
17. CN II 2070; III 3274.
18. CN I 438 and n.
19. N 38 (1829).
20. Sh C II 11. Cf. CN III 3291n and 4181n.
21. Sh C II 12.
22. BL I 202.
23. Introductory Discourse to Chemistry Lectures, 21 Jan 1802. DW II 315.
24. BL II 14.
25. Loc. cit.; DW II 325.
26. BL II 16.
27. BL II 65.
28. Marginal note to *Aurora* in Jacob Boehme, *Works* (1764–81) I 41–2 (BM copy C. 126.k.1).
29. See, e.g. Sh C II 104.

30. CL II 1102 (See below, p. 135).
31. CL II 709.
32. CN II 2355.
33. From his last book, *In the Crucible of Scientific Revolution*.

5. *Coleridge and the Romantic Vision of the World*

1. CL III 518n.
2. CL II 1126.
3. BL I 114.
4. WPW V 1–2; also W Prel XXXVII.
5. BL I 114, 136.
6. BL I 121.
7. BL I 98.
8. W Prel (1805) XI 6–7, 47–8; XII 21.
9. VIII xi; cf. VIII viii.
10. BL I 137.
11. *Friend* I 203n; CL IV 956.
12. R. Kroner, *Von Kant bis Hegel* (Tübingen, 1921–1924) I 1–3.
13. *Kants gesammelte Schriften* (Berlin, 1902 ff.) VII 27 and VI 34, 134–6.
14. C. L. Reinhold, *Briefe über die Kantische Philosophie* (Leipzig, 1790) I 9–16.
15. J. G. Fichte, *Briefwechsel*, ed. Hans Schulz (Leipzig, 1925) I 449–450; to Baggesen, April 1795.
16. *Phänomenologie des Geistes*, ed. Hoffmeister, pp. 563–4.
17. Preface to the *Phenomenology of the Spirit*, tr. Walter Kaufmann, *Hegel* (New York, 1965) p. 380.
18. BL I 137.
19. 'My Mental Development', in *The Philosophy of Bertrand Russell*, ed. P. A. Schilpp (New York, 1963) pp. 10–12.
20. CL III 490.
21. 22 June 1806, CN II 2866.
22. CL III 477.
23. Joseph Warren Beach, 'Coleridge's Borrowings from the German', *Journal of English Literary History* IX (1942) pp. 38n. 50; Fruman 126.
24. John Stuart Mill, 'Coleridge' (1840; *Dissertations and Discussions* 1859) in *Mill on Bentham and Coleridge*, ed. F. R. Leavis (1950) pp. 99–100.
25. Newton, *Opticks* (4th ed.), ed. I. Bernard Cohen and others (New York, 1952) Query 31, p. 400, and Queries 17–23, pp. 347–53.
26. *Ibid.*, Query 31, p. 403 and Query 28, p. 370.
27. 'Conclusion', AR 392–3.
28. *The Statesman's Manual*, LS 96; CL IV 760–761.
29. *Friend* I 94 and n.
30. BL I 188, 196–8.

31. TL 38, 40–2, 51–2, 70.
32. TL 85–6; and PL 179.
33. *Friend* I 520.
34. *The Complete Works of Samuel Taylor Coleridge*, ed. Shedd (New York, 1853) III 709. See Thomas McFarland's thorough study of *Coleridge and the Pantheist Tradition* (Oxford, 1969) especially chap. iii.
35. *Friend* I 519.
36. 20 Jan 1820, CL v 18.
37. *The Statesman's Manual*, in LS 28–31.
38. For example, Hegel, *Phänomenologie des Geistes*, ed. Hoffmeister, pp. xxxviii, 536–44, 549; *Lectures on the Philosophy of Religion*, tr. E. B. Speirs and J. B. Sanderson (New York, 1962) I 20.
39. CL II 961; BL I 98, 137.
40. *The Statesman's Manual* in LS 69–70.
41. LS 49–50.
42. *The Statesman's Manual*, Appendix C (Appendix B in 1839 ed.) in LS 72–3.
43. CT 182.
44. IS 223–4.
45. C & S 233. See also PL 358.
46. LS 30–1; see also 79, and AR 250–5nn.
47. TL 85; CL IV 769.
48. Wallace Stevens, *The Necessary Angel* (1960) pp. 40–1.

6. Coleridge's Anxiety

1. *New Letters of Robert Southey*, ed. K. Curry (New York, 1965) II 117–18.
2. CL VI 910 (to William Worship, May 1832).
3. CL II 1102 (to Davy, Mar 1804).
4. CL II 959 (to Southey, Aug 1803).
5. WLR (1806–11) 399.
6. House 18–19.
7. W. Prel (1805) II 477.
8. CL VI 892 (to Green, 23 Mar 1832).
9. CL VI 769 (to Sotheby, 9 Nov 1828).
10. CL II 710 (to Poole, 24 Mar 1801).
11. 'The Spirit of the Age': HW XI 30.
12. DWJ I 92–3; 103; 107 (21 Dec 1801; 29 Jan and 6 Feb 1802).
13. DWJ I 79 (10 Nov 1801).
14. WLR (1787–1805) 464.
15. BL I 31.
16. Freud XX 144.
17. CL I 310 (to Poole, Mar 1797).
18. WLR (1806–11) 373.

19. E. Betham (ed.), *A House of Letters* (1905) p. 116.
20. Freud XX 89, 90.
21. CL I 347 (to Poole, Oct 1797).
22. D. Beres, 'A Dream, a Vision and a Poem: A Psycho-analytic Study of the Origins of the Rime of the Ancient Mariner', *The International Journal of Psycho-Analysis* (1951) XXXII 97–116.
23. J. D. Campbell, *Samuel Taylor Coleridge* ... (1894) p. 3; J. Gillman, *Life of Coleridge* (1838), p. 7. Cited Beres, loc. cit., 102.
24. Freud XX 84, 133. Cf. XVI 396–7.
25. CL I 63 (to G. L. Tuckett, 6 Feb 1794).
26. CL II 1054 (to Sir G. Beaumont, 1 Feb 1804).
27. Freud XX 138.
28. Ibid., 123.
29. HCR I 446.
30. PW I 191 (gloss of 1815–16).
31. CL I 347–8 (to Poole, Oct 1797).
32. CL II 1054 (1 Feb 1804); 929; 959 (to Southey, 1803). See also below, p. 178.
33. CL VI 984 (to Eliza Nixon, 7 June 1834); CN II 2998.
34. CL I 62 (to G. L. Tuckett, 6 Feb 1794).
35. CL III 498 (to J. Cottle, 27 May 1814).
36. CL I 184 (to Wade, 10 Feb 1796).
37. CN II 2647.
38. CL I 99 (to Southey, 1 Sep 1794).
39. CL I 330 (to Cottle).
40. CL VI 580 (to Cattermole, 25 May 1826) and cf. V 164, VI 607–8 and 804.
41. CN II 2647.
42. CL I 347 (to Poole, Oct 1797).
43. WLR (1787–1805) 338–40; CL II 756, 1124 and III 210.
44. CL I 257 (15 Nov 1796); CL V 255.
45. CL I 491 (6 May 1799); 584 (31 Mar 1800).
46. CL I 80 (to George Coleridge, May 1794).
47. CN II 2860; CN II 2712.
48. CN II 3148.
49. CN II 2726.
50. CL I 334 (to Southey, July 1797); 391 (to Cottle, Mar 1798).
51. CL V 249–50.
52. See Jane Worthington Smyser, 'Coleridge's Use of Wordsworth's Juvenilia', *Publications of the Modern Language Association of America* (1950), LXV 419–26; E. H. W. Meyerstein, 'Wordsworth and Coleridge', *Times Literary Supplement*, 29 Nov 1941, p. 596; 6 Dec 1941, p. 611. For Coleridge's borrowing of 'green radiance', and the composition of his footnote, see Robert Woof, 'Wordsworth and Coleridge: Some Early Matters', *Bicentenary Wordsworth Studies in Memory of John Alban Finch*, ed. Jonathan Wordsworth (Ithaca, N.Y., 1970) pp. 76–91.
53. IS 68; CN I 1679; CL I 519 (to Wedgwood, 21 May 1799).

54. CL I 329 (to Cottle, June 1797).
55. CL I 67 (to George Coleridge, Feb 1794).
56. WLR (1806–11) 399.
57. Freud XX 165. Cf. XVI 395.
58. *Sein und Zeit*, siebente unveränderte Auflage (Tübingen, 1953), p. 186.
59. Ibid., p. 185.
60. Ibid., pp. 186–7.
61. Ibid., pp. 191, 343.
62. J.-P. Sartre, *L'être et le néant; essai d'ontologie phénoménologique* (Paris, 1943) p. 66.
63. *The Concept of Dread*, tr. Walter Lowrie (Princeton, 1957) p. 139. With the translator's 'dread' rendered by me throughout as 'anxiety'.
64. CL I 396 (to George Coleridge, Mar 1798).
65. op. cit., p. 41.
66. Ibid., p. 47.
67. Ibid., p. 38.
68. *Life of Savage*, ed. C. Tracy (Oxford, 1971) pp. 139–40.
69. op. cit., p. 139.
70. Cf. Seneca, *De Providentia* II 6–7.
71. *Friedrich Nietzsche; Werke in drei Bänden*, hrsg. Karl Schlechta (München, 1954–56) II 848.
72. *Hours in a Library* (1909) III 329.
73. HCR I 80.
74. Note in Mr Keymer's album. Quoted E. V. Lucas, *Life of Lamb* (1905) II 266.
75. DQW II 211.
76. WLR (1806–11) 371, 375, 380.
77. op. cit., p. 266.
78. Ibid.
79. 'H. N. Coleridge's Preface', *The Table Talk and Omniana of Samuel Taylor Coleridge*, ed. T. Ashe (1888) p. 13.
80. 'In Search of Goethe from Within', *The Dehumanization of Art and Other Essays on Art, Culture and Literature*, tr. Helene Weyl *et al.* (Princeton, 1968) pp. 143–4.
81. F. R. Leavis, 'Coleridge in Criticism', *Scrutiny* (1940) IX, 69.
82. Cf. Heidegger: '*Am Dasein ist eine ständige "Unganzheit", die mit dem Tod ihr Ende findet, undurchstreichbar*' (op. cit. 242).
83. *Philosophie*, dritte Auflage (Berlin, etc., 1956) III 222–36 *et passim; Von der Wahrheit* (München, 1958), pp. 299, 956.

7. *Coleridge on Powers in Mind and Nature*

1. Introduction to *Biographia Literaria*, ed. G. Sampson (1920) pp. xxiv and xxviii.
2. Carlyle 73.

3. BL II 243.
4. *Coleridge and the Pantheist Tradition* (Oxford 1969) p. 32.
5. LL II 190 (26 April 1816).
6. CL I 260.
7. BL I 202.
8. CN II 2435.
9. BL I 105.
10. CL I 260 (to Thelwall, 19 Nov 1796); CN III 3605. Professor Kathleen Coburn kindly let me see the proofs of the third volume of the *Notebooks*.
11. LS 114.
12. In his *Essay concerning Human Understanding*.
13. BL I 69n.
14. PL 318.
15. CN I 1710.
16. I. A. Richards, *Coleridge on Imagination* (1934) p. 60.
17. CN I 1313.
18. From notes for an Essay on the Passions: IS 67.
19. CN II 2453.
20. Essay on the Principles of Method, *Friend* I 509.
21. CN I 1717.
22. A. N. Whitehead, *Aims of Education* (1932) p. 2.
23. AR 1.
24. *Friend* I 473 (Cf. IS 71).
25. IS 206 (Cf. BL I 34n).
26. F. H. Bradley, *Logic*, Bk III; pt II, ch. iv, p. 591.
27. C & S 14.
28. Cf. 'All the numberless goings-on of life': 'Frost at Midnight', l.12 (PW I 240).
29. LS 72.
30. *Bulletin of the John Rylands Library* (1952) XXXIV 276–95; reprinted *Coleridge*, Twentieth Century Views Series, ed. K. Coburn (Englewood, N.J., 1967) pp. 161–78.
31. (Cambridge, 1970.)
32. TL 94 (quoted Snyder, *Coleridge on Logic and Learning* (New Haven, 1929) p. 22.
33. *Proceedings of the Aristotelian Society* (1948).
34. BL II 258.
35. *Cambridge Essays, by members of the University* (1856) p. 306.
36. CN II 2546 (cf. above, pp. 9, 27–8).
37. BL I 102.
38. CN I 922.
39. CN I 1382.
40. N 51.6.
41. LS 83.
42. Fruman, Part IV.
43. Hort, *Cambridge Essays*, p. 308.
44. *Rousseau and Romanticism* (Boston, 1919) p. 287.

8. *Coleridge and Kant*

1. TT 2 July 1830 (cf. Fruman 114–15 and nn).
2. *Coleridge* (1953) p. 54.
3. Chapters x and xiii.
4. BL I 202.
5. TT 21 Sept 1830.
6. Quoted IS 141.
7. CN I App. B, p. 457.
8. Letter to Place, 6 Dec 1817: Graham Wallas, *Life of Francis Place*(1898) p. 91.
9. Paris, 1970.

9. *Coleridge's Enjoyment of Words*

1. *Coleridge on Shakespeare . . .*, ed. R. A. Foakes (1972) p. 72 (cf. Sh C II 124–5).
2. CL I 250–1 (5 Nov 1796).
3. CL V 409–10; V 790.
4. CL V 222.
5. CL I 295.
6. TT 2 June 1834.
7. IS 106 (cf. above, pp. 33–4).
8. CL I 293.
9. *Friend* II 185 (and elsewhere).
10. BL I 114 and TT 4 April 1832; BL I 49n; LR III 33; CL I 84.
11. CL IV 792.
12. BL I 107.
13. *Paradise Lost* VII 41 (cf. VIII 648).
14. Line 91.
15. *Paradise Lost* I 595.
16. M. Bréal, *Semantics*, tr. M. Cust (1900) p. 129.
17. Andrew Young, *A Retrospect of Flowers* (1950) p. 31.
18. CN I 1387.
19. BM MS Eg. 2826, ff. 403–4.
20. CL I 626.
21. S. W. Alexander, *Space, Time and Deity* (1927) I 12.
22. See his note at end of Swedenborg's *De Equo Albo* (BM copy C. 44.g.5) and my *What Coleridge Thought* (1972) pp. 53ff.
23. BL I 61.
24. CL V 466 (to Gillman).
25. CL V 332.
26. *Friend* I 432–3; TL 36.
27. *Friend* I 457.
28. CL VI 756.
29. Essay on Faith, in *Confessions of an Inquiring Spirit* (1849) p. 109.

30. See above, p. 208.
31. TT 8 July 1827 (both words).
32. BL I 188.
33. CL VI 551.
34. *Friend* I 283 and n, 432; LR III 122.
35. CL V 199.
36. CN I 6 (f6v).
37. LR IV 227.
38. BL I 189.
39. Ibid. (cf. IS 224–5).
40. IS 57.
41. IS 67.
42. AR 219n.
43. TT 2 May 1830.
44. BM MS Eg. 2801 f. 15.
45. C & S passim.
46. See above, p. 207.
47. PW I 77; TT 1 March 1834.
48. CL V 517.
49. CL V 196.
50. CL V 133.
51. IS 106.
52. BL I 61 and 63n.
53. BL II 230 (cf. IS 106).
54. *Friend* I 94n.
55. But see BL I 198.
56. CL II 866–7; and cf. CL VI 570, LS 88.
57. Leigh Hunt, *Autobiography*, ed. R. Ingpen (1903) II 54 (interpolation by T. L. Hunt). Quoted Deschamps 281n.

10.   A *Stream* by *Glimpses: Coleridge's later Imagination*

1. Diary entry of 18 Dec 1836, in Caroline Fox, *Memories of Old Friends* (1882) p. 12.
2. Letter to John Carlyle, 22 Jan 1825, quoted C. R. Sanders, *Coleridge and the Broad Church Movement* (Durham, N.C., 1942) pp. 151–152.
3. LL I 197.
4. Ibid II 191.
5. 'My First Acquaintance with Poets' (HW XVII 115).
6. DQW II 150.
7. WPrW III 469 (cf. 492).
8. Marginal note to *Aurora* in Jacob Boehme, *Works* (1764–81) I Flyleaf (BM copy C. 126.k.1).
9. John Sterling, *Essays and Tales* (1848) I xxv.
10. *Letters of John Keats, 1814–1821*, ed. H. H. Rollins (Cambridge, Mass., 1958) II 88–9.

11. Letter to John Carlyle, 24 June 1824. Quoted C. R. Sanders, *Coleridge and the Broad Church Movement*, p. 150.
12. See Lane Cooper, 'The Power of the Eye in Coleridge', in *Studies Presented to J. M. Hart* (New York, 1901) pp. 78–121. Reprinted in his *Late Harvest* (Ithaca, N.Y., 1952).
13. Ibid.
14. *Friend* II 51.
15. CN I 838.
16. TT 30 April 1830; IS 57–8.
17. AR ix–x, 397.
18. Thomas McFarland, *Coleridge and the Pantheist Tradition* (Oxford, 1969).
19. BL II 230. Cf. CL III 533–4 and n.
20. J. A. Heraud, *Oration on the Death of S. T. Coleridge* ... (1834) pp. 27–8.
21. E. V. Lucas, *Life of Lamb* (1905) II 256.
22. WL (LY) II 710.
23. T. Allsop, *Letters, Conversations and Recollections of S. T. Coleridge* (1836) I 86.
24. See above, note 10.
25. CL I 112.
26. *Letters of Sara Hutchinson*, ed. K. Coburn (1954) p. 428.
27. Sermon LXX, *Sermons*, ed. G. R. Potter and E. M. Simpson (Berkeley & Los Angeles 1957) III 236. Quoted R. Heywood, *The Infinite Hive* (1964) epigraph.

Index

(Items beginning with a lower-case letter are discussed primarily as words in the text)